PRAISE FOR *TOKEN BLACK GIRL*

"With wit and the sharp eye of a woman who has lived through it, Prescod's memoir takes the reader into the places and institutions of privilege where the idea of the Token Black Girl thrives. Literally shrinking herself to conform to the expectations of those around her, Prescod's experience feels both unsettlingly familiar and incendiary. This is an essential read to understand how beauty standards and media industry affect Black women in America."

—Gabrielle Union, author of *You Got Anything Stronger?*

"Sometimes it feels like we are just beginning to discuss the full extent of the Black experience in America, and with a frankness and a brave ability to stare down her own truth, Danielle Prescod has vividly detailed a portrait of Black womanhood that feels so familiar and yet so rarely discussed. It's time! In her firsthand account of what it's like to live as a Black person in the middle of whiteness, Danielle suffers no fools and holds back no punches as she explores the humor, WTFs, and emotional repercussions of coming of age as she did. As a memoirist and cultural critic, she deftly keeps things from feeling like a collection of the aha-ha moments you have in therapy, and instead, through her experience, offers people a way out of their token Black friend role (self-inflicted, structural, or otherwise)."

—Allison P. Davis, senior writer for the Cut

"In an honest, relatable, and enlightening fashion, Danielle eloquently speaks about an experience many of us know too well. This pointed memoir reveals the struggle of being a Black woman in a world that tends to praise everything opposite of what you are. This is necessary reading for all women navigating social constructs while simultaneously learning to love themselves out loud."

—Taylor Rooks, Emmy Award–nominated sports journalist and host of the Bleacher Report

"Danielle Prescod candidly shares her experience from growing up in a predominately white environment to then working in a white-dominant industry and how those experiences impacted her identity formation throughout the years. Her story made me feel seen as it is honest and relatable and will leave you mulling over your own experience with self-discovery in a world where we all strive for perfection and to 'fit in.' *Token Black Girl* is a must-read for anyone who has felt like a 'token' in society."

—Hannah Bronfman, entrepreneur, author, and founder of HBFIT

"With her richly introspective debut, *Token Black Girl*, Danielle Prescod reveals devastating and lingering childhood traumas in evidentiating the racist structures central to the psychological gymnastics that the Black community must navigate in order to exist and thrive in the United States."

—Tamu McPherson, fashion consultant and
All the Pretty Birds founder

Token Black Girl

Token
Black
Girl

A Memoir

Danielle Prescod

Little
a

Published by Little A, New York

www.apub.com

Amazon, the Amazon logo, and Little A are trademarks of Amazon.com, Inc., or its
affiliates.

ISBN-13: 9781542035163 (hardcover)
ISBN-10: 1542035163 (hardcover)

ISBN-13: 9781542035156 (paperback)
ISBN-10: 1542035155 (paperback)

Cover design by Leah Jacobs-Gordon

Printed in the United States of America

First edition

For Grandma and Grandpa Spann:
you both know why.

Who taught you to hate the texture of your hair? Who taught you to hate the color of your skin? . . . Who taught you to hate the shape of your nose and the shape of your lips? . . . Who taught you to hate the race that you belong to? . . . You should ask yourself who taught you to hate being what God made you.

—*Malcolm X, May 1962*

INTRODUCTION

In the summer of 2003, I turned fifteen years old. In July, the very same month of my birthday, *Vanity Fair* released a cover that is infamous within my generation of media obsessives. The cover teased a teen-focused special featuring five of the wealthiest and most popular female representatives of television and movie stardom. Amanda Bynes, Mary-Kate and Ashley Olsen, Mandy Moore, and Hilary Duff posed draped around one another in varying shades of pastel pink. An expansion of the cover, hidden behind a fold, featured blue-eyed brunette Alexis Bledel, broody Evan Rachel Wood, Token Black Girl Raven-Symoné, and token bad girl Lindsay Lohan. The cover line read "It's Totally Raining Teens!," a cheeky nod to youth-speak and *Vanity Fair*'s way of cementing an authoritarian cultural claim on who the "teens" of the times were. Cover expansions are significantly less popular in the modern media landscape, maybe because it's cruel, but perhaps more practically because people are now likelier to see cover images on a screen than in the aisle of their local CVS. At the time, it was a subtle and not-so-subtle way to both include and exclude people, with the message: "We need you, but you're not quite cover material."

Teen Vogue, *Vogue*'s kid sister, would be launched that same year. After a test issue featuring a twenty-year-old Jessica Simpson (blonde) cuddling her then boyfriend, obviously Nick Lachey, debuted in 2000, the magazine promised to be the anti–crush quiz fashion bible teen girls craved. For me, an all-girls-school attendee, it was welcomed and essential reading. But the magazine was published quarterly, and that left a void in the teen fashion landscape for months at a time. The July 2003 issue of *Vanity Fair* satiated some of that thirst. I became an absolute rabid animal in the hunt to get my hands on this issue. I was not, at fifteen, a *Vanity Fair* reader, nor should I have been, as the other cover lines of the issue previewed subjects far outside my interest—hard journalism about the Bush administration, a Hamptons real estate feature, and an author reporting on cold case murder facts—but the cover had been hyped up on all my favorite entertainment news programs, and I was intimately familiar with every single one of those teen girls' faces. I was gently conditioned to already believe these adolescent women were goddesses. In fact, my younger sister and I were such dutiful consumers of all Mary-Kate and Ashley products that, to this day, I refuse to buy anything from The Row, their clothing line, as a twisted attempt to get justice for the money I have already shelled out to them.

You may have noticed that all the girls, now women, featured on that *Vanity Fair* cover are white, and I am not. More specifically, they are all thin, blonde, white girls. Even Mandy Moore, who had an edgy brunette cut at the time of the shoot, had been introduced to the world as a sugary-sweet blonde. No matter what her colorist mixed up, that was how many people still viewed her.

It seems like no accident that the brunette, the bad girl, the redhead, and the lone Black girl were conspicuously absent on the actual cover, instead relegated to the foldout. Alexis Bledel played the smart, safe, and overly anxious Rory Gilmore on *Gilmore Girls*. Evan Rachel Wood starred in the chilling 2003 film *Thirteen*, which was about suburban girls who rebelled by getting tongue piercings and having threesomes. Raven-Symoné, a *Cosby Show* alum, was now a Disney darling, the lead in an eponymous sitcom where she played a high schooler with psychic abilities. And Lindsay Lohan almost needs no introduction, but in 2003, she was not yet a Mykonos club hostess with a troubled family past. Rather, she was the girl who played both starring roles in *The Parent Trap* and was on the cusp of *Mean Girls* celebrity.

Vanity Fair, like most publications at the time, was telling readers who deserved their attention. The inside story featured a more diverse set of "totally teens," including Kyla Pratt, Christina Milian, and Solange Knowles, and was largely unmemorable. The cover is what everyone recalls. A magazine cover is a beacon, mesmerizing the reader with the image it presents. And for many years in fashion media, an upper echelon of publishing, we readers were shown white women and white women only. In the early part of the millennium, critical years of my development, if a coveted cover spot was assigned to someone, it was a blonde girl—extra points for a bony one.

Ignoring the presence of Black women is a massive power flex that exposes the ideologies of the decision makers who determine what celebrity is worthy of a feature. Erasure is a useful tool of oppression, and *Vanity Fair* was not alone in ensuring the erasure of Black women and girls from positions of prominence and honor. The media's compounded interest in either strategically or accidentally reducing the visibility of Black women across the board poisoned my mind for years.

Raven-Symoné must have felt incredibly lonely shooting that *Vanity Fair* cover. To my knowledge, she's never spoken about it. She has met some controversial moments in more recent years, relating in particular to her identity as a Black woman. In 2015, she became a trending topic after her criticism of ethnic Black names on the morning talk show *The View* went viral. Raven and her cohosts opined on whether racial bias affects hiring probability by way of recruiters screening the names of candidates. (Spoiler: it does.) Raven said that she would not hire a woman with the name "Watermelondrea" when that name appeared as number twelve on a list of "sixty of the most ghetto-sounding names." And while hers was an ignorant and harmful comment, I do not think it is a surprising one from a Black woman who seems to me to have been coerced to maintain a degree of self-hatred, one that was ingrained and then nurtured by an environment that prioritizes whiteness in all forms.

In 2003, the public was not prepared to have a conversation about the influences of white supremacy in the mainstream media. I certainly wasn't. I was too busy worrying about how to suck in my lips (true story) and shrink my body so I could conform to my white peers. I imagine in some regard, Raven was too. The previous fourteen years of my life had desensitized me to seeing very few Black faces in the media I consumed. And like an orphaned duckling, I found myself imprinting on girls like the quintet of the *Vanity Fair* cover stars in a desperate attempt to tether my existence to that which was considered desirable and beautiful.

As the Hilarys and Mandys increased in popularity and marketability, a part of me always recognized, shamefully, that I was not the thin, blonde archetype. That fact did not deter me from trying my best to get as close to that archetype as possible. For years, I singed my hair follicles with chemical relaxers to achieve a pin-straight, "nonthreatening" mane. I was acutely aware of how sinful my excess of brown flesh was, so I starved myself, frantic to reduce my size. I took pleasure in my exposed clavicle and hip bones, but no matter how thin I got, I was always outrunning the possibility that I might become "too big," too noticeable, more noticeable than I already was, which was an utterly terrifying potential reality. Despite understanding that I was different—that, like Raven, I was the Token Black Girl—I still felt I needed to fit a profile in which my skin color was my only difference, and not one of many.

You've probably seen the Token Black Girl in many iterations over the years. She's Tootie, played by Kim Fields, on *The Facts of Life*. She's Lisa Turtle, played by Lark Voorhies, on *Saved by the Bell*. She's Jessi Ramsey in The Baby-Sitters Club book series. She's Olympic gymnast Dominique Dawes and then she's Gabby Douglas. She's Stacey Dash's Dion in *Clueless*. She's Gabrielle Union as Katie in *She's All That* and Chastity in *10 Things I Hate About You*. She's the Spice Girls' Scary

Spice, also known as Mel B. She's Normani in Fifth Harmony, and she's Jordyn Woods before getting unceremoniously deleted from the Kardashian-Jenner family group chat. You've seen her, sure, but you don't *know* her because you are not meant to. She is not "the main character," as the kids on TikTok say.

The Token Black Girl is characterized mostly by her proximity to her white peers and her nonthreatening and friendly nature. She is non-threatening because she is almost never the romantic interest, and her primary function is to provide "attitude" and "sass," either as humor or as an attempt to elevate the sex appeal of the otherwise all-white entity. She is a good student because she has to be. She actually feels like she has to be good at everything. She's almost always a good dancer, and even if she's not, it doesn't matter because everyone will still *think* she's a good dancer. She either has or can get the requisite social signifiers of acceptance—everything except white skin, of course. She will be well spoken, well dressed, and well groomed. She likes all the things her friends like, including boys, but they will not like her. She almost never acknowledges her position as the sole Black member of a group because talking about race makes white people uncomfortable. She can never make white people uncomfortable. Her most critical responsibility is providing protection against the "racist" label that might otherwise be hurled at a gaggle of white women devoid of ethnic variety.

While this relative invisibility (as in, being *there* but never being central) dictated the rules of engagement for my life, covers like the July 2003 *Vanity Fair* helped white girls establish the notion that they were the world's most precious gift, an idea reinforced by movies and television, where they saw idealized versions of themselves projected or reflected back. They could pick and choose which elements were worth imitating. That imitation is not necessarily healthy, but as an alternative to complete erasure, it does seem appealing.

Examining beauty standards as a system—one that has adverse effects on all women—is worthwhile. In recent years, the dialogue about fighting these standards has become more emphatic, but like racism, it is a harmful culture that evolves just as quickly as its counterculture. Social media apps have joined magazines in upholding a completely unattainable aesthetic as the singular criteria for beauty, and still, imagery of Black women and subjects pertaining to them are siphoned out of mainstream publications to "ethnic" magazines like *Ebony*, *Jet*, or *Essence*. But at fifteen, I was not an *Essence*, *Jet*, or *Ebony* reader. My tastes were morphed and molded by magazines like *Vogue*, *Teen Vogue*, *Teen People*, and *YM*, publications where Black women were scarce, if present at all. And that scarcity was also totally reflective of my own day-to-day reality.

The media could have been a lifeline to me, a window into a more diverse reality, but that's not how it functions. Insidiously enough, media is often employed to protect and uphold white supremacy, and I'm not just talking about the obvious here, like *Birth of a Nation*— although, yes, that's a big one. In the 2020 book *Stamped: Racism, Antiracism, and You*, authors Jason Reynolds and Ibram X. Kendi reveal that entire film empires, like *Tarzan*, *Planet of the Apes*, and *Rocky*, were built on the idea of specifically preserving the mythic dominance of white masculinity. As I was growing up, women's fashion magazines were doing the same work on me. With their insistence that beauty was to be defined solely through a narrow Eurocentric lens, the magazines accomplished, for white women, what the novels and films of the twentieth century did for white men. But guess what? It all worked so well that I had no idea it was happening.

Primetime TV was no better. Just like *Jet* and *Essence*, there were several Black television programs and movies released when I was young, but none seemed to inspire a devoted fandom among my white friends. There are people my age who now profess their love for *The Fresh Prince of Bel-Air*, but in 1996, every girl I knew had a poster of Jonathan Taylor Thomas, the *Home Improvement* hottie, pinned up somewhere in her room. No images of Will Smith adorned those same walls. I faked a crush on JTT, too, because what else was I to do? But at eight years old, I had never even seen the show that made him a household name. My parents stringently monitored what my sister and I watched on TV, and the shows they approved of, like *The Cosby Show*, *My Wife and Kids*, and *Family Matters*, often played into respectability politics, showing romanticized family structures and successful Black people. But these were not the shows celebrated by my white class-mates and friends. For all I knew, they weren't watching them at all. Preferences were so subtly expressed and communicated that there was no need to explicitly determine what was "good" and what was "bad." I understood that I should not prefer *That's So Raven* to *Lizzie McGuire*. It was BSB, not B2K. Anything Black that existed in my world was bizarrely countercultural and needed to be approached with caution. Black characters on-screen, like the male leads of *Friday* or *South Park's* Token Black, were only ushered into conversation as the butt of jokes, useful for impersonations to generate laughs but never the ones to look like, be like, or love.

When I began to watch shows and movies dictated to me by the whims of my friends, classmates, and sometimes their parents, I had to strain repeatedly to find myself represented at all. And sure, there were some ways I could see myself reflected in Token Black Girl roles, like Nebula, Zenon's Black best friend (played by Raven-Symoné), but the movie is called *Zenon: Girl of the 21st Century*, not *Nebula*. It's not even called *Nebula and Zenon*. I gathered from the treatment of these Black characters that they were not to be the most beloved. They were supporting structures, not the stars. Always made to shine just a little less than whoever the real star was. They are never the love interest or the girl who wins in the end. They help a lot, sure, but they don't dazzle. And so while I was not watching or reading anything with a centralized Black narrative, I was consumed with media that procedurally avoided Black people and continued to celebrate and center white people. As I took in all that media during my formative years, I got the message:

"Sorry, you're not actually lovable." The indoctrination was subtle and absolute. I trained myself to be smaller in the physical and metaphysical sense. I squeezed myself into that narrow lens as much as possible, and I suffocated there.

Mostly because of what I saw, from an early age, I was plagued by the differences in the size, shape, and color of my body, and not just in comparisons to girls on television or in magazines; the comparisons were live and in color between me and my friends and classmates. You could always easily spot me in a photo, at a party, or on a field. I was *the Black one*. I oscillated between the complicated desire to be both visible (wanting to see myself and imagine who I could be) and invisible (in that there was no real difference between me and the people who surrounded me). I picked apart every single aspect of my appearance. This was driven mostly by a desire to integrate imperceptibly into the world of my white friends, and my self-loathing was aimed at all the characteristics that made me stand out. Obviously, my skin made the distinction between us abundantly clear, but I became preoccupied with my other physical features as well. I was conditioned to think that Blackness was a hurdle, something that had to be overcome or conquered. I knew I could not change this notion of Blackness, but I deduced that if I could, perhaps, change *myself*, especially in appearance or behavior, I could change the context of what Blackness meant for me.

At the same time, I saw Black people succeeding in unprecedented areas. I watched Tiger Woods win his first Masters. My tennis-playing little sister and I were constantly "looking like" or "reminding" people of Venus and Serena Williams, who began to dominate professional women's tennis in the '90s. It was a tiresome comparison, and twenty-plus years later, we can predict with stunning accuracy when someone will make a Williams-sisters comment after seeing us on a court. But the momentous achievements of these specially anointed Black figures opened my world to possibility. So I focused my energy on what seemed like the "right" road to go down, never becoming like Sheneneh, the loud, crass, misogynistic, ghettoized caricature on *Martin*—whom my classmates imitated by arching their backs, rolling their necks, and shouting "Giiiiinnnaaaa!" at any opportunity that arose. I, instead, became overzealous about what I could accomplish. It seemed easy enough to avoid being a punch line. I just had to act perfect. And *be* perfect.

I understood that I would need to excel to be accepted. My parents may be somewhat responsible for planting this seed, as they gave me the ubiquitous Black-parent talk: "You'll need to work twice as hard to get half as far." I became obsessed with all markers of achievement: straight As, trophies, blue ribbons, anything I could collect that would designate me as a winner, as better than the next person, proof that I was good enough and belonged. I gained all my confidence from performing as I thought I should, chasing a version of myself that was projected through a white lens. I was attempting not to appear "aggressive," "monstrous," "wild," or "ugly." Never ugly. But, ultimately, I was playing a game that could not be won. All those esteemed magazines existed to drive that home, especially considering that Black women, aside from in their tokenized positions, were nowhere to be seen.

Through youth or delusion, I remained hopeful that my social accession and acceptance were just a makeover away. I simply had to get there. To me, makeover magic and that seminal before and after were sorcery in its purest form. *The Swan*, an addictive show that aired when I was in high school, gave women the ultimate makeover: extensive plastic surgery, hair extensions, and new clothes—all so they could be considered "hot." Someone should maybe check on those contestants now. But when I was entering puberty and going through my first round of excruciating body developments, all I could hope was that, one day, a producer would pluck me out of suburban obscurity and turn me into a perfect plastic television princess. Several Anne Hathaway films later, I had so many fantasies about how all I needed was money and a knowledgeable enough team of experts, and voilà! I would be unstoppable.

My parents were careful enough not to raise my sister and me in a way that prioritized being pretty. I am grateful to them for that, but their fortitude in emphasizing talent, hard work, and inner beauty could not protect us from a world where the best thing a girl could hope to be was both thin and beautiful. And if you can't be beautiful, you must be thin. And more intense still, for a Black girl in a white world, you must be perfect. There's really no other way to avoid the structural mistrust and scrutiny that comes with being Black and a girl, and frankly, even if you're as close to perfect as you can get, someone will still have a problem with how you look or how you are. Constantly running up against this truth was crushing. I felt rejected by the world. I began to notice that all the physical qualities I hated about myself came as the result of being Black. My lips, my nose, my skin, my hair, my ass. They all meant I could never hide.

Thanks to magazines and movies, I believed, really and truly believed on a cellular level, that the best way to cover up my genetic curses would be to ascend to a level of fame and beauty that was acceptable to all people. OK, who am I kidding? To *white* people. This was, of course, before I was conscious of the fact that some people don't even like Beyoncé. These people should be anathematized, but nonetheless, they exist. No matter how perfect you seem to be, or how exquisite your art, or how enormous your dedication, there will always be haters. But I had yet to understand that. So I spent the next three decades of my life suppressing my emotions, stepping into roles I resented, constantly auditioning to find favor with whatever audience was before me, endlessly criticizing my own appearance, literally starving, and drowning in my own misery—but essentially looking amazing while doing so. I was going to succeed, no matter what. I would play the cards I was dealt by the wicked almighty dealer and come out on the other side of life, like Oprah—but my weight would never yo-yo. I would beat racism by becoming beautiful. Isn't that cute?

Becoming pretty as a pathway to social acceptance was a mysterious maze I had to navigate to unlock the best parts of life, but beauty is subjective. It was difficult to "win" at being beautiful, and within the community I grew up in (read: rich, white), I wasn't even in the running. People could see me, yes. They could see I had qualities rooted in white supremacy; I was "well spoken" and "articulate." They could see I was a good dancer and an athlete. When it came to looks, I knew I was subordinate, but because I am nothing if not determined, I came up with a formula I could implement to maximize my chances of acceptance.

First, I knew my body was a critical element. After careful observation of the world's distaste for anybody of substantial size, but particularly women, I knew I had to remain as small as possible. My Black body needed to be slimmed down, dramatically. I was run-of-the-mill thin, but I needed to be exceptionally thin. Standout thin. The kind of skinny that people whisper about. Second, my brown skin presented an inescapable complication: it was quite visible and, therefore, limiting. I would never be able to hide, at least not in the spaces I occupied, so I had to make sure my skin remained unblemished, unscarred, and pristine at all times. (Even at this very moment, my skin is slick with moisture, shiny, and smooth.) My makeup would need to complement my features but not be loud or flamboyant. It would take years of my life to find the right color combinations to achieve that effect. Third, my hair would need to be disciplined out of its unruly natural state to something straight, docile, and cooperative. And the last bit of the equation would be controlling variables like clothing, nails, attitude, inflections in speech, and so forth, so by the time I was in my twenties, I seemed more robotic than human. (I watch the "hosts" on *Westworld* with a familiar acknowledgment.) It all kind of worked for a while. A really long time, actually. But eventually, the whole thing began to crumble. And then, of course, came my major malfunction.

Eventually, I had to get to the bottom of my own deeply buried self-hatred and attempt to claw my way out of that soil so I could, at least, not be so sad. I fell into a deep depression when I uncovered that I was guilty of not only believing the toxic sludge (e.g., cultural erasure, colorism, hair-type hierarchy, diet fixation, etc.) the media insists on distributing daily but also spitting out toxic sludge and making sure the cycle continued by lording these same concepts over others. I was complicit. An active participant, working in media establishments that derive profits from exploiting the insecurities of all women, but in particular, Black women. I hope this book encourages people to understand that there are many factors at work in our mental and social conditioning, and we must cultivate media landscapes that are more inclusive and that celebrate our racial, physical, and external differences frequently and with enthusiasm.

CHAPTER ONE

Like most millennials, I have intentionally crafted over many years a version of myself that is a careful and precise edit. The thing is, when you are assigned roles to play from an early age, whether you want them or not, you learn to play them well. Being confident, expressive, and funny was my assumed persona, and it was easy for me to behave that way because people responded positively to it. For a lot of my adolescence, my peers also responded positively to a cunning brand of cruelty that seemed to be a necessary way to gain respect. Hiding the parts of myself that were ugly, less developed, and socially unacceptable only served me further. And the most hideous part of myself was a deep self-hatred and sense of unworthiness that developed as a by-product of constant anxiety about my own inadequacy due to being Black in a world that acknowledged and celebrated only whiteness. I learned to cover up all my self-loathing with makeup and hair and fancy clothes. I elevated my social and professional status by doing so. This worked for a long time, but in reality, I was a mess. I'm about to tear all that down, and to do that, we have to go to the beginning. Before I had ever even encountered a magazine, before I had ruled the playground with an iron little Machiavellian fist, and before I knew anything really, I had a very regular life.

It feels inappropriate to start any story about me without talking about my family. We are an oddly codependent group and the picture of heteronormative middle-class efficiency. Both of my parents are Black Americans, born and raised in New York City. They met at a tiny liberal arts college less than a mile from the hospital I was born in and married in their midtwenties. All their college friends got married within the same two weeks in 1980. They are all still friends.

An awful lot of planning seemed to go into establishing the Prescod unit. My parents waited eight years before having children. They got a dog first, a yellow Labrador named Apollo. Finally, after those extended honeymooning years, my parents had me. Then, twenty-one months later, they had my sister, Gabrielle. We are so close in age that I cannot remember a life before her arrival. We are constant companions, barely conscious of our individual identities, defined by our relationship to each other. And with her birth, our foursome was complete, perhaps fueled by my parents' obsession with tennis—it is not lost on me that we have a complete doubles group.

My father worked in electrical energy, and my mother, before becoming my mom, was a kindergarten teacher. She has a degree in early childhood education. She dedicated herself to our development and learning in a way that allowed her to utilize her skills as a teacher and a parent. By the time my sister and I arrived, she was a full-time stay-at-home mom. We were never cared for by anyone outside of our family. I never had even a single babysitter. While my cousins had nannies or live-in housekeepers for most of their upbringing, my mom was our everything, and this is perhaps where the codependence set in, because she still is. I feel sick, I call Mommy. I need to know what to put down on a W-9, I call Mommy. I spilled something on the carpet, I call Mommy. In the advent of cellular telephones, my parents got themselves brick-like Nokia devices that my sister and I would regularly ring if we were ever home alone, to the point where, for a good few years, we metaphorically went wherever they went. And to this day, my mom always picks up, no matter what. If she does not answer, rather than wait patiently like a rational person might, I will call her repeatedly until she does.

My father was in the workforce and less accessible to us, so we didn't lean on him as much. Still, while he may not be the one to call in an emergency, my father tailored his work schedule to be able to make it to every recital, graduation ceremony, and major life event with flowers in tow.

My parents were loving but strict. They had traditional ideas about how we should behave and what our responsibilities were as children. Their primary focus was our education, and the expectation was that we would "always do our best," but the subtext was that our best would need to be *the* best, period. Whatever debt we owed them for our relatively stress-free, comfortable lifestyle, we paid in straight As, trophies, and awards. Despite that pressure, my childhood was equal parts privileged and sheltered. I was coddled, surrounded by love and support, and told every day that I was special and capable. I grew up in Westchester County, roughly thirty minutes outside New York City. We lived in an old colonial four-bedroom house with lots of stairs, an attic, and a basement, which was converted into our playroom. It was a white house—but very dirty because my parents never power washed it—with a huge front porch and green trim. And while I did not think of us as "rich" because of the extravagant wealth displayed in our community, I never wanted for anything. I was never hungry or cold. We had birthday parties every year. We went on family vacations. We went to summer camp. We netted obscene amounts of gifts on Christmases and birthdays.

My town was an epicenter for diversity and, historically, was a wonderful place for Black people, which was why my grandparents migrated there from Harlem in the 1960s. According to the 2020 Census, the population breakdown is now 65 percent Black, 20 percent white, and 16 percent Latino. While these numbers suggest that I was surrounded by racial and ethnic diversity, I was not. Growing up, I didn't actually spend much time in my neighborhood. I attended predominantly white private schools in neighboring towns, and my life was the definition of *overscheduled*, shuttling between various sports, hobbies, and activities. My sister and I, instructed early on in the art of competitive extracurriculars, played tennis, soccer, softball, and basketball; danced ballet, tap, jazz, and hip-hop; did gymnastics, figure skating, and horseback riding; and played piano and violin, respectively. I am exhausted even typing all that. Growing up, an extraordinary portion of my life was spent changing outfits in the back seats of cars. My memories of my so-called hometown are limited to trips to the supermarket, bank, post office, or the Black-haircare stores that could not be found anywhere else in Westchester.

Because we went to school and did activities in other towns, we didn't know our neighbors or the other local kids. When we got home at night, we simply did our homework and went to bed, which is why I have difficulty understanding the concept of "hometown"—my hometown is actually many.

In the ninth grade, I transitioned from a small coed Catholic private school to an all-girls Catholic school in Greenwich, Connecticut, an NYC satellite town famous for being a hedge funders' haven. The population of Greenwich is roughly 3 percent Black, and three lonely Black girls staked our representation claim in my high school graduating class of fifty-two. Otherwise, the town is 72 percent white, and the median income hovers around half a million dollars, which is enough to give anyone a complex about money.

The infamous Black conservative troll Candace Owens grew up in Stamford, Connecticut, a town about six and a half miles away from Greenwich. I look at Candace and see a monstrous refraction of what I could have become had I not, at some point, figured out how to embrace my identity. I have always thought of her as a product of our shared environment, and though it may be unpopular, I have empathy for her.

As someone who felt consistently drowned in a sea of Republican hyperbole, let's just say, I get it. Not everyone is able to develop the survival skills that allow them to emerge Black and proud from a place engulfed in white supremacy. It is a struggle that I think deserves patience and grace. As for me, I invented a narrative that I lived in poverty because my white prep school friends had ponies, flew to their vacations on private planes, and never once had to question whether they deserved their place at the top of the food chain. And I, who had plenty but none of that, struggled to find my place among them.

Nearly everyone in our orbit lived the same way. We lived in a house around the corner from the home where my mother grew up. Our world had a lean radius, and I just assumed that *everyone's* lives were quite similar—two parents, two kids (sometimes three), a dog, and a whole host of competitive hobbies. My parents raised us in a way that, I believe, intentionally protected us from trauma. Of course, this is what all parents want for their children, but mine took it to an extreme. My family was both insulated and isolated. My sister and I were each other's playmates and confidants, so the need to attach to other children was reduced by dint of our circumstances. When I started school, Gabrielle snuck into the building so many times at drop-off that she was enrolled in her own daycare program.

On the face of it, our social circles were diverse. My parents' lifelong college friends were an amalgamation of interracial couples. We understood adoption early, as not every family we knew was established traditionally. And yet, of all the various kids we played with, each came from two-parent households with a mother and father who were still married and had similar economic circumstances to my family. It was a bubble. I was in college when I learned that American Girl dolls—a toy line that featured a classic Token Black Girl, the Addy doll—were actually a status symbol of wealth and, for lack of a better word, clout. Every girl I knew growing up had one, and it never even occurred to me that this was unusual. The dolls themselves cost upward of one hundred dollars, but I didn't yet understand that it was an "expensive" toy and what that might mean for a child who could not buy in.

Because I had a very American rearing, many of my interests were about acquiring more stuff—bigger, better, nicer stuff. At the height of the Furby craze, one girl in my fourth-grade class received seven of them—seven Furbys just for her! The acquisitions matured as we did, starting out, innocently enough, with Tamagotchis and, by high school, progressing to Louis Vuitton bags. Most of my friends got cars on their sixteenth birthdays. While I didn't have my own car, there were three in our household that I could request to use at any time. And this capitalist homogeny helped me relate to my peers. We might not have looked the same, but we had the same things and roughly the same experiences.

My parents would often say that they raised us to be "colorblind." They didn't want us to be spooked by the kinds of white people who would inevitably become our friends and school peers. As a family, we never discussed race, Blackness, or identity explicitly, unless the outside world made it absolutely necessary. If something inflammatory was said at school or something culturally relevant was said on TV, we had a talk. In the late 1990s, when I saw a Black man walking down the street and said, "There's a thug!" my mom seemed genuinely horrified. It was language I undoubtedly picked up from the biased news. My mom reprimanded me, telling me never to say that again. She did not, however, launch into any kind of historical retelling of how the representation of Black men as dangerous and criminal has been harmful. She simply told me that using the word *thug* was wrong. In fact, what she said was, "How would you feel if someone called Daddy a 'thug'?" And my answer, coated in naivete, was, "But Daddy looks like a nice man. Why would anyone do that?" Years later, commuting on the train, my father, a "nice-looking" but Black man, was thrown against the wall by NYPD in a mistaken-identity stop and frisk.

As for any discussion of race as it directly related to me, the topic almost always embarrassed me. The subject seemed more taboo than sex. My family had frank discussions about bodies, boundaries, and autonomy, but for whatever reason, I was not able to do the same about race. I sensed that it was an uncomfortable topic for all parties.

Family members, my grandfather in particular, who were born and raised in the Jim Crow South, crafted a narrative around Blackness that frightened me. In his dining room, under the dozens of Ivy League diplomas his children had earned, was a framed poster of a slave ship. And nearly every time my sister and I visited, he would force us to look at it, describing how people were packed on top of each other during the Middle Passage from western Africa to the modern-day United States. I still don't have the language to articulate the way it made me feel, but on some level, I had a phobia that the same fate could befall me. I realize this sounds dramatic. My grandfather was simply an enthusiastic educator. He, like most men of his generation, thought it was of the utmost importance to instill both knowledge and pride into his offspring—and me, a child who was, at best, indifferent about her identity. When I learned that my grandfather's grandparents were slaves, the leap from "that could never be me" to "that is me" narrowed to a small hop, and I did not like that proximity to both suffering and such a humble status. I wanted people—white people especially—to view me as equal, if not superior. I avoided racial discussions entirely. I swallowed my medicine while visiting my grandparents and shook my grandfather's words out of my head when it was time to go back to school. I was terrified to bring white people around him, lest my grandfather start "educating" my friends.

He often retold stories about growing up in Savannah, Georgia, expressing his frustration about being restricted to library usage on only the "colored day," Wednesday, during reduced hours. He wasn't allowed to borrow books, so he had to sit in the library and cram as much enjoyment as he could into three hours. Meanwhile, in my childhood bedroom, I had my own library, so to speak—entire book series spilling off the shelves. I could not and did not want to imagine a world where that wouldn't have been possible.

My grandfather's thirst for learning fueled much of his passion, and he graduated from college after serving in the US Navy. We grandkids called him the Number Giant, as in addition to his signature history lectures, he would also randomly throw math equations at you and expect them to be solved. His kids, my mother and her three brothers, were forced to bring home their schoolbooks every single night and read ahead at his behest. He tried to encourage this in the grandkids as well, but that particular brand of doing the most didn't catch on. My grandmother, his wife, was also a college graduate, and they sent their children to the best schools they could, so they, too, could graduate college, painting an American dream that was our job as the next generation to maintain. I never had the pressure of being "the first" in my family, but the pressure of Black Excellence was certainly ingrained. It was expected that we would perform to a certain standard, especially considering the many obstacles to success that had been removed from our lives. "Your job is school," my father would always say, and we were always handsomely rewarded for both good grades and good behavior.

My mother kept our lives organized and our days structured. By the time I arrived in kindergarten, I could already read. In my earliest years, I went to public school on an accelerated path. In the third grade, I was shuttled to the sixth grade for reading and social studies. This earned me nerd status and marked the beginning of my being a pariah at school. I was teased for my speech pattern and vocabulary, which I didn't mind. I chalked it up to an occupational hazard of being a baby genius. And anyway, I was a snobby little show-off. It never occurred to me that I needed to confront any racial differences between me and my classmates or friends. It was around this age that other children's suggestion that I *thought I was white* began to stick.

In fact, before my grandfather's speeches began, I was one of those children who assumed they were white for an embarrassingly long time, by virtue of being in denial and because I was always looking at white people. I also often interacted with Black people who reflected quintessential elements of whiteness, especially in their mannerisms and dress. In my defense, I hadn't grasped the notion that racial differences existed, or that they could be tied to identity. One of the benefits of having a mind like mine, so anchored in imagination, was the ability to see the world in any way I wanted. What I wanted was a raceless world, and that's what I made. Except in that world, whiteness represented neutrality, and *raceless* meant white. My understanding of myself as an individual was one that was firmly anchored in whiteness. When my mom was excited to see my kindergarten self-portrait on her class visit, she found, instead, a life-size blonde-haired, blue-eyed cartoon rendering with the name "Danielle P." under it.

That portrait has become somewhat of a running joke in our family. My mother, circa 1993, asked me how she would know how to find my portrait, and I confidently responded, "You'll know!" I'd been so sure of both my artistic prowess and my accurate depiction of reality. She was shocked and confused seeing a me who did not look anything like me. It's a story that I still get teased about at home. My mom, with all her early childhood expertise, gently said, "Is this what you look like?" To which I replied, "Of course, Mommy." Mercifully, she did not use that moment to rock my little world. I imagine that in the same way you don't cruelly reveal to a six-year-old that Santa Claus doesn't exist (apologies if this is news to you), it is difficult to clarify the complexities of race and identity to an otherwise naive mind.

My parents are practical people, not emotional ones, and their decision to disengage with my fantasy was not rooted in some psychological strategy. They expected, and they were right, that I would simply grow out of it. So, since no one told me differently, I went on believing that I must have looked like the things I saw and most liked: my best friends (white), Disney princesses (mostly white), and news anchors (don't ask, and also white). Even years later, when I actually did begin to recognize and acknowledge my brown skin, I still struggled to choose what would be the most appropriate crayon. Am I Burnt Sienna, Sepia, or Chestnut? The colors from the giant 120 Crayola pack gave me panic sweats in art class.

In a 2018 article for the *Outline*, writer Melinda Fakuade describes the self-portrait tradition as it applies to children of color in school. Understanding the concept of self is paramount to the kindergarten educational experience, and being able to express it artistically means that a child has developed a concept of themselves as an individual. She writes:

> The kids are meant to select the colors of their choice to create the best reflection of themselves that their baby brains can muster. It's an odd exercise for children of color, who have likely already begun internalizing the idea that they look different in a way that is rarely celebrated. Their parents, teachers, and friends may praise them, but the surrounding world is heavily filled with images where beauty is communicated as a mostly white ideal. How should they illustrate how they feel on the inside? It's an often undetectable, but present conflict for young kids of color: draw yourself with ethnic features, and admit belonging to a group of "others," or draw yourself as with Caucasian features, in order to more closely align with a so-called image of beauty.

Ignorance, truly, in this case, was bliss, and the adults in my life let me float on in the world, not bothering to interrupt my peaceful reverie about how I looked until I was unexpectedly shoved into the deep end of race relations. And no one had bothered to teach me how to swim.

At the start of fourth grade, I transferred to a new school, a private one a few towns away, with roughly twenty kids in my class, all of them white, save for one Indian boy and one other Black girl. I was an extremely shy kid, never wanting to draw attention to myself unless I was in complete control of the situation (I rehearsed ballet until my feet bled—that kind of control), but I never had a problem making friends. I acclimated to my new environment quickly and was accepted by the so-called popular girls in my class. This put a target on my back, and some of the other girls set out to knock me down a few pegs. I became the victim of a three-way-call attack, a phenomenon made infamous by *Mean Girls* years later. I was ahead of the curve, I suppose. In three-way-call warfare, two people talk on the phone and a third person secretly listens in. The objective is to gather information. Among preteen girls, secrets are valuable currency. The motivation is almost always sinister. The conversation, as it was relayed to me, went something like this:

Girl 1: Do you like that new girl, Danielle P.?

Girl 2: I don't like her because she's Black.

Girl 3: (silently scheming on the phone to destroy Girl 2 with this information later)

The gossip spread slowly through the entire class. Finally, Leslie—one of the girls on the call—feigning concern, relayed to me that Kristen did not like me because I was Black. I gave a lackluster response because I had no idea how I should react. It was the first time I had been called "Black," and I couldn't comprehend what it meant. I gathered that I was supposed to be upset, angered even, but I was so numb to the truth that I had no reaction at all. I didn't know how I got to be Black, and I didn't know how to not be Black. But I gathered that Black must be negative, especially if it was a reason not to like someone. I also understood that it must somehow be specific to me. *"Don't like her because she's Black."* *Because* and *Black*. Well, by any straightforward logic, this clearly meant that I should just undo it. At least then I could be liked, which was all I ever wanted anyway. As soon as I figured out what Black was and how to undo it to myself, I would be fine, back to fitting in seamlessly at school, and otherwise enjoying my life.

Months later, wiser to the intricacies of female friendships, I discovered the whole thing had little to do with me and everything to do with a power struggle between Kristen and Leslie, who were enemies vying for a position as queen bee. News of "The Call" became the scandal of the fourth grade. Parents, teachers, and even the principal got involved, and if I didn't care before, I cared then. There were several calls and meetings among the parents. All three girls involved had to apologize to me, which was hopelessly awkward and did nothing to change the chasm of inequality that had formed between us. They sheepishly approached me one by one, under the guidance of our teacher. I don't think any of us held eye contact. I kept my eyes fixed on the floor, and so did they, as they apologized and I whispered, "OK," in response. I was the harmed party and, somehow, I felt sorry. I felt shame. They were white. I was Black. They had the power to like or not like me because I was Black. And I had been working with this new vocabulary for only a few days.

It was humiliating to know that everyone at school had been talking about me, and embarrassment is one of my top three least favorite emotions. I couldn't believe everyone had known I was Black *but* me, but I was especially miffed to find myself in such an unfavorable minority. Since it became clear to me that I had no hope of correcting being Black and returning to the blissful, widespread popularity I had gained, I was in distress. I had enjoyed being "the new girl." I did not enjoy being "the Black girl." It tinged my social standing with negativity and drew attention to something I could not control. As a control freak, this was a nightmare. I became insistent on rejecting Blackness wherever I could.

I shut down pretty quickly after that three-way call sent a sonic boom through the fourth grade. It was my first experience truly being lonely. My parents did their best to explain what was happening, finally forced to confront my delusions with the enormously cumbersome subject of race. They were tentative at first, asking me mostly how I felt about the situation, but I didn't want to talk about it. At all. I didn't know how to tell them how uncomfortable and embarrassed I was. My parents wanted to use this unfortunate event as a teaching opportunity and tried to fill our home with more Black traditions and imagery. Over the next few months, they flew into Black-and-proud mode, hoping to get me to claim Blackness in a positive way. They took my sister and me to a local store in White Plains called That Old Black Magic, where Black artwork and iconography were in abundance. We started celebrating Kwanzaa, which I snubbed so adamantly that my father bribed us with one hundred dollar bills to participate. I still would not. By that time, my opinion of Blackness as something shameful had already been nurtured and solidified. I became extremely resistant. I learned the phrase "I'm fine" and employed it ad nauseam. I was very much not fine, but I did not know how to say that. I didn't know how to tell my Black parents that the thing that made us alike, the thing they seemed to be proud of, I didn't want. And so my rebellion manifested in the way that it often does for spoiled children: a bad attitude.

Whatever positive associations my parents were trying to build at home were not being replicated at school, and this inconsistency did nothing to improve my personal feelings on being Black. In the early and mid-1990s, there was no such thing as Black Girl Magic, or there was, but we did not have a way to express it. I didn't. We did not have hashtags and digital communities built on uplifting one another. I didn't know where I could find anyone who could relate to my particular issues. This is part of the isolation of tokenism. In school, we did not make a point of studying Black heroes on a regular basis. When popular books, shows, and movies depicted Blackness, they did so negatively, as something to be avoided. It is difficult for Black children to align themselves with positive associations that the outside world is not supporting. Dr. Dena Phillips Swanson, a professor from the University of Rochester, points out in the same *Outline* article, "Our curriculum in school does not validate black children's sense of self-worth." As a result, children are left with glimpses of Blackness through an already racist lens. She continues, "Our youth are left to make inferences on their own in terms of what it means to be black, based on other experiences and exposure they may have." And while schools might have the opportunity to do this at present, they are too busy finding ways to outlaw critical race theory to make it a real priority. For my own experience, my school completed requisite Black History Month education and nothing beyond that. We learned about Martin Luther King Jr. and no one else. If a boy wanted to report on a sports figure like Jackie Robinson, for example, we would hear his interpretation of Robinson's life, but why would any of them bother when there was Babe Ruth?

In 1940, Doctors Kenneth and Mamie Clark performed a study to demonstrate the negative effects of segregation on school-age children, commonly known as the Doll Test. The doctors presented Black children aged three to seven with dolls that were identical in every way except for skin color, then proceeded to ask the children questions like, "Which doll is most like you?," "Which doll do you prefer?," and "What race is this doll?" Overwhelmingly, the children preferred the lighter-skinned dolls. In a 1985 PBS interview, Dr. Kenneth Clark said, "The Dolls [sic] Test was an attempt on the part of my wife and me to study the development of the sense of self-esteem in children. We worked with Negro children—I'll call black children—to see the extent to which their color, their sense of their own race and status influenced their judgment about themselves, self-esteem."

This inferiority complex, uncovered in 1940 in a study that was then repeated several times and as recently as 2010, is a time-honored phenomenon, thanks in no small part to the influence of white supremacy and the media itself. Most children's worlds are small. They are home, they go to school, and they occasionally run errands or do activities. For the most part, they are not exposed to much outside their immediate surroundings. How is it, then, that a child as young as four comes to determine that a white doll is more preferable than a Black doll? They can learn this concept in direct ways, through racist parents or grandparents, for example, or they can learn it in roundabout ways, from how children are depicted in books and on television to what their own dolls and community look like. From this study, it is evident that Black children adapt to a preference for whiteness, and this preference might dictate how they feel about themselves and others.

After the conversation from the phone call was revealed to me, I remember that the reality of Blackness settled onto me like a terminal illness. I desperately wondered how I could get rid of it so I could just be like everyone else. It distressed me that I would never be "cured" of it and could never escape it. And it would always be outwardly visible. Blackness had painfully ostracized me, at least at school, which, at nine years old, was my entire world. Over the next year or so, I submissively accepted my fate and dealt with it by attempting to minimize what I saw as my own personal plight as much as possible. I never spoke of race to my friends. It was an invisible canyon that hung between us. I would stiffen myself every Black History Month, the one time of year we discussed the struggles and accomplishments of Black people at any considerable length, meaning roughly the twenty days we were in school out of twenty-eight.

Around this age, I explored many ways of altering my appearance. I started trying "diets"—really just refusing to eat certain foods. I took a greater interest in my clothing choices and hairstyles. It brought me immense comfort to be in control of the way I looked, but the one thing I could never control or change was my skin. My skin, this thing I was newly aware I was living in, was a sadistic tower to which I was confined for life. In contrast, I don't believe my white friends thought very much about their skin at all, and as an adult, I've come to realize that this encompasses the thorny concept of privilege. I saw my skin as a massive disadvantage. Even though I never felt I was in grave danger because of it, it plagued me every day of my life as a child, and it was something my white friends never even had to think about.

Now that I have more Black friends and people in my life, they grill me on the delusion that I could have ever been anything but Black. In a 2019 article for the *Atlantic* on Black children's attendance at predominantly white schools, Dani McClain writes, "Not all children so gracefully develop survival strategies that allow them to participate in predominantly white schools while also resisting and even transforming the culture." Aya de Leon, an activist and parent, is one of the many mothers quoted in the same story: "In these white environments, you're being harmed, and you don't even know it because you think there is something wrong with you. [You think] if only you could get these white people to like you, then everything would be OK." This was the exact methodology I was compelled to adopt. I have considered this often over the years, and the only explanation I can muster is this: you can believe anything you want to believe; a creative person's most practical talent is getting other people to see things their way, no matter what the truth is. I found myself blessed with the gift of persuasion, and I directed the world around me to be exactly what I wanted. Eventually, of course, the magnitude of the truth will crush whatever silly fantasy has been nurtured, but until that fatal point, anything is possible.

Once I had to accept reality, I did the only thing I thought I could do: I minimized the importance of race in my life and sought to assimilate by worshipping at the altars of the same things my white friends did. It was fundamental to my social survival that I fit in by whatever means necessary. Then I did the second-best thing: I diverted the attention.

In this same fourth-grade class, we had journals we were supposed to write in every day. Our entries were intended to be about school assignments, but I guess you could have written whatever you wanted. Each student's journal was kept in a stack on a shelf in our classroom. I waited for my opportunity, and one day, at the end of class, I slipped James's journal inside my backpack and took it home. A thin, white, nerdy boy who was regularly picked on, James was an easy target. In my bedroom, I let the pages of his marble notebook spread out on my pale pink carpet. Inside was a goldmine of his most precious secrets. One entry in particular caught my attention, about how much he liked the tallest girl in our class—easily the most mismatched pair that could ever be. I absorbed all the contents, all his deepest desires, then went back to school the next day, slipped the notebook back on its shelf, and told absolutely everyone what I'd read. I started spilling first to the girls I considered my best friends, a quintet that usually controlled the energetic temperature of the class. Then we told the boys. The tall girl was on the fringes of the social circle, and in both physical stature and interests, she stood out. We decided to clue her in by asking her if she liked James back, giving her an opportunity to reject James while gaining some social cache in being on the receiving end of a crush. We also informed her that she was a topic of a class-wide discussion, the very thing I was running from. It was a terrible thing to do, but I needed to create a target that wasn't myself. I needed to escape the negative attention that was coming my way as a result of The Call. And I also wanted to feel powerful. My power had been taken, and I wanted some back.

The fallout of this was *epic*. Word spread fast, and someone told James that his crush was not returned. He cried. Sobbed, really. The teasing that resulted was monstrous. His mom called everyone—our teacher, the principal, my mom. I got in so much trouble. My parents were disappointed that I would do something so cruel, and I was disappointed that I got caught. I was not, however, sorry. My mom always favored the kind of discipline that comes from conversation, but my father was in favor of the corporal kind. I got spanked. The intention was to teach me a lesson—not to steal, not to snoop, and not to share secrets. I suspect everyone might have been forgetting that *Harriet the Spy* was adapted into a film starring Michelle Trachtenberg just a year prior; I was obviously taking my cues from somewhere. In the end, I may have been punished, but I got what I wanted. The class moved on to a new scandalous subject and forgot all about my Blackness. And from there, I didn't get nicer. I just got smarter.

CHAPTER TWO

If it's not clear by now, the way I grew up was substantially centered around whiteness. Busy trying—at all costs—to avoid the unwanted pressure of being one of two Black girls at school, you'd think I might have sought out avenues that presented a more diverse world. But all the books I read and movies and television programs I watched heavily featured white characters. It felt jarring to read a book where a character was identified as Black. In the 1990s, any time "African American" characters were called out, it was with stilted and formal language, but aside from calling out the fact of their race, few other details about those characters were deemed significant enough to be mentioned. I know this because I read and watched *a lot*. I read a lot because reading was encouraged by my parents and teachers, and I watched a lot of anything my parents approved of. For getting straight As, we were taken to Blockbuster and allowed to check out any age-appropriate movies we wanted, and everything else, I watched in secret. When I was eight, the film adaptation of the Roald Dahl book *Matilda* was released. I've always thought of myself as a witch, but wow, being a witchy genius seemed fab. After witnessing Matilda's Mensa status, I forced my mom to get me the book *Moby-Dick* so I, just like Matilda before me, could read it. I slogged through the tome for months, retaining almost nothing because it was published in 1851 and I was in the third grade, but

I was not going to be bested by Matilda Wormwood, so I finished it. While Herman Melville is not an easy, breezy read, I devoured books like Louisa May Alcott's *Little Women* or anything Beverly Cleary wrote. My white friends were consuming the same media and were also using it to develop their opinions of themselves and of the world as a whole. Many of them didn't know any people of another race, save for the few of us kids of color they interacted with at school. While it wasn't fair to place the representation of an entire group of people on a child, no matter—movies, TV, and books were there to pick up the slack. The inequalities my peers perceived in real life were then hammered home by various forms of media. Each of us formed opinions of ourselves and one another that were dictated by racism.

The group of friends I hung out with were all "horse girls," and we devoured an incredibly niche series called Thoroughbred about girls growing up on horse-racing farms in Kentucky. I would spend my birthday money acquiring between five and eight of the books at a time, whenever there were newly issued additions to the neatly numbered set. And my group of friends would race each other to get the most current editions because, of course, even leisurely reading was a competition.

We were obsessed with Francine Pascal's Sweet Valley High books as well. Sweet Valley, the fictional town in California where the over 150 Sweet Valley High novels take place, is an implied utopia. Anything wrong in Sweet Valley can be solved in two hundred pages or fewer. It is a sterile, protected world where the Wakefield sisters, Jessica and Elizabeth—twin girls with "shoulder-length blond hair, blue-green eyes, and perfect California tans"—are the centers of their respective universes. The language was upbeat and romantic. I wanted to get lost in this world, over and over again. I just never saw myself in it. The books emphasize the sisters' Aryan physicality and top the description off with a flourish: "Each wore a gold lavaliere around her neck—matching presents from their parents on their sixteenth birthday." Their sartorial differences are emblematic of their personalities. "Elizabeth's style was more sophisticated and preppy, while Jessica's was up-to-the-minute trendy." But the real kicker is why Jessica did not wear a watch, while Elizabeth did: "Time was never a problem for Jessica. She always felt that things didn't really start until she arrived." The sisters are depicted as bastions of beauty, wealth, and confidence. The books telegraph that the internal brilliance of these twins was deserved because of their outward appearance and simultaneously fortified by it.

When I got a bit older and became more driven by curiosity, I sought out books that featured Black characters on the covers. One day, I made the mistake of reading *Rain* by V. C. Andrews, who uses soap opera–like plotlines and scandal to drive her narratives. I picked up *Rain* from the library after seeing a girl with brown skin and big, curly hair on the cover. I thought she was beautiful.

Rain Arnold was one of the first Black protagonists I ever encountered. She speaks of herself with a detached, almost scientific quality: "Some of the girls resented me anyway because of my looks . . . My hair was straighter, richer than most. I had a creamy caramel complexion, never bothered much by acne. I also had light brown eyes, more toward almond, with long eyelashes." The important subtext of this description is that Rain is mixed race. To a mature reader, the red flags of colorism are apparent. The climax of the story comes with the revelation that Rain is biracial when she discovers the true origin of her family. A white woman wrote that description, which largely recalls Eurocentric beauty ideals: straight hair, light skin, almond eyes. It whispers to the reader, just as Francine Pascal did while describing the Wakefield twins, "Value this." Rain's looks ostracize her in the Black community and even in her family, to the point that she is fearful and timid—the opposite of what Jessica and Elizabeth experience in their white community. Rain says, "I was afraid to wish for anything good. Nice things had to happen to us accidentally, by surprise. If you wish for something too hard, I thought, it was like holding a balloon too tightly. It would simply burst, splattering your dream into pieces of nothing."

At age ten or eleven, Rain's general lack of confidence, her rejection of good fortune, and her discomfort with her own appearance were a nightmare that felt so familiar. The Wakefield twins presented themselves as the center of the world, while Rain shrank into hers. It was too real for me, already a shy kid. I needed to learn how to show up in the world, not how to hide from it.

Rain's younger sister, Beni, has darker skin, a different hair texture, and a bigger body. Andrews goes on to describe her with subtly coded language: "She had a bigger bust than I did and liked to keep a button or two undone or wear tighter clothes," and "she was wider in the hips," a trait that made another character identify her as a "tramp." As for Rain, her "lips were thinner" and her "nose was straighter and more narrow," undoubtedly a nod to her more elegant Caucasian heritage. Beni, we come to understand, does not think she is pretty at all. In fact, neither girl thinks of herself as pretty, and by the way, the darker, curvier sister is a "tramp." Awesome. If this is triggering in any way, I apologize. It is for me too. It is, effectively, the road map of how I learned to hate myself.

Compared to Jessica Wakefield exploring her own reflection in the Sweet Valley High book *Secrets*, the difference is startling: "Her shoulder-length blond hair looked perfect, not a strand out of place, and her new blue eyeliner really brought out her stunning Pacific blue eyes . . . She looked perfect today, she *knew*." The repetition of the word *perfect* is telling. Jessica looked perfect and she knew it; meanwhile, Rain could barely make eye contact with anyone. The distance between these characters was more than geographical, and I knew exactly who I had to emulate.

In stark contrast to the sunny privilege of Sweet Valley, the connection Andrews forged between Black characters and poverty disturbed me, though I had no idea that it was, perhaps, a reflection of how a white author interpreted Black life. All I knew was the Wakefield sisters made me feel happy and hopeful. They had boyfriends and cars and their own phone lines. The Arnold sisters made me feel sad. They had nothing. I was dealing with my own preteen angst, and if my diary from that time is to be believed, I was already suffering enough. It's no wonder I dissociated from Black characters.

In my fifth-grade class, we had to read according to a monthly theme and present a book report to our fellow students. I was already reading more than your average kid, so this was not an issue for me. I loved bookstores. Going to Borders or Barnes & Noble felt special, and I was always satisfied with my purchases. My mother did not like these kinds of chores. She was never someone who seemed to get high off the pleasures of consumerism; it was as if she was immune to the euphoria of a successful shopping trip, except for at the supermarket. My best friend's mother mentioned that she was going to Borders and could pick up a book for me to read. The stay-at-home moms did things for each other like this: bought bulk shin guards when it was soccer season, stocked up on poster board to share, just in case. I overheard my mother tell this woman to make sure to buy me a book written by someone Black. Our class had been instructed to read an autobiography, so while most girls would probably do something like *The Diary of Anne Frank*, my mother ensured that my report would be, at the very least, culturally educational for me.

I was given the book *The Diary of Latoya Hunter: My First Year of Junior High School*. I likely would have selected something different— something centering a white person, no doubt. Gravitating toward whiteness was already an unconscious habit of mine, but since I was denied the opportunity to choose for myself, I became destined to read about Latoya. The book was the first-person account of a girl living in the Bronx and her experiences entering a new school. Since I, too, would be entering middle school the next year, it was valid to assume that I would enjoy a preview of what it might be like. Except I thought junior high might be like *Saved by the Bell*. Granted, Scarsdale, an East Coast standard "village," where my school was located, was nothing like television's sunny Californian Bayside, but the depiction of Latoya Hunter's Bronx school both stunned and terrified me. I imagine it would have been easier for me to digest the Anne Frank autobiography. If nothing else, at least so much more time had passed since World War II. Latoya's story was literally and figuratively too close to *my* home.

The diary was written by a girl, almost the same age as I was at the time, in a place less than twenty miles from where I read it. I had been to the Bronx many times; my paternal grandmother lived there. I hadn't understood it to be a dangerous place. One day, when I was around eight, my grandmother let my sister and me walk to the bodega on the corner alone, and when we later proudly recounted our exercise in independence to our mother, she flew into a rage, the likes of which I hadn't seen before and haven't seen again since. My mother was furious that my grandmother would take such a reckless risk. "But we aren't babies!" I said, urgently pressing for my mom to see us as mature beings, capable of running a simple errand. A few years later, a teenage girl was kidnapped in front of that same store. She was snatched by strangers and thrown into a car. Call it generational trauma, but my absolute worst fear—and it still lingers in me today—is being taken. After reading through Latoya's experiences, I finally saw some of the dangers my mother feared.

Latoya's story required a lot of unpacking. Her unmarried teenage sister got pregnant and had a baby over the course of the year she spent writing. I wasn't fully clued in to the mechanics of sex yet, but I definitely knew it was a naughty thing to do, and especially salacious if you weren't married. Latoya went to a party in Brooklyn for "under twenty-five" youths, which sounded intense for someone not even in high school. She stayed out until 5:00 a.m., whereas I could barely keep my eyes open until midnight on New Year's. My own diary features an entry from when I was twelve and tried to convince my parents to let me go to the movies without adult supervision. I still can't recall when they amended those rules.

Latoya's description of her house made me flinch, just like reading about Rain's life did. And mostly because her unhappiness is palpable. "I live on a street where everything seems so ugly to me. The sidewalks, the houses, even my own house. From the outside, it looks really broken down. It needs everything done to it to improve it. The inside is really small. It has three bedrooms, the smallest one mine. I can hardly move around in it. I would say it's the best the family could do right now, but I don't believe it. I'm sure there's a better place for us; it's just no one seems to be looking for it right now."

Latoya had a hyperbolic way of looking at the world, typical of teenage girls, especially when writing in their diary. A clamorous chorus of *me, me, me* reverberated through her writing as she detailed her frustrations and feelings. The deepest embers of my Leo soul were fanned by that, but her homelife was ultimately too foreign to my own experience, and I found it deeply troubling. She spoke of intense violence with a chilling nonchalance: "My friend Lisa wasn't as lucky with brothers as I was. Her brother was shot 12 times just the other day." Latoya's own father was held at gunpoint, a neighbor stabbed. It is unfathomable to think of a twelve-year-old processing so much trauma, yet the diary was an account of her everyday. I was the kind of kid who did not want to read about anything ugly—why would I when I could just read about nice things instead? And, frankly, the possibility that her life could be my life shook me forcefully. I turned on her, and I hated the book. I had, by this point, begun to realize that when people thought about the lives of Black girls, Latoya's was what they imagined.

I understand now that this was an exercise in empathy by my mother, an attempt to get me to relate to a Black girl the way I did to, say, Ashleigh, the lead in the Thoroughbred books. My identity crisis was unnerving to observe, I am sure. It distressed me, though, to be connected to this much pain and suffering, especially with no triumphant story arc that sees Latoya sprung from the Bronx into the big house she dreams of. I guess I was supposed to understand that not everyone lives like the girls in Stoneybrook, Connecticut, or Scarsdale, New York. But I did not want to understand this. I wanted to bury it. Even more problematically, I had to report on this book to a class composed almost entirely of white students led by a white teacher, of course, giving them a glimpse at a Black experience that I did not know how to reconcile, and perhaps providing them with the only example of a Black girl that they might encounter, besides me, for a while. The cover jacket featured a description that read, "Her story is, of course, typical of girls like her, and it is also unique. It is affirmative, inspiring, moving, human, real." I had no idea that the covert messaging of the phrase "girls like her" meant girls like *me*. There was no room for a layered Black experience; it was all the same: tragic and traumatic. And in Latoya's case, it didn't happen in 1942; it was happening in real time, in my time, just next door.

The effect of this literature was not simply to make me feel bad about myself and my Blackness—it did, but that's not the point. The point is the literature I was exposed to established a world where white was good and Black was bad, then used multiple channels to reinforce that over and over again. And since these kinds of stories are produced, edited, and consumed by white people as well as Black people, it becomes a mechanism for white people to further prove and reinforce the idea that they are superior to everyone else. Black characters and their stories were an alternative universe to whiteness, and there was no crossover in the Venn diagram like my life had. The message was clear: look at how poor, how sad, how ugly the Blacks are. Our only value in those stories was that of a cautionary tale. And if audiences are never provided with alternative narratives, with a representation of the true breadth and expansiveness of the Black experience, that is what they will continue to believe.

CHAPTER THREE

As a kid who read a lot and came of age in the "new millennium," I predictably found my way to the Harry Potter universe. I first discovered the Harry Potter books while I was stuck at home from school, recovering from a surgery. The year was 2000, and the first three books dominated international bestseller lists, while the Hogwarts hive waited for the forthcoming fourth addition to arrive in the summer. I spent the next two decades extremely invested in all things Potter, naming our family dog after Harry and even writing many pages of this book wearing Hogwarts sweatpants.

Harry Potter was reimagined for a live-action play in 2015, and the casting of a Black actress as a grown-up Hermione Granger sent shock waves through the internet. The topic raged like a wildfire, with voracious fans digging up the most obscure citations from the entire anthology to prove that it would be literally impossible to see Hermione as anything but white. The arguments among fans over Black Hermione bubbled up so aggressively that author J. K. Rowling took to Twitter to attempt mediation. Twitter is a volatile medium and can prove to be a creative's friend or foe. For the most part, Rowling managed to wrangle fans on her side, but in the middle of 2020, she found herself the recipient of intense backlash after she used the platform—where she has upward of thirteen million followers—to publicly reveal transphobic opinions, much to the dismay of her adoring and devoted audience, myself included. My current gripe, however, is about a tweet she sent five years prior.

Rowling has often revealed new things about characters years after publishing the books. She has taken time to explain details that might be hinted at but are otherwise not explicit—Dumbledore's sexuality, for example: he's gay. This is something you would likely not have assumed had Rowling not clarified. On December 21, 2015, to shut down the petty fighting over Black Hermione once and for all, Rowling tweeted, "Canon: brown eyes, frizzy hair, and very clever. White skin was never specified. Rowling loves black Hermione."

The tweet itself was revelatory, in that it forced people to consider that perhaps they had imagined Hermione wrong all along. White fans hated this.

Rowling's description of Hermione could have been doubly repurposed to characterize me as a child, but growing up, I still saw her as white, and my vision was then solidified by Emma Watson's casting in the films. What I found most curious about Rowling's tweet is, while she says, "white skin is never specified," it rarely is when it refers to white characters. Rowling wrote several Black characters into her book series, and they are each emphatically described as Black. In the first book, *Harry Potter and the Sorcerer's Stone*, she refers to the character Dean Thomas as "a black boy even taller than Ron." And later, readers meet Angelina Johnson, "a tall black girl who played Chaser on the Gryffindor Quidditch team" and is teased by a Slytherin for her hair, which readers can assume is in braids. White skin, on the other hand, is simply the default in the books. The assumption is that a character will always be white, and it would only be necessary to describe skin that was not white, the skin of the *other*.

This is a long-winded Pottermore way of saying that if Rowling had wanted us to know Hermione was Black, we would know. That's not to say she *could* not be Black, but establishing her race almost two decades later seems feeble. Either way, the outcry from fans was an irrational response. For them, changing Hermione's race in 2015 seemed to change something fundamental about her character. Race is never discussed in Harry Potter, except for those brief signifiers to establish diversity, and ironically, it is clear that we are to come away from the Harry Potter books having a deeper understanding of how a hopeless obsession with bloodlines can destroy a society. Still, it matters very, very much to people that Hermione is white.

Apparently, it is too difficult for people—white people—to imagine themselves as embodied by a Black character, but Black children are forced to do the reverse constantly. I pretended to be white characters so often as a kid that I've become an expert. I am uncomfortably old for the *Frozen* movies, but when I saw the animated film in my late twenties, I couldn't help but translate the Elsa-and-Anna dynamic to how I interacted with my own sister. It didn't hurt that, at the time, my sister was in a doomed relationship with a potential psychopath, and I coldheartedly told her that their relationship was both cursed and senseless. Would I have liked that sister pair to have been Black? Yes, it would have been thrilling to watch, but their whiteness did not stop me from being able to relate to the story. I had been doing that my entire life. It is, I suppose, for whatever reason, not possible for white people to do the same. That must be why, when news of the casting of Halle Bailey in the new Disney live-action *The Little Mermaid* was released, riots broke out online. Black Hollywood rushed to her defense, but the anger over the suggestion that an extremely deserving and talented Black girl would be cast as one of the Disney canon's most beloved characters could have very well been the spark that started a race war.

The funny thing is most people consider themselves to be "not racist" because they would not be outraged over a Black Ariel, yet most of them will have a harder time relating to or enjoying Ariel if she is played by a Black girl. Ariel, Hermione, whoever—those characters must be white and remain so. White supremacy demands an expansive dominance over everything, a surety that whatever is not white will ultimately bow to whatever is, producing an inveterate need to see and know characters are white—everyone else must mold themselves around this view. It is restrictive and damaging, placing unrealistic boundaries on what the world really looks like. With media that is made for children, that adherence to the status quo forces young, malleable minds to participate in the erasure of narratives and characters that are not white, and if they themselves are not white, they are made to erase themselves. That's how I ended up drawing a blonde-haired, blue-eyed self-portrait at five. I saw what I liked. I saw what the world liked. I made myself into that.

One of my favorite movies was *A Little Princess*. The live-action film came out in 1995. I was seven years old. The main character, Sara Crewe, was a stylish but benevolent heroine, so generous that she becomes a Jesus-like figure among her boarding school classmates—that is to say, devoutly loved and followed. Goals. In the movie, Sara is portrayed by real-life heiress Liesel Pritzker Simmons (stage name Liesel Matthews), who acted in two subsequent films, then never again. That fact still haunts me. Her performance of Sara was so compelling, I wish she hadn't abandoned her craft, but ultimately, she doesn't need to work at all, so whatever.

If you're unfamiliar with the classic story, here's the SparkNotes version: a young girl, Sara, is sent to a New York boarding school when her wealthy father volunteers to fight in World War I. Sara is given the fanciest suite at school, but she makes a concerted effort to be kind to her jealous schoolmates. Sara's father goes missing and cannot pay her tuition. Instead of throwing her out on the street—since she's a child—the wicked headmistress allows her to stay, but she must work as a servant to pay off her debt.

All the students at the school are white. The story takes place during the early twentieth century, so this isn't historically inaccurate. However, in the film version, there is one Black character: a girl named Becky who is Sara's age and a servant. Becky lives in the attic, dresses in rags, and scrubs the floors after the other girls ruin it with their careless muddy footsteps. Her hair is unkempt, and even worse, she is so abused by the other students and staff of the school that, for most of the movie, her head and eyes remain downcast in contrite genuflection. When Sara is demoted from student to servant, she bunks in the attic with Becky and serves her former classmates. She does so without complaint, and she and Becky form a friendship in their shabby attic retreat.

In the end, Sara's father miraculously returns, adopts Becky, and they ride away from the school in matching white dresses with bows in their neat hair. At this point, I found Becky to be an acceptable character—after the makeover, of course, not before. It is not lost on me that Becky was saved from her lowly station by only the kindness of a wealthy white benefactor, and perhaps this plot element encouraged me to be content in my pet status as the Token Black Girl. I was repulsed by the idea that Becky had to clean up after girls her own age, and again, if this is the only view of Blackness you ever see, it distorts your ability to see otherwise.

That view meant that when I showed up to my friend and neighbor's Upper East Side apartment wearing leggings and carrying a Whole Foods bag, I was asked by the doorman to use the service entrance. As a child, I thought it meant I would have to act in service to my friends. It was a problem magnified by the fact that Addy Walker, the singular Black doll of the American Girl doll universe, was also a slave. How would that Black doll ever be preferable to a white one? Why would I voluntarily pick the slave if I could choose otherwise? I always chose otherwise.

My friends and I so often acted out things from books or movies in the games we would play that I always felt in danger of being assigned roles like Becky, and however limited my power, I pushed so hard against this kind of potential typecasting in how I presented myself that I could have pulled a muscle. Still, I knew there was a limit to how much I could fight. Becky escaped her unfortunate fate by making a useful alliance and upgrading her appearance. That's not too bad. Her trajectory taught me a lot, even though I was haunted by the material reality that I could become Becky at any minute through an unchallenged impulse of one of my peers. I drew the somewhat reasonable conclusion that looking "presentable" would and could serve as protection against both a lifetime of servitude and potential bullying. I never wanted to be Becky, ever. I wanted only to be Sara.

My friends found many ways to make my skin useful. I could play the resident Scary Spice if we were pretending to be the Spice Girls. No matter that I more closely identified with Ginger or Baby—I was to be "Scary" because, duh, the only Black one. I begrudgingly agreed. This same experience was documented on the 2019 Hulu show *PEN15*, where Maya, the singular person of color, is forced by her classmates to be "Scary" and also their "servant" at the same time. At sleepovers, my friends and I would study Spice Girls videos for choreographed dances, and my friends would tease my hair out just to see how big it could get. If this sounds like bullying, it shouldn't. At least, I didn't think of it that way. I knew this was the role I needed to play. I made a silent agreement when I resigned myself to the Token Black Girl role within my friend group, and it often included doing whatever my friends wanted.

In his 1903 book, *The Souls of Black Folk*, W.E.B. DuBois comes to terms with his own Black identity in his New England school. He recalls that he and his classmates bought cheap cards to exchange with each other in a ritual that sounds a lot like what might happen at an insurance conference: "The exchange was merry, till one girl, a tall newcomer, refused my card, refused it peremptorily, with a glance. Then it dawned upon me with a certain suddenness that I was different from the others; or like, mayhap, in heart and life and longing, but shut out from their world by a vast veil." This veil, race, separates him from his friends and classmates, isolating him but fueling his desire for success. DuBois continues after this anecdote to present one of his most famous ideas, double-consciousness: "It is a peculiar sensation . . . this sense of always looking at one's self through the eyes of others, of measuring one's soul by the tape of a world that looks on in amused contempt and pity. One ever feels his two-ness, an American, a Negro; two souls, two thoughts, two unreconciled strivings; two warring ideals in one dark body, whose dogged strength alone keeps it from being torn asunder." Feeling a two-ness is a lot for a kid, and it's much easier to delay those emotions by feeling nothing, to simply continue playing your ascribed role. Assessing yourself through the eyes of white people is a dangerous game, the outcome of which only gets worse the more you play.

When it was time to switch gears from Spice Girls to The Baby-Sitters Club, I was cast as Jessi—a junior club member—who at eleven years old, was two years younger than the main cast of characters. I suppose I was somewhat grateful for this sliver of representation, even though I felt that my personality landed somewhere between Mary Anne and Kristy. But it was better to be Jessi than to be no one at all or to be told that I couldn't participate since no one looked like me. The books tell the junior club members' stories through the different perspectives of the core group of club members, and Jessi was given protagonist status several times over the course of Ann M. Martin's The Baby-Sitters Club series. I actually recognized many of her struggles in my own, but I didn't love the "junior member" status emphasis. Still, I played the parts I was asked to play, resigned to what I was "supposed to be" rather than what I wanted to be. I never said a thing. I didn't believe I deserved anything different. I never felt comfortable enough to properly advocate for myself in a healthy way. Being the only Black girl among all white girls established such a disproportionate imbalance of power that I felt I needed to deny race altogether and accept whatever was offered to me. I didn't begin to find a voice for speaking about my identity until I was well into my twenties, when years of pent-up frustration came roaring to a head and I finally realized I was angry.

The fusion of Blackness with ugliness, poverty, and general negativity was pervasive in all media forms, and I continued to absorb it over and over again, further driving my desire to put distance between myself and being Black. It meant everything to me that I was accepted among my white classmates, that I was seen as "one of them," even though I never really could be. Many girls I grew up with had never had a Black friend before me and probably don't have any Black friends now. I know they would not seek out a friendship with someone Black and that ours were relationships of convenience, much like Becky and Sara in the attic, in that we occupied the same place at the same time. And when they needed me, I was the Token Black Girl. Their worlds do not otherwise intersect with Blackness, and they do not need to.

Growing up, I was told many times that I was not "*Black*," which, loosely translated, means that I am visibly Black but don't have the myriad negative qualities associated with being Black. I was exempt from these qualities in many people's eyes, and this made me swell with corrupt pride. *Thank God*, I would think. *It's all working.* I was being rewarded for my good behavior and my dedication to beauty with the acceptance I craved.

Even as I managed to advantageously disguise my feelings, I developed a certain frustration in being repeatedly assigned roles that I did not ask for, especially ones I didn't feel personally aligned with. I was not able to be myself, or the version of myself I saw as natural, because my skin prison would not let me.

I have a loud laugh. I shriek if I am excited. I had to train myself out of those habits, as doing either in an all-white environment would almost always yield a negative reaction. Try to notice the ways white people look at a group of young Black people in public. Through the collection of that kind of feedback, I learned to just be quieter in general. The difficult thing was that I felt I had no choice in the matter. If I had suggested to one of my white friends that they be Scary Spice or Jessi, well, that would have been laughable. Why would they put themselves in such an impossible box when I was there to be the perfect fit? The fog of privilege made it unfeasible for them to find themselves in any Black character when I was constantly finding myself, no matter how implausible, in white ones.

Oddly enough, considering how hard it was for my white friends to imagine taking on Black roles in childhood, it seems like, now, not a single Halloween or costumed event passes by without the subject of Blackface being raised. The argument that Blackface is not offensive when it is done in celebration and not in mockery is prevalent among white people who darken their skin to become Diana Ross or Michael Jordan for a night. Hideous historical context aside, the practical application of the "Blackface is OK" stance is at the very least faulty because it is wholly nonreciprocal. There is no opposite. The concept of "whiteface" is not even possible. No matter how grand my costume, makeup, or imaginative capacity, I could never have been seen as a white character. It reinforces the presumptions of white supremacy that someone white can try on a new race for a night out, but a Black person can never escape their reality. Blackness is permanent. No matter what, I would always have to explain. "I'm Baby Spice" would have sounded absurd. There was never any question of which role I would play, and I was pretending so constantly that it became oppressive. Since I was good at my roles, though, my despair was imperceptible.

CHAPTER FOUR

My parents signed me up for my first ballet class at three. I was extremely enthusiastic about donning my pink tights, leotard, and slippers. The class itself was recess with musical accompaniment: children struggling to pay attention with limited dexterity and limb control. If you've never witnessed a littles ballet class, it's chaotic, but dance teachers do their best to give it structure and regulation. As you get older, you learn things like the positions, proper French names for steps, differences in music, and how to coordinate your legs to do one thing and your arms to do another. Ballet teaches discipline, spatial and body awareness, and that practice and hard work are critical values for success.

In ballet, one thing quickly becomes clear: there is literally no room for dissent. A strict adherence to a certain standard in looks and performance is essential to how ballet is taught. Similar to martial arts, the uniform you wear for dance class can indicate your skill level, and even novice children are expected to have the same exact tights, leotards, and shoes. For most "littles," this means a ballet-pink bodysuit, tights, and slippers. Ballet pink is a "nude" tone; it's intended to disappear on your flesh. Ballet-pink slippers are supposed to look like an extension of your own foot. When you graduate to pointe shoes, the same principle applies. This, of course, works only if you're white. If you're Black, the color difference shows up starkly and awkwardly, making you unintentionally stand out when the idea is to blend in.

Aside from the attire, a big part of the ballet uniformity comes down to body and hair. George Balanchine, the late ballet genius, is largely responsible for the underweight and bony aesthetic. But from a practical perspective, dancers are generally small because in order to partner properly, you must be lifted. It is much easier to lift a small girl than a large one—that's just physics. The other factor is that size uniformity on stage is considered to be less distracting than having several different body types, and castings are usually skewed to ensure that everyone is the same shape and size. Furthermore, dancers often wear the costume of a performer who came before them, and it's easier to take something in than it is to let something out. The desired body shape is long and lean, and this has been universally accepted as the ideal ballet aesthetic. Many people extend this requisite uniformity to race as well, which is why there are still many stories of Black dancers who are asked to paint themselves white so they don't break continuity with their fellow company members.

Early on in my life, ballet established a necessity to be the same size, shape, and color as my peers. And there was one last area of non-negotiable compliance: hair. Most ballet parents receive a handbook of guidelines for how to best prepare their child for class, and this includes rules about how dancers' hair should be worn. Rules about hair in ballet class are as follows: Hair must be worn in a bun—no bangs. If a dancer has bangs, they must be clipped back or gelled away from the face. The intention is to create an elegant line for the head and neck and to ensure invariability in dancers. Hair accessories are not allowed.

Most dancers—or parents of dancers—will recognize this language. These requirements present a challenge for children who have hair that is not easily manipulated into a traditional ballet bun. Braided or natural hairstyles are strongly discouraged and, in some cases, not acceptable at all. The New York Academy of Ballet, in defense of their rules, notes on their website that "Simplicity is one of the distinguishing characteristics of a truly fine dancer." Strength, technique, and tangible skills are taught in class, but their importance is supported by "being simple in dress." Dance institutions that consider themselves competitive have requirements like these, as these programs are marketed as preparation for dance careers. As the New York Academy of Ballet says, "Showing respect for our art in conduct as well as dress code helps foster the required discipline it takes to learn a classical art." You may think this language is exclusive, and yes, it is. Most dance institutions are. Like schools, prestige is dictated by who you keep out just as much as who you let in. Because of that, students understand that it is their responsibility to follow these rules to the letter. They learn to monitor themselves and their peers. If you are the same size and color, and if you have the same hair texture as everyone else, your anxiety about being able to successfully blend in is greatly reduced. But if your body and hair don't conform, consequences help students understand what is appropriate and what is not. Students who fail dress code or hair inspections can and will be asked to leave class.

Teachers were sometimes offered up as volunteer hairdressers to demonstrate how to make a bun the right way, but that worked only if they already knew how to style the hair in question. All my dance teachers were white. Imagine the humiliation of being asked to leave class because your hair is not properly secured in a bun or having an instructor who has no background in Black hair try to fix yours to fit in. That threat hung over me, so I learned I always needed to show up looking perfect. Further justification of hair restrictions reveals that loose hair is a safety concern: "A proper bun secured tightly to the head is important, especially when turning in class. Hair that is falling out is disruptive to the learning process and is also a safety hazard as pins can fall to the floor." This was pulled from a 2021 iteration of the New York Academy of Ballet website. I don't imagine the message would have been any softer in 1992. So for many years, every single day, my hair was always secured, as to not be "disruptive," in a high bun or a ponytail that I could easily turn into a bun myself. I attended dance classes multiple times a week, so this style became my non-dance look as well. Later, the stress of the elastics started to erode the health of my hair, especially once I started chemically relaxing it so it could be straight all the time.

My mother, bless her, was the one who repeatedly struggled to make me "presentable" for dance. The ritual of haircare is a cherished bonding experience between mothers and daughters, and is an especially tender ritual for *Black* mothers and daughters. I have sat in between several pairs of knees over my lifetime, and that is where I learned the ineffable skills of stillness, pain tolerance, and patience. Perseverance and hard work eventually produced a result one could be proud of. My mother did hair for my sister and me, and I know she had her hair done for her, as did my grandmother before her, and so on. The common thread is that it's an affectionate expression of self-care among women. But it's also a form of education: handing down knowledge about personal grooming and appearance and the importance of both in relation to your gender. It's also a way of communicating that obedience and submission are cherished qualities for women.

I have spent so much time sitting to get my hair done that the number of hours I have logged should surely be repaid to me at some point. Not to mention the countless hours of labor the women who were actually working on my hair logged while I sat there distracted by television, a movie, book, or magazine. It is remarkable to think about how much time I have dedicated to making my hair look a certain way, often manipulating it far past its natural state, and it's hard to say exactly why. It also should be clear by this point that I am somewhat unwilling to change this behavior. Over the years, I have started to value my time more, forgoing hours-long weaves, relaxers, and complicated braid patterns in favor of styles that are simpler and "easier," but no matter what I do, it all takes precious time. Time out of my morning and nightly routines, my pre- and post-workout rituals, my weekends, and sometimes my workdays.

It can take an entire day to wash, dry, and style my hair, and like a beast whose bite I fear, I give it whatever it wants—to a point. And even though I feel like I have rebelled considerably against the requisite sacrifices for my hair, I still would, and I still *do*, alter my behavior to protect my hair.

My first memories of the hair ritual take place in my living room, where my mother bribed my sister and me to sit on tiny plastic play chairs while she wrestled our kinks into something more practical. We had swim lessons every Saturday, and after the pool was the dreaded hair wash and blow-dry. In the 1990s, the tools and products available for Black hair were considerably less sophisticated, so the methods were crude. They were also extremely painful. We fought our mother, constantly squirming, wincing, and yelping as the smoke from the blow-dryer billowed out in a hazy cloud, smelling of leave-in conditioner and burning follicles. We incurred burns from combs heated directly on the fire of the gas stove. Eventually, my sister and I developed our capacity for compliance and learned to be both still and quiet. I learned what it felt like to have braids so tight that your scalp bubbled from the stress of the tension. I learned what it felt like to be burned by a hot comb. I learned what it felt like to have a tangled knot so big, it needed to be cut out of your head. The beauty industry has mercifully made some serious advancements in haircare, so I am not worried for my future daughters, but they really will have no idea what they missed.

Having your hair "done," and the idea that your hair should be "undisruptive" for your appearance to be acceptable, is a concept that extends far past ballet class. While watching the 1996 cult favorite *The Craft*—a movie beloved by the style obsessed and those who identify as witches—I learned that my hair was wrong and needed to be fixed. I saw the movie when I was ten, about two years after it was released, and I was amused to see the character Rochelle attending a school that looked very much like mine. Rochelle, played by Rachel True, is a star on the diving team and the only Black girl in her school. She's a target for bullying, and the main guilty party is Laura, a blonde who constantly tries to sabotage

Rochelle's diving performance and mentally rattle her. Rochelle makes the grave error of wearing her naturally curly hair to school, and predictably, it doesn't go great for her. In the scene that haunts my nightmares, the girls are in the bathroom when Laura says, while picking up her hairbrush, "Oh God, look! There is a pubic hair in my brush!" She pauses for effect before delivering a lethal blow: "Oh no, wait . . . that's just one of Rochelle's little nappy hairs." Rochelle tries to defend herself in the moment, but Laura brushes her off, telling her, "I don't like negroids" before casually leaving the restroom. It was a grounding interpretation of the potential things a white girl could think or say in regard to natural Black hair. At the time, my hair was often just back in a bun or ponytail, springing free only when I might need it to transform me into Mel B. Don't worry, though; Rochelle gets the last laugh, casting a spell to make Laura go bald, which is the ultimate revenge fantasy. Magical as I am, I knew the likelihood of me nailing a spell like that would be slim, so I decided to perform the only kind of magic I knew—I changed my hair to make sure no one at school would say it was nappy. Also, to this day, I make sure to clean out my shower before my housekeeper comes, lest she think any of my natural hairs are pubic ones.

I grew increasingly frustrated with how different my hair looked from the images I loved to look at in advertisements and print editorials. Images of flaxen, silky, straight hair always ran with copy on how to reduce "frizz" and give your hair "hold." The fact that an entire day at the salon could be undone by one sweaty night's sleep—exactly what happened to me the night before school picture day in the fifth grade—was an unbearable injustice. My mom did her best to replicate how my hair had looked when I left the salon, but the shrinkage and texture at the roots bested us during a morning that was already a time crunch. Those school portraits were never seen again, and whatever I did with them in a fit of blackout rage remains unknown, even to me. I thought my hair in its natural state was "not done." That belief was reinforced by the way every special occasion required a wash and press.

The idea that some people can just rise up from their bed and leave their home without first removing their bonnet or sleep scarf and fixing their hair is still remarkable to me. The "just woke up" thing doesn't exist for Black girls; there are just too many things that must be done to our hair between waking up and leaving our homes.

At some point, I learned what a relaxer was—a perm, as we called it—and began to routinely pressure my mom into letting me get one. How I even discovered the concept is still mysterious. I had no other Black friends to speak of, and I can't remember any snappy television commercial advertising silky-smooth hair as the result of lye either. I must have, at some point, overheard the concept in an adult conversation, and I immediately became a zealot. Sure, I had no idea about the intricacies of the process or the potential side effects, but who cared? I was ten years old and ready to cannonball straight into a pool of mystery chemicals if they gave me what I wanted. All I knew was that a relaxer had the ability to transform my hair from poofy and rough to smooth and straight (so long as it remained dry), and it seemed like the answer to my prayers. I even loved the way the girls looked on the boxes: grinning, with their hair neatly divided into several ponytails fixed with bobbles—a typical Black-girl hairstyle that I banned my mother from giving me, as I was the only one of my friends who would be wearing it. The differentiation was intolerable. One ponytail was fine.

A perm was it. A perm would solve everything. Even more than a Giga Pet, Skechers, and a VTech walkie-talkie shaped like a cell phone, this thing I absolutely *had* to have. My mother was resistant at first. She encouraged me to be satisfied with the washes and presses I was already getting, but since I was constantly in danger of upending the results of a wash and press in a routine gym class, I was desperate for a more permanent solution. I think eventually the promised ease of the perm was the factor that wore my mom down. She had started working part-time, and getting two girls ready for school in the morning could not have been simple. I eventually got what I wanted. My mother agreed to let ten-year-old me and my eight-year-old little sister perm our hair. For years, that age discrepancy plagued me. I had a militant sense of justice. Why wouldn't my sister be required to wait the two additional years that I had to? It seemed that once I crossed a milestone, she immediately was able to do the same.

So we both got our perms on the same day. And for the next ten years, roughly every eight weeks, we would repeat the experience. The first perm was truly like watching magic unfurl. We got our hair done at a friend's cousin's home, about twenty minutes away from where we lived. Eventually, that hairdresser's drug problem became progressively more clear, and we moved on, finding someone else through word of mouth. I always forget what life was like before Google and Yelp. Without a system of stars and reviews, you ended up having your perm done in a living room, where the occasional roach scurried by. I used to ask my mom why I couldn't go to a "nice salon," like a lot of my friends who started getting bangs and layer cuts when we were tweens. My friends and I would sometimes go out for pizza or ice cream near where they got their hair done, and they would point out these places to me, leaving me burning with jealousy. Logic told me those salons were far superior. Unlike where we went to have our hair relaxed, these places had storefronts and receptionists, a setup that actually seemed like you should pay to get your hair done there. I didn't know anyone else who huddled in a tiny plastic chair while Maury Povich blared from the TV screen and a young grandmother chain-smoked in the next room. It felt shameful. I would have been humiliated if I'd ever been found out. I have thoroughly repressed the memory of how I ever even answered the question "Where do you get your hair done?"

For that first perm, though, it didn't matter to me where it happened. I was finally doing it. I was getting a *perm*—the critical key to unlocking an introductory level of beauty, one that I was wolfishly hungry for. There's really nothing like the first time, and since there was no YouTube yet, I had no idea what to expect. Watching the perm potion come together, it was unclear to me whether I was supposed to eat it or spread it on like lotion. Anything was possible! In the end, petroleum jelly was generously applied to my scalp, followed by copious amounts of a thick white substance. The minutes ticked by as I waited to transform before my very own eyes. "The longer you sit with this, the straighter your hair will be. And make sure to tell me when your scalp starts tingling," the hairdresser said. I focused on the words *longer* and *straighter*. I would sit there as long as it took. Turns out, it doesn't take that long. Fifteen minutes and two segments of Maury later, my time was up. I was led over to the kitchen sink, where I had to stand on a booster stool to be able to bend my shoulders and head under the faucet. This was where the transformation would be revealed. Cool water rinsed out the thick white cream and simultaneously erased all my tight, spry, stubborn coils, and in their place fell long, thin strands of perfectly straight hair. I could have peed myself from excitement. It was like a baptism but better. Filled with the holy spirit, I wanted to shout, "I BELIEVE!" If I'd had a more mature mind, I would have understood why people fuss over being reborn. In my limited reality, a new hair texture was life changing. I was led to the makeshift dryer back in the living room and stationed there for an hour. I fantasized about the new life I would have with my straight hair.

I tried to will myself not to sweat under the dryer, knowing that any perspiration could turn this insubstantial dream back into a nightmare. When the dryer dinged off, the hairdresser retrieved me and led me to another chair in the kitchen, where, this time, a hot comb and curling iron were heating on a stove top. My hair singed as it was flattened into submission even further. The stylist gave me a prissy undercurl that took my straight hair and made it incredibly babyish, but I was just ten—an actual baby. But in that moment, I was ecstatic. I had finally achieved a seemingly impossible task: forcing my hair to be perfectly straight. I could not wait for school on Monday. I was finally free to become pretty, and I was thrilled.

CHAPTER FIVE

I vibrated with excitement in my bed that Sunday night. I woke up and prepped for school, gingerly touching my newly straight hair to make sure it was still straight. I was amazed that it actually remained so. I imagined the reaction I would garner when I stepped onto campus. I rehearsed feigning humility and nonchalance. I was sure everyone would be wowed by my new look and impressed with the fact that I had convinced my mom to agree to me getting a perm. A *perm*!

When I arrived at school with my new straight hair, there was absolutely zero fanfare. It was infuriating. After all that stress and effort, not a single person bothered to notice my accomplishment, which was only achieved by the impressive depth of my perseverance and will. White people can be so hard to please. Perhaps they didn't notice, or they just assumed I'd done what I was supposed to do and trained my hair. I was undeterred. I knew the perm was the right decision, and I committed myself forevermore to keeping my hair as straight as possible. This also meant that I developed a distaste for rain, for water of any kind, including but not limited to being splashed, being sprayed, jumping or diving into pools, and water balloons. Whenever we were going on a family vacation anywhere near a body of water, I got my hair braided and felt a sense of freedom in being able to do anything I wanted. With those braids, my activities were not limited by whether they would get my hair wet. My perm allowed me freedom in a specific and limited sense, but I was ill equipped to anticipate the ways in which it would also imprison me.

The upkeep, for one, was intense. The perm needed to be redone every two months, religiously. I could push the edges of this limit if I had no other choice, but it was not recommended because obstinate new growth would sprout at my roots, threatening to expose the whole straight-hair thing as a facade. Over the years, through extensive trial and error, I learned to manipulate my hair to strategically hide new growth if necessary. Additionally, my hair needed to be washed weekly, and every time I washed it, the roots got a little less straight. The exact limitations of a perm's permanence were disappointing. It wasn't going to last forever, and it wasn't ever going to be easy, but for me, nothing in beauty was. Besides, knowing I had to work hard for what I wanted had become a cornerstone of my belief system, so I was happy to put in effort where required if it meant I would get results.

I could tell it confused my friends at sleepovers when I would arrive with a shower cap to cover my hair when I bathed. They constantly questioned it. "So you, like, never wash your hair?" As if daily-washed hair were a new badge I needed to get in Girl Scouts. I tried to explain to them that I washed it once a week, but they thought hair needed to be washed every day. I had unwittingly revealed something unsavory about my hygiene. This gave me a brand-new insecurity, but I wouldn't ruin the perm for anything, so I accepted my new fate: now I was dirty. I just tried my best to make my hair look as good as it possibly could.

My utter determination wasn't always enough to overcome the material reality of having Black hair. "The Rachel," a haircut popularized by a 1995 episode of *Friends*, was a look that would plague my orbit for years. In 1997, before my first perm, it felt like I was living in the apex of Rachel-mania, named for Jennifer Aniston's character. Even though I didn't watch the show, by sheer osmosis, I knew what the haircut looked like. Rachel was the pinnacle of 1990s beauty, and that haircut was the only thing anyone could talk about for several years. It was as if the hallways were incessantly whispering, "The Rachel."

Girls my age started experimenting with "highlights" and "layers" to give them an edge of maturity. When I was still reeling from the emotion of having my hair straightened, The Rachel added a level of pressure to do even more, and it sent me into a virtual tailspin. I knew I could never have The Rachel, so I turned on it, enraged by the mere existence of the thing. The idea of blunt, choppy layers is just not something that translates to a 4C curl pattern without chemical treatment and even more grueling daily management, or extensions. In essence, it would require such extensive manipulation of natural Black hair to achieve it that it could cause long-term hair damage or hair loss.

Who knows what effects The Rachel had on the Monicas and Phoebes of the world. Perhaps it's best that we not celebrate any one woman's beauty over another, but that is not a realistic expectation. As we have developed more awareness and language around the structures and systems that encourage this singular beauty behavior, the culture around comparing and criticizing women's appearances has somewhat improved. But the instinct to compare will never disappear from our culture completely. It is buried so deep in me that I worry it might be embedded in my genetic code. That compulsion to routinely compare threatens to undermine my own feminist sensibilities. And since I was relentlessly served Jennifer Aniston as the ultimate beauty icon, knowing it would be impossible for me to emulate her, I began to hate her. Through no fault of her own and from thousands of miles and several tax brackets removed, she became my enemy. I had no weapons (yet) with which to fight her and what I felt she represented, but that didn't mean I wouldn't go down swinging. I still had to show up as close to perfect as I could. I would breathe several sighs of relief when, in 1999, Aaliyah Haughton debuted in *Romeo Must Die* and sang on the corresponding soundtrack, and I found a beauty archetype I could follow. I cut myself a dramatic side bang.

For most of elementary school, I dictated what I wanted my hair to look like to my mother. A lot of the style choices were limited because of the activities I participated in—like ballet—but my chemically relaxed hair made doing my own hair a lot easier and more practical. After I became a person with a perm, I was able to fully take over that aspect of my morning routine. I also developed an addiction to getting my hair as straight as possible. If I waited too long between relaxers, the new growth would come in, betraying my natural hair texture. After a few years of regular perming, my hair began to thin and "break off," meaning my hair growth was slowed and my hair was not healthy. My hair was, essentially, falling out, but could I revert back to my natural texture? At thirteen? Are you nuts? I determinedly surged ahead with my perm routine, ignoring the searing pain in my scalp as the chemicals literally burned me.

You're not supposed to scratch your head when you have a perm. When Beyoncé sings, "Pat your weave, ladies," in "Get Me Bodied," she's referring to the fact that those of us with a perm shouldn't scratch our heads but, instead, should pat our hair if it becomes itchy. I didn't know that in 1998, so I scratched my head freely, as any normal person might as soon as their head itches. It was especially itchy after physical activity or at night. I found out why you don't scratch the hard way. "Have you been itching?" became a procedural question asked at the beginning of every perm I got. I deduced from the tone of the question that my answer should be no, so that's what I said. Scratching the scalp drastically reduces its natural protections against perm chemicals, and that delightful tingle I felt the first time I had those chemicals on my hair soon became an excruciating burn. It burns twice as much when the hairdresser washes it out and your bleeding scalp comes under the water. The relief I was hoping for never came. Then patches of my scalp started to scab over, and the scabs fell out along with my hair. It took me years to change my answer to the "Have you been itching?" question from "No" to "A little," which meant the hairdresser would slightly vary the degree of intensity of the perm, but tremendous damage had already been done, and I kept scratching for a decade longer.

On eighth-grade graduation day, when I had two weave tracks braided and sewn into the back of my head, I felt I had achieved another step on my beauty-ascension ladder. I was giving a speech as the salutatorian. Everyone was so proud. I was very specific about the hairstyle I wanted for that day: the front twisted up into neat lines, arranged in a crown at the top of my head, and the back of my hair down. It's shameful to admit, but I was inspired by a style I had seen in the Mary-Kate and Ashley Olsen vacation movie *Holiday in the Sun*—and it was not on any Black actress. The gag is, of course, that it was a copy of a Black hairstyle, but Black people were just totally erased from the movie narrative, even though it took place on a Caribbean island and "borrowed" style inspiration from the same people it pretended didn't exist.

My hairstylist had some leftover tracks from a weave she had done and she asked me if I wanted to "add some length." I'd witnessed the weave being placed in another client's hair in the living room beauty shop. From my viewing angle, I had no way of knowing that the tracks were being sewn into braids. I was horrified as I watched this curved needle being threaded repeatedly in and out of her scalp while this woman did not flinch at all. I held my breath, watching the hairdresser move the needle with methodic exactitude while the woman and our mutual hairstylist casually gossiped. Forty minutes later, I was asked if I wanted her leftover extension scraps and to be subjected to a similar form of torture myself. I practically sweat out my fresh perm in anticipation of the pain alone.

Sitting there, when it was finally my turn, I decided that whatever was in store for me was a compulsory step to becoming beautiful, and if I wanted to improve the look of my hair, this new torture was what I needed to do. I gulped as the hairstylist applied pressure to the back of my head, forcing my chin down and tipping it to the side. Then she started braiding. I don't know what ingredient I was short-changed during my creation process, but as a kid, I found it impossible to ask questions of adults, authority figures, and essentially anyone I deemed superior to me, even if it pertained directly to my own body and well-being. So I sat there silently, having no earthly clue what was about to happen. She finished braiding two neat horizontal braids across the back of my head, then began to thread a curved thick needle. Still, I did not utter a word, and I fully expected that she was about to use it to pierce my skin directly. The cocktail of emotions that coursed through my little body when she spiked the needle through the braid and not my already significantly abused scalp gave over to intense relief. And despite not being sewn together like a little brown Frankenstein doll, I think I held my breath for the entire process. When it was all over, my new length fell just a bit past my shoulders, and the added thickness of the new hair instantly made me feel more mature. While I still have a difficult time saying *beautiful* when it comes to my own appearance, I at least felt closer to beauty than I had when I arrived.

When I left the hairdresser's that day, I had started a new part of a mysterious journey. That feeling, as if I were inching closer to beauty, fueled an addiction so strong and pervasive that I'm still not sure I'll ever fully recover. My perm, the extensions, and my new attitude opened a gateway of possibilities. I loved the confidence boost my new hair afforded me. And, like any addiction, the dosage needed to be upped every so often for the desired high. The ecstasy of my perm two years earlier was wearing as thin as my natural hair, so extensions were a welcomed improvement. The added excitement of having them for a special occasion introduced an obsession with events and outings. I would insist that each event was just as important as the last, until something as benign as a suburban birthday party could produce the same level of stress and anxiety as, say, the Met Gala. Years later, I actually *did* go to the Met Gala and nearly fainted from starvation, but I looked good, so who cares, right?

The amount of attention and financial backing—new dress, new shoes, new hair—that my middle school graduation ceremony got from my parents solidified a worrisome pattern of behavior.

Over the years, as I permed more, my need for extensions increased and I started requiring them for every single perm appointment. I would not and could not imagine reverting back to my natural hair, especially since its health was diminishing slowly but surely. The tracks allowed me to cover up my hair loss while continuing to perm my hair. It seemed like an ideal solution, so long as no one found out and no one *ever* touched my hair, which is tough when you spend a lot of time among other girls. By the time I was in high school, I had a plug-in hot comb I would use to straighten my hair every single day. Most people wake up to the scent of coffee beans; for me, it was the scent of burning hair. I was using as many as five to six tracks to add length to my hair and was pugnacious about no one ever touching it and never getting it wet.

The tracks increased the price of my hair appointments, and of course, since I was doing it, my sister began to get them too. I can't imagine what an enormous expense it was for my parents to raise my sister and me, but my commitment to being beautiful at any cost certainly did not help the equation. As we transitioned to our new high school in Greenwich, Connecticut, and settled into a more exclusive shiny, white bubble, the hair conversation became even more complicated. In this new environment, it was increasingly essential that our hair be straight, long, and pretty. You might assume that an all-girls community would alleviate the compulsion to look a certain way, but for me, it felt like a microscope and another arena in which to compete. As the constant underdog, the literal Black sheep, I felt an unbearable pressure to always rise to the occasion. I think I wore makeup every single day from the age of fourteen to the age of thirty.

You couldn't convince me that hair and makeup were not necessities. Carefully reinforced by all the media I regularly consumed—television, magazines, blogs—I deduced that beauty was an essential part of being female, inextricably linked to your biological composition, like having a period is to having ovaries. It just came with the territory.

CHAPTER SIX

If you can believe it, there was a point in my life where I directly and purposely exposed myself to the sun. I was adamantly against wearing sunscreen as a child, peeved at the way that applying it subtracted from my precious minutes in the water. My mother was an SPF devotee decades before it was trendy, but I truly didn't see the purpose of sunscreen. It seemed to me to be a really poorly functioning lotion, but instead of moisturizing skin, it produced a creepy gray cast, like I was permanently ashy. Why? Because sunscreen was not formulated for people with melanin. For years, I would pretend to put on sunscreen and straight up lie when I was asked about it, or drop the pretense and forgo it altogether. I loved the sun. I could tell it loved me back. I watched it singe the skin of my friends, turning them into little raw, red tomatoes before my eyes. They would wince, nurse their blisters with aloe vera, then peel like a snake in the next few days. I found it fascinating. I didn't get a sunburn until I was in my twenties, and that was only because retinol creams left me vulnerable to the rays of my longtime ally. After that, I could agree: that shit hurts. But as a child, me and the sun were entirely copacetic.

The summer before I turned thirteen, I sat in my tankini at the pool club—an extension of one of the local golf clubs but much more casual.

(It sounds fancier than it was, I think.) My friends and I had just finished a raucous game of Marco Polo and some underwater handstands when Kristen, my three-way-call tormentor from the fourth grade, in her bikini—string bikini, actually—did some more emotional damage to me. By this point, we had become frenemies, tolerating each other's presence, but we were never really close. Our class was only twelve kids, so there was only so much bickering you could do before you ended up having to work as science partners. For utility's sake, we had to at least maintain a cordial relationship, but this did not keep us from our tenuous competition for leverage and influence over our social circle. She was an only child raised by the only single mother in the group, so she was both extremely spoiled and extremely invested in performing maturity. That day, she lathered herself in baby oil and announced that she was in rabid pursuit of the tannest summer of her life. I'm sure you know where this is going. She held her arm next to mine and said, "I will be darker than you by August. Watch." I didn't know what to say to this, except that I knew it was impossible. I said nothing and sat in dazed silence. I replay scenes like this from my youth often, and I worry that I was weak, that I should have done more to stand up for myself and should have been able to identify microaggressions like this. Even if I didn't know what a microaggression was at the time, I knew it made me feel weird. But I was alone. I was the only one. I didn't have the vocabulary or knowledge to craft the response I would use now. And the risk of further isolating myself, of alerting the group to my otherness and possibly forever altering our fragile dynamic, filled me with an unspeakable anxiety. So instead I tucked my feelings away. And there her comment sat, burrowing deep and far into the recesses of my mind, another thing I threw into my grave of emotion because I couldn't access the confidence, the logic, or the passion to push back.

What I needed was a book or a show to demonstrate what I should do. I had a playbook for peer pressure and being offered "dope." I knew bullet-point responses for dealing with a boy who got too handsy or a friend who wanted to cheat on a test. But there was nothing to tell me how to deal with a friend who, years before, had claimed to not like me for being Black and now claimed she wanted to be darker than me. Instinctually, I knew some code was being spoken. I just didn't yet have the key to decipher it. Being dark was OK for her since she was so clearly white with straight, long hair and thin lips she would later inject with fillers. Me, though . . . I was born in my skin, a birthright that, in her eyes, made me inferior. I was also visibly Black beyond just my skin tone, with my hair in braids, my flat nose, and the curves I was trying to hide in my modest swimwear threatening to expose themselves. We were not the same. And I wouldn't be able to turn around in the winter and say, "Soon, I will be as pale as you." I feel disappointed that I couldn't come up with a snappy comeback, but I also knew she was delivering a barb to me that I could never challenge. In the end, of course, the sun got her good, burning her like an overcooked Hot Pocket. My evil side smirked while she nursed her wounds. She complained for days about the discomfort. Eventually, to my great disappointment, it *did* turn to a tan, but it was a bitch getting there. Maybe there was an element of achievement in that for her, earning her tan from that pain. Unfortunately, I knew what that was like. I still know. There is a depraved honor in celebrating agony for beauty, like emphasizing that coal becomes a diamond only under intense pressure.

Kristen would later pay weekly visits to a tanning salon and brag about the deepness of her "base" to anyone of fairer complexion. Some of my other friends would too. Slowly, all around me, I noticed white people doggedly chasing darker skin. It became a fixation and a prerequisite for being hot. "Ugh, I can't wear shorts, my legs are so pale," "Pre-prom tan," and "I'm doing fourteen minutes" all became sanctioned refrains when talking about must-do beauty rituals. Yet another practice that I could not engage in—at least not actively. "Do you want to lay out?" was added to this chorus, and though it was not something originally in my vernacular, I quickly discovered that it meant my friends would gather to do absolutely nothing but lie in the sun. Natural sun, of course, was better than artificial, which should be used only if one was not able to take quarterly vacations to tropical destinations. Living in the temperate Northeast presents a certain set of challenges to getting optimal sunlight, especially if your main objective in life is to remain tan. My friends and I would read magazines or gossip, but mostly the point was just that, laying out. I participated since intense FOMO served as an incentive for doing such things, as wack as it was. While it erased the unpleasant paleness of my friends, I can't say it was that useful for me. I browned quickly and deeply, always. Moving my bathing suit straps aside revealed a much richer brown than whatever brown I had begun the day with, prompting my friends to ooh and aah in awe over the speed with which I could soak up the sun.

But this ceremony took a turn for me: while my friends got darker and therefore became more attractive, as I got darker, I became less attractive. I began to hear messaging that being darker was a bad thing. Older family members would call my sister and me "tar babies," which was to say that we were so dark, we resembled tar. That same message was extremely apparent in the media. Light-skinned Black women were routinely cast as the love interests, securing modeling campaigns and just generally winning at life. My parents are the same complexion as my sister and I, but all three of my mother's brothers, high-earning Ivy League grads, are married to light-skinned Black women, which was also revelatory: the preference for lighter skin existed even within the Black community.

In 1932, Zora Neale Hurston wrote in her autobiography, "If it was so honorable and glorious to be Black, why was it the yellow-skinned people among us had so much prestige? The light-skinned children were always the angels, fairies, and queens of school plays." Hurston writes of what she observed from her school life, and though she was raised in a strictly Black community, the principles of colorism invaded even here and, in some ways, may have been more hurtful than the outright and more expected forms of racism. The mystifying spite that exists for darker-skinned people within the Black community presents another layer of our limitations for loving ourselves.

Eighty-five years after Hurston's observations, ex–professional basketball player and amateur internet troll Gilbert Arenas commented on an Instagram photo, a designed graphic featuring the phrase "You don't have to be mixed to be beautiful," writing, "Not to be funny, can you name a beautiful black woman on the outside . . . not brown skin . . . like Tyrese black." The inspirational quote was an obvious response to patterns of colorism that are quite prevalent on social media. Arenas then followed up by saying, "As for Lupita she ain't cute to me sorry . . . just like I'm not cute to 95% of you." Arenas was referencing famous Kenyan actress and Academy Award winner Lupita Nyong'o who, in 2019, released a children's book called *Sulwe*, an autobiographical account of her own self-hatred for her dark skin. Of all the women that came forward about being harassed by Harvey Weinstein, Lupita Nyong'o was the only one whose account he felt compelled to directly and publicly deny. She speaks readily and often about the discrimination she has faced because of her skin and hair—racism from the outside and colorism from all sides.

There was an unmistakable "before" and "after" to my life—as if I had eaten from the tree of knowledge—when I learned I was Black. Once I became aware of my skin, its color, and what it meant, it began to taint my otherwise innocent viewpoints. Racism, and its stringent hierarchy, became so normalized for me that I began to develop a deference and reverence for whiteness. I learned to accept that my skin could not be changed, but that didn't mean I wasn't resentful or that

I didn't wish it could be different. Still, I knew what I was supposed to do to have the life I wanted. I understood the constraints of my complexion and behaved accordingly. I adopted a new way of being, doing anything and everything necessary to find even tiny morsels of acceptance. I think a lot about who I have become and how different it seems from the girl I was, but I know that the choice I made early on was one born of a desire to both survive and achieve what I so desperately craved: perfection.

CHAPTER SEVEN

My middle name is Aisha. It's one of those "about me" facts that almost no one knows, not even people close to me, because I was told it was "so weird" so many times in middle school that I just stopped using it altogether. In fact, it appears only on my passport, an official document that my parents gave to me when I was too young to have an actual say in the matter. Aisha is otherwise absent from all other official identifications; it's not on my driver's license, or my apartment lease, or even the cover of this book. All my monograms say DP, not DAP. I am not ashamed of the name now, but I spent so long reflexively hiding it because I didn't want to have to explain or defend it; it just became easier to erase it completely. Assimilation to white dominance at its finest: the renaming of yourself to make things easier for white people and, by extension, for yourself. Making things easier for white people is a preeminent responsibility of a Token Black Girl, and one that I learned to take extremely seriously.

One of the crucial ways the Token Black Girl makes things easier for white people is the "you're not racist" cosign, a critical function of Blackness in white spaces. I have been featured in the brochure or on the website of every school I have ever attended. I had assumed, for most of my life, that this was because I am extremely photogenic. Turns out that is only partially true. While I do take a nice picture, the other part of the truth is that I made a very nice Token Black Girl, a perfect addition to any campus or organization, because I looked right, and I was quiet. My comfort level was almost never taken into consideration. I was not asked nor did I ask to be in that kind of spotlight, but it became another piece of evidence for Black people to determine that I was a sellout or, worse, a coon performing all my essential duties for the white man. Really, I was just trying my best.

By now, you're probably trying to figure out why I didn't have any Black friends. The reason is simple and twofold: the few Black kids I knew through family friends did not attend school with me, so our interactions were limited to summertime or weekend socializing; and if and when I got the opportunity to meet other Black kids, they usually made it clear that they did not like me. Because I am not interested in painting myself as an ideal victim in this narrative, I am conscious of the ways that my behaviors and attitudes could have been interpreted as, well, stuck up. And, because I was so partial to whiteness, I adopted behavior, language, and mannerisms that operationally supported white supremacy, even in situations where no white person was present. White supremacy has an omnipresence, and my devotion to staging, functioning, and behaving always for the white gaze likely made my presence both threatening and unwelcome to other Black kids. In other words, I was an Op. They weren't wrong. Sometimes, Black people have an uncannily intuitive sense that alerts them to who among them may or may not be self-hating. In more recent years, Twitter has made it easier to identify people with these tendencies, but in the time before Twitter, you just had to go on gut instinct. The O. J. Simpson attitude of "I'm not Black, I'm O. J." can manifest in a variety of ways, and each one of them is harmful to the idea that Blackness can be nuanced and still be Black.

As a child, all I knew was that the Black children I met in passing at parks for playtime, or the Black kids at summer camp, teased me for the way I did, well, everything, but especially the way I spoke. They were convinced that I thought I was white. But based on what happened to me in the fourth grade, I knew for sure I was not. It made me extraordinarily self-conscious and fueled an intense anxiety. What *was* wrong with me? Why *did* I "talk white"? Admittedly, I have a vocal fry and a habit of up-speak that intensifies when I'm nervous. The characteristics and mannerisms I had been conditioned to perform, as prescribed by my role as the Token Black Girl, were obviously off-putting to the young members of my own community.

As for interacting with Black children who were more like me—prep school students hypnotized by white culture—I was encouraged to attend Jack and Jill events. Jack and Jill, a national, members-only club, was founded in the early twentieth century by Black mothers who wanted to further educational opportunities for Black children. Over the years, it morphed into kind of a social club, a who's who of affluent Black communities, where kids were encouraged to network. Though the members were other prep school kids like me, none of the Jack and Jill kids went to my school, and the events happened so infrequently that every interaction required an awkward and painful warming-up period. It didn't feel natural, and those relationships didn't last.

I was constantly on edge when I knew I had to interact with other Black kids. I feared their ridicule and judgment. There was often a massive lack of understanding between us, and I felt rejected by Black children. I was already shy, and I developed a deeper shyness as a means of protection.

I've researched the reception of Token Black Girls by the Black community. All you need to do is turn to Twitter comments to see all kinds of statements that gatekeep Black identity and invalidate an individual's Blackness based on their perceived relationship to whiteness. I searched Nia Sioux Frazier, the only Black cast member of the reality show *Dance Moms*, and discovered commentary like, "You are not talented and are basically a fat black girl wanting to be white" and "that girl Nia on dance mom is a white girl trapped in a black girl body!!!" In

2014, after Kerry Washington made history starring in Shonda Rhimes's *Scandal*, Twitter users commented, "Kerry Washington could do voiceover work as a white sorority girl" and "Kerry Washington is such a white girl. Love her tho!" Willow Smith, Will and Jada Pinkett Smith's daughter, is similarly called out: "Willow Smith sounds like a white girl," "Willow Smith is a white girl trapped in a black body," and last, "Willow Smith irks me; her voice is like a fourteen-year-old white girl from the valley. Jada is from BMore, why the kids ain't hood??!" Each of those comments feels uncomfortably familiar to me. Having a certain hobby or speech pattern does not automatically make someone an agent in service to whiteness, especially at an age where, developmentally, it is not necessarily a conscious choice. The estimation that Black girls who grow up in environments like Nia Frazier in "Trump Country," Pennsylvania, Kerry Washington at The Spence School in New York City, or Willow Smith in Calabasas are somehow less Black is harmful to their ability to access their full selves. Every person is a product of their environment. They *know* they are not white, and it is fruitless to suggest that they are not Black because of circumstances outside their control.

White supremacy exerts a stranglehold over every culture that is not exclusively white and flattens Blackness, producing a mythic monolith of Black culture, one that commands there is a singular way to be Black. And, in response, Blackness seeks to protect itself from the supremacist suggestion that the dominant image of Black is a bad way to be. It becomes necessary, in that way, to ensure the survival of the culture by fortifying it against interlopers, even those from within.

The rejection I felt from other Black children was swift and bitter. We were the same but not, and even more distressing, I would never be on equal footing with my white friends either. I was conditionally accepted at school based on my ability to assimilate, and those same qualities made me conditionally rejected by children of my own race. Even Whitney Houston was traumatized by the Black community rejecting her at the beginning of her career. The documentary *Whitney* delves into the aftermath of Houston being booed by the Black audience at the 1989 Soul Train Music Awards. She was already a Grammy winner and had the bestselling debut album of any single female artist in history, but some Black radio stations refused to play her songs, and she was frozen out by her own people. Whitney Houston, born and raised in New Jersey, was strictly middle class. She was thin, smiling, exceptionally talented, yet humble. An iconic Leo. Whitney's career blossomed when artists were being manufactured by record label A&R divisions to an aggressive degree. Aside from Houston's divine musical talent, she was also extremely beautiful, a working model before she made it big as a singer. Her ability to conform within the white beauty standard almost certainly contributed to the way she was marketed by Arista Records and then CEO Clive Davis at nineteen years old. The result was massive commercial success and limited acceptance from Black people. Prominent Black leader Reverend Al Sharpton is even on the record harshly referring to her as "Whitey" Houston. She seemed genuinely haunted by her rejection at the hands of the wider Black community, and her difficulty in managing the Token Black Girl role in American popular music, a role she never asked for, breaks my heart. I empathize with that pressure on the tiniest fraction of that scale.

I needed to unofficially referee between white and Black communities, and it was a taxing assignment. For white people, I was a representative of Blackness who they could quiz on slang terminology. For Black people, I was the sad lost sheep who needed to eject the Backstreet Boys from my boom box and come home. I had to hide my likes and dislikes and constantly mediate my personality to fit whatever group I was with. This required a splintering of myself so drastic that I still feel uncomfortable admitting that I cannot jump double Dutch, that I didn't listen to rap music until I was sixteen years old, and that I detest collard greens. I knew how other Black kids wanted me to act, and to me, that always felt unnatural. This Black self that they wanted, or the

Black self that I learned was expected, took studying and work, and who had the time? One could flip channels back and forth between *TRL* and *106 and Park*, but not in real life.

My Blackness also gave me a cool pass that I certainly didn't earn. As an adult, when I meet new people, I find myself overemphasizing that I am *not* cool, just in case they see me and assume otherwise. I might have cool clothes, the right hairstyle, cool friends, and so on, but at my core, I am nerdy and uncool. My anxiety won't let me be anything else. I overthink everything. I try to anticipate behavior so I can respond in a way that will elicit the most favorable reactions.

At some point, I began to notice that, around my white friends, my Blackness made me an authority. I was shocked. In high school, a girl said "fo' shizzle, my nizzle" when I was in earshot and, later, came to apologize to me. "I shouldn't have said that," she said with her head lowered in contrition. I shrugged and said, "OK!" Not because I was excited to give her a racism pass—like I was so used to doing—but because I didn't realize that *nizzle* was Snoop Dogg speak for *nigga*. Literally, I had no clue. But she assumed, because I was Black, that I not only would have known but also would have been offended by her use of the word. It couldn't have been more confusing to me. By extension of my Blackness, in addition to decoding slang, I was asked to instruct my friends on popular dance moves and—this is my favorite because I know absolutely nothing about music—explain song lyrics. None of it made much sense or played to my personal strengths, but I was excited to have the social cache, however it came.

Being around other Black kids threatened to upend this charade. They knew! They knew I wasn't cool, for sure. This added to my hesitation to really and sincerely engage with them. They could expose me, and that was dangerous. I couldn't let that happen. What if they started actually speaking in slang terms I didn't know! I felt that my social position was so fragile, I developed an aversion to other Black kids. I was convinced they were competition, and my survival banked on the fact that I was *the* Token Black Girl. I had to keep away from *them* at all costs. On top of that, the more time I spent with Black kids, the less I might be accepted by my white friends. For them, one Black girl was OK—ideal even. Five Black girls? That was a gang. I saw how my white friends and their families evaluated groups of Black people. There were certain places—school dances or other spots where kids gathered—places disproportionately inhabited by Black and brown people, where we simply were not allowed to go. We called them "sketchy" or "ghetto"—language, unlike the word *thug*, that was more inconspicuously coded and took decades longer to stamp out of my vocabulary. I remained in denial that *I* would be categorized as "sketchy" had I been in one of these places surrounded by other Black girls. I couldn't imagine being seen as one of *them* and not one of *us*, an "us" I was only conditionally accepted into based on nothing but random chance, the happy coincidence that my parents chose to place me in a certain school at a certain time.

It was an impossible situation. My identity was called into question daily, and there weren't any guidelines for what to do about it. I adopted a passive persona simply because I had no rubric of dos and don'ts for dealing with issues surrounding race.

In the fall of 2002, my best friend called me up after a dance she had attended without me to report on the number of boys she had danced with. She wanted to tell me the "craziest" story. A Black boy had grabbed her and pulled her toward him. This was a very pre-#MeToo mating ritual. In my youth, consent, in the modern sense, was mythical. We were not so much asked to dance as pounced upon. She told him she didn't want to dance with him and pushed him away. As male egos go, this was a huge blow. He got upset. He said she was racist and that she didn't want to dance with him because he was Black. She was telling me, of course, because I was her best friend in the world. Her response to him was classic: "That is definitely not true. My best friend is Black." Ugh, I know. *I know!* Guys, I know. But you know what I did, right?

I agreed with her and I defended her, knowing our friendship was the realest, confirming that she was most definitely not racist. We are still friendly to this day, and I am pretty sure I am still her only Black friend. Does this mean she is racist? Not quite. It's not as simple as that, but her behavior made me feel something I didn't know how to articulate. In that moment, I stepped into a new role, one I had played before, even if I didn't realize it yet: a protective buffer against the label "racist."

I could do this only because of the inherently racist ideologies that anointed me as the acceptable Black girl. I was polite and well spoken, had enough money, had straight hair, and most importantly, I was there. Adjacency and convenience, both total happenstance, were the factors that my social position hinged upon. If I embodied a single negative stereotype, would I have the friends I had? Would I have the life I had? My acceptance was contingent upon me looking and acting a certain way, that much I knew from television shows and movies, even if they didn't give me any help in handling this specific situation. The mannerisms and language I had adopted were those of the oppressor. I was forged in the fires of white supremacy, then sent out to further its mission by evangelizing to other Black people. I was, indeed, hyperaware of the way I spoke, but I was not aware that it was a weapon. I did not realize that my very adjacency to whiteness, my compliance within the framework of white supremacy, was helping uphold negative stereotypes about Blackness. I carefully played the role I was supposed to play, and in that moment, my role was to reassure my friend that she was categorically not racist and that I, Token Black Girl, could vouch for that.

Of course, I can see now what this looks like: it looks like I did my duty as the good little negro and bolstered my white friend, as opposed to saying, "Actually, that whole story is racist." I was just trying to be a good friend. I wanted to maintain our relationship more than I wanted to confront the fact that she probably *did* reject that boy because he was Black. I was straddling the need to please two groups of people who had radically different expectations. Black kids thought my code-switching switch had malfunctioned. They were confused and perhaps betrayed by the way I operated in service of whiteness. And as positive reinforcement, white kids constantly said I wasn't "really Black," a racist assessment. I existed outside my friends' narrow view of what it meant to be Black. I had done all the things literally required of me in handbooks and dress codes to effectively stamp out the characteristics of my Blackness, but I was still visibly Black. And that visibility was an asset to white people as long as I was willing to appear on their terms.

CHAPTER EIGHT

Last year, I sent a group photo to my mom—a picture of her and her friends at a recent college reunion—which she then shared with the rest of the ladies in the photograph via text. "God, I look so fat," Lisa responded right away, an echo of something I had listened to her say my entire life. She had never once, at least not that I'd heard, said anything positive about her body. Occasionally other women would join in, but Lisa was always the harshest, comparing herself to hippos or elephants. I feel the pathological need to emphasize that she was probably a solid size two for most of my life and, as she's approached sixty, has edged up maybe two sizes. I wondered how much this intense body criticism was a generational condition, like perhaps we have been so brainwashed by the influx of media putting skinny and beautiful on an impossible-to-reach pedestal that this desire to be thin never goes away.

I wasn't sure how Lisa could ever see herself as fat, but as I got older, I became sucked into the same distorted fun house mirror. I looked at myself once, decided I was fat, and could never see anything different. The amount of brain space that was occupied by thinking about my body, thinking about changing or improving my body, thinking about how others think of my body, and thinking about how my body has let me down would be alarming to any person who has more normal thought patterns. I remember reading some statistic about how the human brain thinks about sex six times a minute, and I thought it was so strange because my brain was constantly in overdrive thinking about how wrong my body was. There was no time to ever think about sex.

Mean Girls, starring none other than the aforementioned Lindsay Lohan, covers this ritual of self-criticism flawlessly. I was a high school sophomore when it came out. In one particular scene that's a bit too on the nose, Karen looks in the mirror and says, "God, my hips are *huge*."

"Oh please, I *hate* my calves," Gretchen adds before joining her at the mirror.

And last, the queen bee herself, Regina, brings it home with, "At least you guys can wear halters. I've got man shoulders."

The girls continue berating their reflections, covering everything from hairlines to pore size. In unison, their heads snap toward Cady, the white African newcomer who hasn't yet offered up her most intimate insecurities. Awkwardly, she confesses, "I have really bad breath in the morning," to which they all respond, "Ew."

Strangely enough, when I got Black friends in adulthood, I discovered this was not a universal practice. I have since wondered if perhaps this brand of self-examination was a particular white-girl ritual that doesn't cross over to Black women, who are already perpetually judged by the world. They might not have any need to voice these criticisms aloud themselves. I began thinking about it this way only after encountering observations Black writers made about white culture. I was so entrenched in white culture that I didn't notice it. I learned those behaviors early and participated in them often. I watched Cady's plight in *Mean Girls* with unrelenting criticism. I did not understand why she couldn't just *get it*, why she couldn't learn how to assimilate faster, especially when the stakes were so high. I readily offered up everything I thought was wrong with me and laid it at the altar of my tribe.

By the time middle school came around, it became easier to express my displeasure with my body, as I noticed other girls in my environment were similarly dissatisfied with their appearance. We would hate-bond with each other, picking ourselves apart and laying our contempt before the group as a peace offering that seemed to say, "I, too, am one of you." Some friends were more accepting of self-criticism, and I began to identify subtle differences in these relationships over the years. I had my friends who would tolerate extensive discussions of calories and fitness tips and those who would not. The extra level of intimacy that self-loathing requires became quite critical to a lot of my female friendships. We tended to our own cesspool, dumping on ourselves for the good of the group, then targeting other people so we were constantly in a state of observance. The element of self-hatred was the lynchpin in guaranteeing the success of the system. And that self-hatred made it all the more natural to internalize criticism from friends as well.

In the fifth grade, I begged my mom to buy me a Spice Girls T-shirt. It would be the final frontier of my Spice fandom. I had the Chupa Chups lollipops. I had worn my parents down to buy me platform Skechers. I could recite *Spice World: The Movie* from memory, and I was in possession of two Spice Girls CDs. And duh, I had done my due diligence as "Scary." But I had to complete my pyramid of worship, which included merch. I needed to publicly display my devotion. Then one day, I spotted a Spice Girls T-shirt *on sale* and knew it had to be mine. Much to my delight, my mother acquiesced, and I planned when I could debut the shirt for the maximum desired effect.

I debuted it at my best friend's birthday sleepover, where, just the year before, I was pinned down while my hair was brushed out into a gigantic afro so we could perform "Wannabe" approximately seventeen million times for a camcorder. I packed my T-shirt for my next-day outfit, planning to nonchalantly debut it before everyone's moms pulled through to pick them up. I had nailed the pajamas look, wearing a favorite frilly seafoam-green set. The next morning, finally, it was time for me to change into my marquee outfit.

I paired the Spice Girls tee with biker shorts, ankle socks, and Keds sneakers. It was, by my own personal metrics, a winning look, until Kristen decided otherwise. Three-way-call, Tanning-gate Kristen scoffed as soon as I entered the room. It appeared that I had worn the wrong thing. "Ew, do you still like them?" she said and motioned to my T-shirt with the Spice Girls positioned front and center, just like on their "Wannabe" single cover. "We are *so* over them," she followed up while I scrambled for a response. Kristen was too mature for ten. Her mom was loose with rules, and Kristen was always the first to do or have anything. She and I often battled for the coveted right-hand position to the leader of our group, and our relationship often flamed up.

I set my jaw determinedly and said as flippantly as possible, "Oh, well, this is an old shirt," hating myself for the lie but also hating myself for not having known that the Spice Girls had become uncool.

In that moment, I made a vow to myself that I would become the person who makes the call on what's in or out, what clothing is acceptable, and would never again be caught in the inglorious crosshairs of being out of touch with what's popular. To combat this feeling, I hardened. You know how the Vibranium suit in *Black Panther* physically absorbs the shocks of hits and then uses them as ammunition for enemies? I did that with all my hurt feelings and powerlessness. I hardened so much that I became manipulative, calculating, and mean. I was desperate to gain some modicum of control, and to do that, I constantly doled out criticisms, gossiped, and stirred up petty drama. I developed a haughty affect that I employed for both passing judgment and my own protection. And I relied on this manufactured persona until adulthood, where I used it for the same reasons.

I don't think there is enough scholarship or discourse around the trope of the Black mean girl. The mammy archetype and Black Venus have been analyzed to death, but it seems to me there's a need for a new investigation into the making of a mean girl—one who is Black. In my case, it was a survival mechanism. At least it started out that way. And then it became an addiction. The 2019 film *Selah and the Spades* spends a little time examining this. The plot follows the eponymous character,

Selah, a Black girl, as she acquires and maintains social dominance while navigating her life as a boarding-school bully. These days, we're in the habit of collectively criticizing girls who bully—mean girls—but many people forget that's what a lot of us were encouraged to be. In some cases, these personalities formed as a direct reaction to an environment that was already hostile and unsafe. I've never gotten into a physical altercation in my life, but I've still had to fight. I just did so with psychological and emotional warfare. As Black girls are slut-shamed, belittled, and discredited, we have to consider, what if the resulting response is not one of cowering submission but one of premeditated rage? Personally, I picked the latter.

The 2021 YA novel *Ace of Spades* (I guess everyone creating on this topic got a card deck memo) also dissects a power-hungry, popularity-obsessed Black girl. The story centers around Chiamaka, one of two Black students at an all-white prep school. Chiamaka is ruthless in her social and academic pursuits, to the point where the word *intense* sounds a bit lazy. She keeps people at arm's length while using and abusing them to increase her public capital—a means of outlasting, outshining, and invalidating her white classmates. She is extreme, of course, but there is an underlying desperation to her actions, one that suggests she has learned to strike first, before she is struck. It's not the kind of character we're used to seeing. If you google "Iconic Mean Girls," you will be served with results that are exclusively white. The mean white girl, the Blair Waldorfs, the Heathers, the Kathryn Merteuils—we are trained to understand her, and to some degree, her attitude is admirable. We know she feels neglected by her parents or has some underlying daddy issue that makes her lash out in a brutal and unrelenting fashion. But we do not yet have a framework for understanding the Black girl who adopts meanness as an armor. The bitchy-Black-woman stereotype has been done to death—not the mean Black girl. But only Black women have to negotiate the liability of their Blackness and, therefore, must labor against any indications that they have even the most minor of character flaws. And there is a point—in adolescence, I think—where you can make a choice. A choice to stop feeling so apologetic, to stop feeling so bad all the time. That choice was to go on the offense and be the deciding voice in who and what curries favor. I picked that choice. It's a skill set that is useful for becoming a fashion editor.

While I can vividly recall the agony of being singled out by Kristen and mocked for wearing something so unacceptable, I spent the next decade or so doing the same thing to other people. I did things like make PowerPoint presentations on "rules" of appearance to coach the girls around me on how they should look, reenacting the ways television and magazines instructed me. I sought out social control through manipulation and coercion. I was in dogged pursuit of an imagined sense power, and was very mean in doing so. And I strengthened the muscle of my meanness so I could eventually flex it with little effort. But I wonder now if I was always meanest to myself.

CHAPTER NINE

I have wanted a different body since I learned what a body was and that mine was mine. I cannot say it was any one thing in particular that caused me to consider the shell that I lived in to be wrong. In truth, I had an average body, probably more on the skinny side. But I always, always, always wanted to be as small as possible. Perhaps I wanted to disappear, to become so insignificant that I was not noticeable at all. This instinct worked in direct opposition to my desire to be celebrated as exceptional, so it was a hard line to toe. My sister, only twenty-one months my junior, is extremely skinny. She had what I assumed was the "right" body, while I had the wrong one. As children, we were constantly compared. In elementary school, our Italian school principal would playfully marvel at how thin our little legs were. "Your legs are like spaghetti," he would say to me. I knew what spaghetti was. I liked spaghetti. "But *your* legs," he would say to my sister, "are like vermicelli. Do you know what that is?" We didn't because why would we? He would then proceed to explain that vermicelli is "the thinnest pasta noodle! So thin that it just disappears! You can't even see it." He would amuse himself like this over and over, multiple times a week. The verdict is still out on the creep factor here, but the propriety of the commentary is not the point. The point is conditioning girls to accept their bodies being compared to each other and scrutinized so closely.

This kind of comparison becomes second nature for women, and even if it's projected in the most harmless way, it can still have disastrous consequences. Eventually, it revealed to me that my legs were big and my sister's legs were small, and visibly so.

In 2015, writer Kelsey Miller published an article for Refinery29 about dieting in young children. She wrote, "Last week, a new study from Common Sense Media made headlines by reporting that 80% of 10-year-old girls have been on a diet. Furthermore, this 'horrifying new research' found that more than half of girls and one-third of boys ages six to eight want thinner bodies." Miller goes on to describe that as early as the 1970s, studies have revealed body dissatisfaction in young children, mostly girls, and that it eventually results in an indoctrination into diet culture.

For me, this repeated interaction with my principal set up a world where *bigger* in any sense was bad. My legs were spaghetti—bad. I needed for them to become vermicelli. But for the most part, as a child, I was somewhat unconscious of my desire to be thinner. It was present, but it had not yet completely taken over my thought patterns. Over time, I began to understand that "fat" was a monster to be outrun by any means necessary, and it represented the absolute most undesirable and shameful characteristic that could be bestowed upon a Black woman: laziness. In a moment of desperation, I wrote to Santa Claus to ask him that I be put on Weight Watchers and gifted a NordicTrack for Christmas.

Fatphobia and anti-Blackness are fused concepts. Fatness is associated with laziness, ineptitude, and ugliness, which are all colleagues of anti-Black ideas. I assumed by avoiding fatness, I would be able to avoid the other negative affiliations of anti-Blackness. It was fine for me to be the Black one, but being the fat one or the fat *and* Black one would be a fate too hopeless and forlorn to overcome.

The fusion of the concept of thin and beautiful with whiteness can be historically traced as an element of the white-supremacist beauty standard. Yet, as with feminism, white women have become the face and voice of "body acceptance," which began as a radical concept for Black women, a means of compensating for generations of exclusion and ridicule at the hands of white supremacy. In 2020, singer Lizzo called out the app TikTok for removing her videos and claiming that her body in a bikini abused the community guidelines. As TikTok relies on videos generating likes, you can be assured that there is no shortage of bodies in bikinis on the app. One body was a problem, though.

The idea that valuing "skinny" is a white concept is thorny. It could be argued that prizing thinness is an ideology adopted by people of color, or Black people, merely as a tool to navigate white supremacy. Many Black members of the modeling and fashion industry say that, growing up, their slim figures were derided in their communities of Caribbean or African descent, declaring that female bodies with pronounced butts and breasts were always preferred. In my family, this was never the case. My paternal grandmother was militant about food consumption, serving us only what she thought we could eat and then, if we asked for more, forcing us to finish the entire dish, no matter what. Eating a meal with her felt like playing blackjack. My father was the product of her homegrown fatphobia, constantly commenting on the bodies of people on television, encouraging his children to stay fit by doing crunches, and making his displeasure for overweight people—women specifically—widely known. He is a seventy-year-old retiree who still rises at 5:00 a.m. to do his exercises before he starts the day, a forever athlete undoubtedly convinced that the opposite of laziness is a visibly fit body. While we were never put on diets, it was not uncommon for him to say things like "You have to watch your figure" or simply express so much disdain for an alternative body type that we absorbed the message: never become that. It was an implied urging rather than a direct one, aided and abetted by the media and sustained at home.

My mom joined Weight Watchers and did Jane Fonda tapes in our living room. By the time the Tae Bo craze came around, my sister and I were participating in her fitness routine. As someone who has been diagnosed with a disorder, I don't think my mom had one, but she did seem to be perpetually on a diet, swayed by diet culture, Weight Watchers, and SlimFast. She rarely allowed fast food, rebranding McDonald's as her homemade healthy alternative, "Mommy Burgers." Her friends were always discussing weight loss and diets. I would catch snippets of these conversations at playdates.

Growing up, women, including my mother, would tell me that dieting was not something I needed to be concerned with. Then someone would add a "*yet*," and all the women would laugh, knowing that eventually calorie counting was in my future. It was in all our futures.

By the time I was twelve, I was consciously and obsessively monitoring my food intake. I focused an incredible amount of energy on never becoming fat. I think this is the literal definition of fatphobia. And so much of my own behavior and the content I have produced has been colored by that ideal. I regret the role I've played in giving buoyancy and life to this cultural sickness, one that I believe needs to be eradicated, but I also recognize that it has grown deep roots within my own thinking. I've been in therapy for years, and in treatment and recovery from my eating disorder for two years, but that doesn't mean I am cured. I just have to try my best to catch regressive thinking patterns when they pop up and make sure I do not disseminate and spread that poison further to people who listen to and watch what I do. I'm hesitant to describe the methodology and mechanics behind my dieting tactics because they could become prescriptive for anyone who is not yet healed, but I cannot overemphasize the amount of brain space I have dedicated over the years to thinking about how to become skinnier or how my body is fundamentally wrong and must be improved or fixed. I have tried any- and everything as a way of losing weight. To paint a clearer picture, I will say that I have never considered myself to be particularly proficient at math. I frequently use my phone calculator to help me do simple percentages for tipping at restaurants. However, if you asked me to calculate how long I would need to be on a treadmill to burn enough calories to be able to eat a cupcake, I could give you an accurate answer down to the second. If you asked me when train A was going to crash into train B, I would have no idea. These thoughts started in childhood and then became second nature—such a force of habit that I no longer had to work to conjure them. At a certain point, those demons were just always there.

A surreptitious source of these demons was the mall. I grew up in suburbia, and online shopping hadn't really caught on, so there weren't many places to get underwear. The department stores were fine, but they skewed mature (read: old lady). Victoria's Secret became a sort of mecca, offering a preview of what it might be like to be an adult woman, a grown-up. The Angels were everything, stunning beacons guiding us willing disciples to true womanhood. Their larger-than-life images were plastered all over the stores. My friends and I obsessed over them, needing to know their names, ages, and countries of origin. Klum "The Body," 30, Germany. Banks, 30, USA. Ambrosio, 22, Brazil. We tuned in to the annual Victoria's Secret Fashion Show with the rapt attention of eager protégés.

Victoria's Secret capitalized on its expert messaging with cheap body sprays and pajamas printed with phrases like "I'm with the Angels." The brand determined what sexy was for an entire generation of girls and boys. Men were not immune to this messaging either. They might not have been programmed to be preoccupied with body minutiae, like collarbones and "pit tit," but they were effectively trained to see women as attractive or not based on the standards set by the lovely minds in marketing and advertising. If you're coming of age watching your crush lust after a Victoria's Secret model, chances are good that you'll try to emulate that Victoria's Secret model.

When I was thirteen, girls became obsessed with wearing thongs seemingly overnight. Panty lines were an abominable offense and had to be avoided at all costs. Acquiring a thong was tricky. For one thing, I was a child, and therefore wearing a thong shouldn't have been a concern of mine. And for another, I lived with my parents (see point one), and my mom did my laundry, so there was no way I could hide wearing a thong from her. My solution was to wear one and then throw it away. A thong felt secretive and naughty.

Victoria's Secret underwear is pretty cheap, so a thirteen-year-old with access to money would have no problem cleaning up there, especially during the semiannual sale, which, despite the name, seemed to happen at least once a month. I memorized their sale schedule because I always wanted to make sure I could go to the counter with dozens of new panties and bras, satisfied with my single-use spoils.

Before puberty, I had always been the same size as my friends, and it was common for us to share clothing. We would often swap items from Limited Too and the juniors section of Nordstrom. But puberty hit me hard, and my body began to change—in my opinion, for the worse. There was a day in eighth grade when I could no longer fit into my best friend's pants. They wouldn't go past my thighs. Size twelve was too small. For some reason, I had an insane superstition that your clothing size needed to coordinate perfectly with your age. The realization that there was no size thirteen was crushing. *What now?* I felt let down by my body. I assumed that I had done something wrong to grow past that juniors sizing. I didn't know how I could correct my mistake, but I did know, more importantly, that I had to hide that shameful truth from everyone. I became obsessed with making sure that my weight stayed under one hundred pounds. The number was arbitrary, but I was sure that crossing over into triple digits would mean certain death. I just knew it. I became seriously curious about how to diet. I figured that by restricting my food intake, I could stop my body from betraying me.

I started throwing away food when no one was looking. I busied myself with other things while food was being served or claimed I had homework so I could "eat" alone. It was an obsession that continued to fester over the years, intensified by the fact that it had to be kept secret. I knew that not eating wasn't acceptable behavior and that it would disappoint many people, people I needed to have positive opinions of me. A page from my middle school diary dated December 29, 2000, reads, "It's later. Almost dinner. Actually, I'm not hungry. Well I am, but sometimes I feel fat. Like I should be skinnier. My parents are like 'Oh, you should exercise' and all, but maybe not eating is the answer. My parents will always make me eat. I haven't told them how I feel, but they wouldn't go for it. I was even doing sit-ups so I won't look like a fool at Kristen's bday party." (Yes, I hated Kristen, but she always had a fancy birthday party at a hotel, and I would not be missing that.) In December 2000, I was twelve years old, and I'd already been record-ing these types of furtive thoughts for years. I continued on like that, privately documenting my self-loathing and monitoring my calories.

The resolute devotion to making sure I was the same size as my friends made shopping at Victoria's Secret a personal hell. My friends were all tiny. They wore size extra small because we were children and because they were actually small. Plus, as they were all white, they didn't get the butt I did when the freight train of puberty screeched into town. They would buy thongs in their sizes, and I, too embarrassed to admit that a thong that size felt like a torture device, bought the same size. Let the record show that I wear a large in underwear, a medium sometimes. But I squeezed myself into size extra small thongs. I assumed, for years, that like my perm or eyebrow threading or dieting or any other thing meant to outwardly define femininity, thongs were supposed to hurt. I dreaded any occasion that would require me to wear a thong, knowing just how palpably miserable I would be. I also dreaded being exposed for not wearing a thong. How anyone might find out about my under-wear at thirteen never occurred to me, but still, just in case, I made sure to do my duty because being caught wearing or doing the wrong thing was potentially way worse than wearing too-small underwear.

In seventh grade, the first boy I ever kissed finally drew the decisive bridge between being loved and being thin. It happened during a rowdy game of truth or dare. My coed class of twelve had eight girls and four boys, all of whom wanted a chance to sample what it might be like to kiss our classmates, so the boys invented a spin-the-bottle-like game. It was dressed up like truth or dare, except dare was the only option, and the dare was always to kiss someone. The rotation was at the discretion of the onlookers, an attempt to make sure the kissing playing field was equalized. It was pretty unromantic, but I didn't have much interaction with boys, so I took what I could get. When it was my turn, I assumed that the boy selected for me was at the very least approving of my physical appearance because he did not refuse the kiss. I had seen some other people get painfully rejected during the game, and since that had not happened to me, it must have meant that I looked OK. We kissed. Everyone cheered and clapped appropriately, and we seemed to move on with our lives. I had no feelings about him either way, but he told his friend (who told my friend over Nextel bleep) that—and this is a direct quote, seared into my memory so deep that it will probably be etched into my tombstone—"Danielle's butt is so big, it always looks like she's wearing a diaper."

Well, there it was. This will be hard for younger people to imagine, but there was once a cultural landscape where not everyone was praising derrieres as peaches, where having a "big butt" was a punch line, not a prize. I had certainly noticed my ballooning bottom, but I was hoping that no one else had. I'd begun to resent being in leotards in dance class because I could see that the sway of my back was exaggerated and that my butt stuck out in a way that none of the other little dancers' did. I wore a sweatshirt tied around my waist, which I marketed as a stylistic choice, but the reality was that it was purely functional. I constantly tucked my pelvis forward, clenching my glutes, hoping this might help reduce their size. Obviously, none of this worked, but I hoped the stupid thing people said about concerning yourself with things no one else sees was actually true. It's not. People see. And people saw my butt. But not just any people. I thought that boy had kissed me because he favored how I looked. What a fatal miscalculation that proved to be.

That pivotal moment was the beginning of the end. Once I heard the comment, I knew I had no choice but to reduce my butt or suffer a fate of loneliness and social isolation for the rest of my life. I did not want to be the girl who "always looks like she's wearing a diaper!" I was wearing agonizing thongs, and I wanted the credit for it.

By the time I got to high school, *the* butt, *my* butt, was beginning to incur an uncomfortable amount of notoriety. People noticed no matter what I did. We all started listening to hip-hop and rap, and any song that mentioned a butt made me physically ill. "Oh my God, it's for you!" my friends would squeal as Sir Mix-a-Lot's infamous "Baby Got Back" would play at school dances. Hands would find the small of my back and shove me toward the center of a circle, where I would unenthusiastically shake my hips since sprinting away wasn't really an option. The lyrics of that song haunted me.

Before Sir-Mix-a-Lot begins rapping, a hyperbolic conversation between two white women plays. They say, quite famously, "Oh my God, Becky, look at her butt! It's so big." This has become somewhat of a quirky quip, in part thanks to Nicki Minaj remixing it in her 2014 hit "Anaconda." However, the rest of the conversation is not easily called to memory: "She looks like one of those rap guys' girlfriends. But, ya know, who understands those rap guys? They only talk to her because she looks like a total prostitute, k? I mean her butt is just so big. I can't believe it's so round. It's like out there. I mean, gross, look. She's just so . . . black." This is clearly meant to be a satirical conversation, but I have heard girls talk like this. I myself participated in conversations like this, identifying women as tacky or slutty if they showed off certain body parts. I, of course, had nothing to say in the race department, but

I'm sure it must have come up among people I knew. Many of these conversations happened in front of me, so who knows what went on behind my enormous butt?

At fourteen, about a year into my experimentation with what I will call "extreme dieting," my parents came to pick me up from school when I passed out and fell down the steps. My high school's original building was in an old mansion, so let's just say, it was a lot of steps to tumble down. I lay sprawled out at the bottom, thankful I always wore shorts under my uniform skirt, but unconscious nonetheless. The ambulance came and escorted me to Greenwich Hospital, where I regained consciousness.

I was in shock. Everyone started asking "What happened?" and I had to confess that I hadn't eaten all day, probably for the past few days. I left the hospital with a slight concussion and an inexplicable stutter that lasted for months. Well, that did it. I'd scared myself. I made sure to eat close to regularly for at least a year. But eventually, after I regained my speech and got back to a more normal routine, the old fears about gaining weight returned. Once I was healthy again, I could freely concern myself with the width of my still-developing hips.

The hierarchy of human needs is a tricky beast. All my immediate needs were taken care of, leaving space and time for superficial anxieties to make their way to the surface. This is the common reasoning behind the pervasive idea that eating disorders affect only white women. There is a statistical basis for eating disorders being more prevalent in the white community—but only because eating disorders are typically only studied in white women. It's dangerous to assume that food issues can be explained away as a symptom of being white and rich. And racial bias in medicine often prevents discovery and exploration of conditions that specifically affect Black people. In recent years, data has exposed the fact that Black women suffer from bulimia at a higher rate than previously recorded. Black women have also become more vocal about suffering from eating disorders. We might have a different point of origin driving us toward disordered eating, but the resulting pathology is the same.

In 2019, female rapper CupcakKe went viral after showing off the results of her monthlong water fast. Most people were alarmed by the results of what someone might look like after ingesting only water for one month straight. And yet, almost no one suggested she seek treatment for an eating disorder. Many commenters, too many, were mesmerized by CupcakKe's transformation and wanted to try it themselves. I had similar inquiries when I documented my frequent "fasting" on social media and, even before, when diet tips were passed by word of mouth. Disguising eating disorders as "cleanses" or "detoxes" is how these behaviors slip by mostly unnoticed.

After my fall, I was assaulted by a series of anxiety-inducing questions that I had no answers to, like "Why didn't you eat?" and "Why would you do that?" It was devastating that people knew I had fallen because I wasn't eating. I began to make my eating a performance, deliberately making a show of my meals, always ensuring there was an audience. Being someone who "never ate" indicated a weakness in character. It was usually associated with girls who were excessively interested in clothes—think Emily in *The Devil Wears Prada*. (And by the way, after seeing that movie, I started eating a little nibble of cheese instead of a full meal every time I got hungry.) Even though I was a girl interested in clothes, I didn't want to appear shallow. For the time being, it was essential that whatever I had going on with food, it had to be kept completely secret.

CHAPTER TEN

For a lot of people, "Baby Got Back" served as affirmation of the existence of women with butts and men who, well, liked them. Finally, they got an anthem that acknowledged what they knew to be true: men like big butts and they cannot lie. In fact, between the years of 1810 and 1815, Saartjie Baartman, a woman who came to be known as the "Hottentot Venus," was kidnapped from modern-day South Africa by a European doctor and literally put on display for up to ten hours per day in cities like London and Paris because white people were so mesmerized by what they considered to be her exaggerated backside and genitalia. Her body was viewed as grotesque. And yet, in 1870, almost sixty years after Baartman was violated for white people's entertainment, the first Victorian bustle appeared. For those not well versed in fashion history, a bustle is essentially an undergarment worn beneath skirts in order to give a woman a backside that looks uncannily like Saartjie Baartman's body. In recent years, scholars have drawn a connection between Baartman's involuntary popularity and the advent of the bustle in white high society. The look that became a cornerstone and defining characteristic of nineteenth-century fashion was—like so many things—stolen from a Black woman who was shamed, ostracized, and fetishized because of her body. It's the blueprint for appropriation, and it is still in practice today. Currently, we call these Brazilian butt lifts, a surgical bustle.

But back to Sir Mix-a-Lot. For butts to be considered sexually desirable, and for them to be celebrated so brazenly out in the open, was a major problem for me. It left me vulnerable to girls who had previously assumed that my Blackness took me out of competition for boys' attention—white boys' attention, specifically. The DUFF—also known as the Designated Ugly Fat Friend—and the Token Black Girl were one and the same: totally unthreatening in terms of romantic competition. Why would some guy, let's call him Chad, go for me when he could have a white girl like Becky? This song opened the floodgates for the possibility that Chad might consider me and my big butt sexually preferable to Becky. Listen, I did not want that smoke.

I knew if I expressed any pride in my anatomy, the other girls would destroy it with one sentence or less. I never learned how to twerk or properly utilize what many saw as a natural gift because it brought me so much shame and embarrassment. When you're the only Black girl in a sea of white ones, your best hope is to try to fit in. It will make everything infinitely easier. In 2011, at the royal wedding of Prince William and (now Duchess) Kate Middleton, Middleton's younger sister stole the spotlight on an international scale, and every single headline was about . . . her butt. If you look at this image now, ten years later, you might ask yourself, as I did at the time, "What butt?" Pippa Middleton's dress was neither tight nor indecent, but the fervor created by the press over her tiny, tiny booty was sickening. Imagine what it is like for someone with an actual butt to watch this go down. My adolescence, trying to make my escape whenever "Bootylicious" or "Baby Got Back" blared out of a sound system, came flying back to me.

Plus, however exaggerated the conversation around Pippa's rear end, or the one mimicked in the Sir Mix-a-Lot song, that is still pretty much the way women talk about themselves and each other. "Slut shaming," now a widely criticized practice, was so common, it was instinctual. If you had boobs or a butt, you knew not to draw extra attention to it, or you'd risk the wrath and judgment of your female peers. I still second-guess myself often when getting dressed. The residual shame of a Catholic education constantly reminds me that I am potentially being a desperate slut.

In 2020, *Vogue* published a Met Gala retrospective where former *Vogue* creative director Sally Singer reminisced, "One year, Jessica Simpson was there with John Mayer. She was wearing Michael Kors and her breasts maybe fell out of her dress, and then at dinner it was suddenly like, whoa, Jessica Simpson's breasts are across from me at the dinner table and they are on a platter and I am looking at them." This was printed in cancel-happy 2020, not the "anything goes" media era of 2002. And it's a derogatory statement about a very rich white woman, albeit one who fashion was always kind of reluctant to accept. Nonetheless, it's the way fashion people speak about women's bodies then and now. It's problematic that these are the voices behind what teenage girls are reading. It warps their thoughts, painting any body that is not rail-thin and prepubescent as skanky.

"She's spilling out," "She's asking for it," and "She's doing too much" are all phrases we are trained to think and say, knowing exactly how to supervise ourselves and others. I spent years trying to talk myself into wearing shorts, knowing the combination of my butt and thighs would garner so much negative attention and judgment that I instead just opted to sweat.

I preferred jeans that flattened out my butt. And if you thought my thong-shopping experience was bad, trust me when I say jeans shopping was way worse. In the early 2000s, the only butt in town was JLo's, and even she was not exempt from the denim limitations of the era. Brands like Apple Bottoms, House of Deréon, and Baby Phat catered to a curvier, more urban audience, but donning those brands in Greenwich, Connecticut, would have been the social equivalent of wearing a bikini to play ice hockey. It just wasn't done. So I suffered, stuffing myself into jeans that pushed my ass flesh out the top, spending countless hours hiking up my pants. The bigger my butt got, the bigger my jean size had to be, and to my dismay, despite a moderate number of calories and an excessive amount of exercise, I still grew, and so did it. I was wearing up to a denim size twenty-nine and thirty when I was sixteen, just to be able to accommodate my hips and butt. Stretch denim was simply not a thing back then. All my friends wore size twenty-five and twenty-six, so the messaging that I was fat became even louder. I felt like it was being shouted at me all the time. I was constantly bombarded with reminders that my body was wrong. I felt enormous compared to everyone else, and I couldn't see a world where my body would ever be acceptable.

I was so terrified of becoming fat that I went into hyperdrive, always running from something. I carefully recorded the ways girls would speak about other girls whose bodies they found unacceptable. I listened even more intently to the way boys coded girls' bodies. No matter what, "fat" was an insult, an absolutely unacceptable thing that I could never become. But since I already saw myself as fat, the best I could hope for was to disguise it, just as I had thought I was doing with my butt before it busted free and double-crossed me. My commitment to dieting increased substantially.

While over the last decade it seems that everyone is interested in having an ass, dangerously so if the BBL data reports are to be believed, obscure physical features like "back dimples," little dents of bone that showed just above the waistband of low-rise jeans, were everything in the early part of the millennium. I did not have these. Along with the back dimples I didn't have, I was also introduced to the concept of a "thigh gap." We didn't have a name for it back in 2004, but we knew, all the same, that thighs were never to touch. Friends would coach me on how to stand in photos to appear as if I had a thigh gap even when I didn't. We were constantly thinking and talking about what to do to avoid our thighs rubbing together, as if that would be the absolute worst thing in the world. I felt sorry for girls whose thighs touched, and it's still something I notice, even when I don't want to. As depressing as it is to admit, it is still my personal barometer for whether I have gained too much weight. Do I understand what a colossal waste of time and energy it is to be concerned with the minuscule distance in between your thighs? Absolutely. But once an idea like that is planted and establishes roots, a girl needs a whole lot of herbicide if she's ever going to eradicate it. Unfortunately for me, I had only fertilizer for these kinds of toxic ideas, so they blossomed inside me like a twisted garden, killing whatever semblance of self-esteem I had and making sure I was aware they were in control, not me.

In dark corners of the internet during my teenage years, I'd visit sites that existed solely to promote recklessly thin bodies. They were sometimes called pro-ana or pro-mia sites, aptly named for the diseases they nursed and endorsed. These sites featured images of girls who showed off their bones—shoulders, ribs, hips—making the skeleton an emblem of victory. I used to visit these sites to get "diet tips," which were little more than bizarre, disordered habits we passed to one another. I admired the diligence and discipline that I knew were required to have that kind of body. I never posted on the sites because, even when I found myself under 20 percent body fat, I was still too ashamed of my softness to participate. I always looked just a bit too healthy.

When I was fourteen, I got invited to a casual hang in Chappaqua, the town the Clintons run, so to speak, in upper Westchester. The gathering was a typical parents-upstairs, kids-downstairs kind of thing at the house of one of my closest friends. My friend was white, of course. Another friend was in attendance—a petite but overweight girl who floated by on her affable personality—and as the evening was ending, her brother came to pick her up. He ended up sitting next to me on a couch and we started talking. From my recollection, it was an innocent conversation. I wasn't comfortable enough at fourteen to flirt with anyone, but that didn't matter. When my friend saw me talking to her brother, she yanked him up by the arm. "Stop talking to her," she told him. I was completely taken aback. While I was still seated, she put her face in front of mine and said, "I don't want you talking to my brother because you are a slut." My cheeks and neck burned. Even though she was talking to only me, I was sure other people could hear.

I was immediately confused. For one, I never considered myself attractive, but I did do my best to present myself in a way that was conventionally acceptable. It was a weekend, so I was most likely in a combination of a denim miniskirt and a T-shirt or tank top with sneakers, an exact replica of everyone else's outfits. But still, I was labeled a slut. I had somehow unknowingly released sexy pheromones that were a threat to my friend and a danger to me. No part of me wanted this girl's brother, and no part of me wanted to be labeled a slut, either, but I accidentally got both. I knew it had something to do with both how I was dressed and how I was seen, so from that moment on, I tried not to overtly communicate sex. I wore ballet flats to many dances because I, one, was taller than a lot of the boys; two, did not want to seem like I was doing "too much;" and three, recognized that high heels were inherently sexy and therefore probably should not be worn. I became more and more devoted to fashion and took on what I will generously label as a more avant-garde aesthetic because boys hated that kind of thing.

The next year, I met a white boy at a dance. He was moderately attractive but kind of geeky and greasy in the way that underdeveloped teenage boys often are. It was not easy to meet boys when you went to an all-girls school, so interactions with them became monumental events. He was an enthusiastic "grinder," a mating ritual only millennials will understand, and expressed his feelings for me by rubbing his crotch against my backside. My best friend, a Latina girl, was engaged in a similar flirtation with one of his friends. To cement our newfound status, we tried to find excuses to hang out with these guys on the weekends, in addition to connecting with them regularly over stress-inducing texts and AIM.

Somehow, one of us managed to coordinate everyone's schedules so we would get hours of time with this group of boys on a Saturday afternoon and evening. It took so much clever manipulation and pure serendipity, but we'd managed to pair everyone up with a potential partner that would result in a "hookup." To our group in 2005, that meant sloppy kissing and light petting. I had successfully orchestrated a match with that same thin white boy from the dance, who was taller than me (truly the only metric that mattered since I was insecure about my height). Due to my limited interaction with the opposite sex, every exchange was extremely high stakes, and I had more or less convinced myself that I loved him. That afternoon, we made out in a bathroom, and I was sure that the subtle physical touches and hints throughout the night were meant to communicate that he liked me.

A few days later, my best friend and his were officially in a confirmed "relationship," whatever that meant for two kids who didn't live anywhere near each other and couldn't even drive. I had heard nothing from the boy I'd kissed, aside from a "Sup" message that came through to my pink Razr on the following Sunday night. I was conscious that I was still in the audition phase, that nothing had been solidified between us, but I figured we had a healthy enough foundation to build upon. Plus, our friends were "dating," so that should make it easier for him to ask me to be his girlfriend. I agonized over it for days. I thought of nothing but committing our every word and touch to memory. I wanted to make sure I could analyze all potential clues so I could guess what he was thinking about me.

As it turns out, I really couldn't. One night, my best friend called my landline (you used to get charged for minutes, so it was best for long conversations to happen the old-fashioned way) to tell me that she had an update to deliver about my crush. She was clearly nervous, talking fast and trying to explain a lot. "Don't be mad," she said. Blood rushed through my ears; my intuition told me what was coming.

"I'm not," I said, the requisite response.

"OK, well, [my crush] told [her boyfriend] that he can't date you because . . ." She hesitated and let the sentence hover for a moment, but my hammering heartbeat told me I already knew the rest.

"Because I'm Black," I finished for her with an assist.

"Yes." She exhaled, clearly relieved that she didn't have to be the one to say it.

I cannot explain how I knew this was the reason; I just knew. Four years later, in 2010, John Mayer, another Fairfield County–born-and-raised white man, would give a notorious interview to *Playboy* where he said he had a "nigger pass" and then likened his sexual preferences to David Duke, former grand wizard of the KKK. Based on his popularity within the Black community, Mayer was asked by the interviewer if "Black women were throwing themselves" at him, to which he replied, "I don't think I open myself to it. My dick is sort of like a white supremacist. I've got a Benetton heart and a fuckin' David Duke cock. I'm going to start dating separately from my dick." He then went on to list the Black women he found attractive: Holly Robinson Peete, Hilary Banks (played by Karyn Parsons Rockwell), and Kerry Washington, the latter of whom he referred to as "white girl crazy."

In a *Newsweek* opinion piece in response to his interview, Allison Samuels wrote, "My guess is Mayer will suffer little for his comments. And the reason is very simple. He clearly said out loud what a large majority of mainstream men in power feel in private. I'm referring to those invisible men in the corner offices with the influence and power to put women in movies, on magazine covers, and on television shows. The ones who decide what beauty looks like, how much it weighs, and what age it should be. The ones who, just like John Mayer, have deemed black women as just not good enough." Samuels went on to say, "He and his peers' lack of interest in African-American women doesn't just impact us on date night, it impacts important decisions about how we are viewed all over the world. And it determines whether those sightings are balanced and diverse." And this is the reason why Black people care about likability in the eyes of white people in the first place.

White men are largely in control of who gets hired and fired and what art gets made and seen. It's gross, but overcoming this color barrier can be a means of increasing your access to opportunities.

I think it is worth noting that Mayer's upbringing in the liberal North and the fact that his childhood best friend was Black professional tennis player James Blake did absolutely nothing to squash out the dormant racism of American white men. It was an extremely damaging interview, but nonetheless, John Mayer persists, doesn't he? And he is representative of a lot of white men, giving them a voice and legitimacy. Tell me there were different conversations happening at frats. I dare you.

Mayer was also, in some measure, a local hero. In fact, many of my friends wanted to see him on tour years after the interview ran. I guess not everyone had the same memory for that kind of thing that I did. Yet I held on to that quote the same way I held the memory of being rejected by another Fairfield County–raised bigot because I was Black. You may be thinking I should have sought out Black love interests, and I would have had that been a real, plausible option for me, but I simply did not have access to a pool of Black boys. When I met Black boys later on, they expressed their displeasure for my personality, not looks, by and large telling me that I was a spoiled princess. Go figure!

On some level, I felt comforted with the knowledge. At least now I knew. I wouldn't have to dream up excuses for the way he was icing me out. It became something of a pastime of mine: finding and falling in love with white boys who were clearly uninterested in me. I couldn't help but re-create this traumatic rejection over and over again into adulthood. I sought out ways to prove to myself that I was both wanted and unwanted by seeking out these types of partners and collecting data from our romantic interactions. That particular guy moved to New York City, too, and our circles of friends remained tangentially related. After high school, he went to Cornell. He, unsurprisingly, works in finance and has a very white, very blonde, and very skinny girlfriend. They might be engaged.

I never really considered the effect those comments and incidents had on my self-worth until other Black women with similar experiences began to discuss those experiences more publicly. In the summer of 2020, actress Thandiwe Newton gave an interview to *Vulture* in which she details how her invisibility as the only Black girl affected her ability to have healthy adult romantic relationships: "We didn't talk about it at the time, but the damage was so done. It just made me super-vulnerable to predators. That's the truth. Because there's so much about not having a sense of my value. I suffered quite badly for a couple of years from anorexia, and it all feeds into this. Just wanting to disappear. What happened for me was I had a very complicated relationship with [sexual relationships] I never chose. I let other people do the choosing for me. That saddens me. It was like I had to give something back for being noticed. You get predators and sexual abusers, they can smell it a mile off."

The "damage" Thandiwe refers to is her desperate desire to be both recognized and accepted. She never won awards at school and was never given solos in her dance class, and that pattern eventually festered into a work ethic that had both positive and negative consequences on her. I relate to the anorexia part, surely, but also the vulnerability that being ignored creates. I was convinced that I had to work for and earn affection. In romantic relationships, affection wasn't something that would be readily offered, so I knew that just like with grades or sports or dance, I would have to put in the time and effort to be loved. I assumed that nearly all that necessary effort had to do with how I looked. I sought out relationships with men who displayed indifference or even disdain for me. I would contort myself for their attention, changing little and big things about how I looked, dressed, or behaved. Even now, I find it difficult to trust anyone who admits to being attracted to me. A sizable "why?" hovers in the air. I cannot wrap my head around simply being liked for who I am, and a large part of that stems back to that moment of being told I wasn't datable simply because I am Black.

There wasn't much I could do about that guy, but I'd be damned if I let the same thing happen to me again. I vowed to embody the apex of physical perfection—to the best of my ability, anyway. And thus, I doubled down on my quest to transcend my race by becoming as attractive and successful as possible.

CHAPTER ELEVEN

Buried in the commitment to being beautiful is an understanding that certain necessary sacrifices must be made. When a person starts wearing skirts or heels, for example, they do so with the understanding that those items may limit their free movement. Activities where a person might become sweaty or otherwise undone are no longer suitable; they will tarnish the carefully crafted veneer of a pristine exterior. As the ideal of beauty and the subsequent maintenance of beauty increases in importance, so, too, does avoiding anything that could impede this new, weighty occupation.

My high school had a pool in a basement under the auditorium. Yes, indeed, *The Craft* flashbacks. It was where our swim team practiced, but it was also used for PE classes during the winter. Physical education, colloquially known as "gym class," is not an elective. It is, in fact, a state-required element of a comprehensive education. Because I played a varsity sport, I was excused from gym, but only during the spring and fall trimesters. During winter, I was expected to attend. I knew the class affected not only my grade point average—a numerical value with influence over my life that was surpassed by only my weight—but also my ability to progress to the next grade, or even graduate. Passing gym was nonnegotiable. Unfortunately for me, so was never ever getting into that pool. I knew my precious perm would come undone the second

I submerged myself underwater, and I also knew I could not possibly reveal my natural hair texture at school. The time it would take for me to shower and set my hair properly after a swim would be akin to a whole afternoon. It's called "wash day," not "wash thirty minutes"—I would miss the remainder of the day's classes. My white classmates were able to shower in the locker room and return to class with damp hair, comfortable that it would dry in a way that was still acceptable, if not ideal. I was sure that if I ever got in that pool, my life would be over.

Of course, this feels absurd almost twenty years later, and it pains me that other young girls might still be grappling with these same kinds of feelings, that one day *my own daughter* might sacrifice her academic standing by opting out of swimming in gym class. But I also remember fruitlessly begging my mother to send us to sleepaway camp. Later, upon finding out that my mother had attended sleepaway camp as a girl, I demanded an explanation as to why we had been denied the same pleasure. She said with a shudder, "There was no one there that could do my hair. That was the worst summer of my life." Her answer was sufficient enough to stop my line of questioning. I couldn't imagine any experience, no matter how great, would make me want to abandon haircare completely.

So I spent four years of my life conjuring excuses to get out of swimming. I had my period a few times, and when that excuse was implausible—as gym was every week for three months—I had injuries. I was ill. I was anything I needed to be as long as I wasn't in that pool. Miraculously, it worked. My gym teacher, of course, grew tired of me. One winter, she snapped at me during the last class, "We wear tampons, you know," alluding to her knowledge that a period should not actually keep someone out of a pool. I flinched like I'd been hit. It killed me to displease anyone. The issue itself was not swimming, which I would have gladly explained to her. In fact, I am an excellent swimmer. But "I have to protect my straight hair, no matter what" was not something I could say to my gym teacher, who seemed exempt from the curses of vanity. So I endured the consequences of skipping out on the swim requirement. It doesn't have any effect on my life now, similar to how the SATs were everything and then they were nothing after all was said and done. But what does still haunt me is the fact that I would continue to make exceptions to my schedule, my goals, and my comfort because I needed to look a certain way, all in order to fit into a context that wasn't meant for me. Really, my commitment to beauty was never just about beauty.

I didn't have the agency to defend myself against my teacher's judgment. There was a gulf of understanding between us that I didn't have the tools or language to cross, a distance that existed not just between me and my teachers, but also between me and my peers. Though it would be a long time before I learned how to name them, microaggressions from friends and classmates happened regularly, each one chipping away a little more of my sense of who I was.

Penny was a great tennis player—shrewd and competitive. She was also an imaginative storyteller—some might even say a liar—reckless, and a bit mean, but at the same time, she was really fun. She was a year older than me after repeating a grade, so she got her driver's license earlier than everyone else in our class. Because we were tennis partners and the only two freshmen on the team, we spent a lot of time together. She was obsessed with history and status, and she often bragged about being a "daughter of the revolution." She said she had ancestors who came to America on the *Mayflower*. This, of course, could have been true, but it was questionable because it was widely known that Penny had been adopted.

Penny would often badger people about their family's origins until she got an answer she was satisfied with. One day, after we had sped down the dirt and gravel path from the main school building to the tennis courts for practice, a trail of dust lingering behind her Jeep, she asked me where my family was from. I dreaded hearing this question because the truth was I didn't really know. I also didn't want to ask my parents because I loathed discussing historical topics with them, knowing it would lead to an unpleasant lecture about adversity and hardship. I still hate this question, but for different reasons. It is a shameless way to attempt to assess people's value. What I wanted to say was, "My family crawled themselves from the blood-drenched soil of the South and resolutely worked and worked and worked for half of the pay and even less of the glory of your family so we could both end up in the very same place." That's not what I said, though.

I knew Penny would never let the question drop. I had watched her badger too many people with it but had always managed to successfully elude the question myself. On that day, we were not alone in Penny's car; her best friend, Noelle, also Black, accompanied us to practice. I felt a special kinship with Noelle, even though many of our white classmates refused to tell us apart and frequently interchanged our names despite our looking nothing alike. Noelle's father was natively Jamaican. He had a strong accent, and though she was raised in New York, she could clearly pinpoint "where she came from," unlike me. In a sadistic way, I think Penny understood this when she finally cornered me that day.

"As you know, my family came over on the *Mayflower* . . ." Penny began. I selectively tuned out the rest. I had heard this overly rehearsed play so many times that I could silently mouth her lines. "Where's your family from?" she asked when she was satisfied with the retelling of her family history. She spun around to look at me in the back seat.

To this day, I can't say what possessed me to answer the way I did. I can only hypothesize that years of acrimonious silences and pro-longed bitterness made me snap like a branch holding too much snow. "Your family probably owned my family," I replied, with no inflection in my voice. I had never been more honest. I had never suggested out loud that I was a descendant of slaves. I also understood that in this exchange, I was meant to be denied any pride in being Black. The point of it all was to shame me.

Of course, there was no way to know whether her family owned slaves, but statistically speaking, if a white family had come on the

Mayflower and settled somewhere in the original thirteen colonies, it was highly probable that, over several generations, somebody owned slaves. I didn't know enough about my family history to say either way, but I wanted to shock her and diminish her invalid pride in an ancestry that didn't even belong to her.

Penny was unmoved. She shrugged and said, "Yeah, but I am sure they were, like, the nice kind. Like probably your great-great-great-grandmother and mine were friends." Noelle said nothing, and neither did I. There was nothing to say. White people's belief that slavery was an unfortunate thing that happened a long time ago and has nothing to do with them is cardinal to maintaining the mythos around whiteness. I was a child and had yet to really begin to understand the cruelty and brutality of slavery and its punishing, long-lasting trauma.

In 2019, I took a DNA test and discovered atrocities still lingering in my bloodstream to the tune of 20 percent European DNA. It must have been that "friends" thing Penny was talking about.

Penny finally knew where to place me in her lineage hierarchy. In some way, I knew where to place myself too. And it was critical that I maintain the performance of my role at all times, an imagined necessity that extended to any and all areas of my life.

By that time in my life, eating had become a performative act. It is obviously necessary for survival, and the unfavorable view of those with visible eating disorders was enough for me to know that I needed to keep this shit locked up tight in the closet. So I carefully planned how I would display to the world that I was a girl who ate. When I began to live on my own, my freedom expanded exponentially. As a college student, I was no longer confined to the strict timetables that school and family dinner provided, and I was able to disguise my eating disorder by busying myself in work, saying I was too busy to eat. Token Black Girl representative Kerry Washington, an alum of the prestigious Spence School, describes her relationship to eating and her body the same way. While promoting the 2004 film *Ray*, Washington told *O, The*

Oprah Magazine, "In college, I began over-exercising and under-eating, convinced that a perfect figure would ensure my success as an actor. In a profession where rejection happened daily and my fate was always in the hands of others, my body became the one thing that I could control."

Environments where women feel as if many things are out of their control can produce a psychology that is linked to eating disorders. And any environment that rewards either hard work or perfection is a breeding ground. Washington continues, "I always became a prettier, smarter, taller, and thinner Kerry. My disease of perfectionism began early, and the myth of 'I'm not enough' only flourished with time." By the time Washington was enrolled in college at George Washington University, she was sneaking away from her friends to binge and purge.

Finding convincing excuses is essential for maintaining an eating disorder. In my case, having a study commitment was seamless since being a "driven woman" is a positive quality. I adapted this same excuse later in life when I entered the working world. When I could no longer stand the hunger and I needed to "crack" and eat something, I would binge-drink on top of eating and then throw up, using the alcohol as a cover for bulimia. When you've been drinking as a college student, you can easily throw up in public, and no one will think anything of it. I found it incredibly humiliating to throw up after eating, but being drunk eliminated my inhibitions.

Being an alcoholic was totally acceptable. Fun, even. Being a bulimic was not. I stopped drinking about six years ago and stopped puking maybe three years after that. People question me about why I don't drink all the time, asking if I will ever "be fun again." I don't know what to say. I know drinking will almost certainly make me want to start throwing up my food. Partying and purging are too closely related for me. One almost always followed the other. It was just too easy. Escaping to the bathroom during dinner is a telltale sign of something being amiss. Escaping to the bathroom during a party is a telltale sign of a good evening. I became the poster girl for booting and rallying, and no one had any idea I was booting because I was actually sick with something else.

The basic idea that being hungry means you should feed yourself and give your body what it wants is a difficult concept for me. I spent so much energy ignoring basic cues that are useful for survival. Self-discipline became my superpower. I can override nearly any itch, desire, or even necessity. All-nighters for studying? No problem. No time to stop and go to the bathroom? Easy for me. Impossibly high heels for ten hours a day? Me! All these toxic behaviors flawlessly executed with no chemical enhancements, just adrenaline and sheer self-hate.

More than anything, I craved that sense of control. I not only wanted to carefully orchestrate how others saw me but also wanted to fundamentally control what went in and out of my body because only I could. Just as I made many quality-of-life sacrifices for my hair, I began to make decisions based on how they might affect my weight. I would never smoke weed because I heard it could make you hungry. I didn't go on birth control until I got an IUD in my late twenties because I was terrified that it might make me gain weight. For the same reason, I resisted antidepressants I was prescribed. I exercised obsessively. I was at the gym every day, no matter what. I ran because it was free and convenient and felt like terrible punishment.

It was hugely important for me to be social, so I found a way to attend group dinners and order only a soup and salad. It would be preferable for people to think I was cheap than to think I was pathetically obsessed with my weight. But I was doubly encouraged by both the fashion industry that I wanted to be a part of and the internet to continue on this path. In a 2009 interview with *WWD*, supermodel Kate Moss was asked if she had any personal mantras. "Nothing tastes as good as skinny feels," she said. I snatched up this nugget and ran with it, reciting it like a prayer, posting it to Facebook, and keeping it with me at all times as confirmation that starvation was a precious virtue.

CHAPTER TWELVE

In the wake of my rapidly changing body, I felt immense comfort in the fact that my school uniform meant I could still live in a simulation of sameness. I wore a uniform for most of my life, and though it made me want to push the boundaries of self-expression, it also delineated me as the same as my peers, a status that I obviously coveted. These days, when I am stumped for an outfit, I almost always reach for a miniskirt and a sweater, an iteration of what I wore to school every day for twelve or so years. In the spring, it was a light-blue skirt with three pleats or a traditional kilt. In the fall and winter, it was heavy navy and forest-green plaid in the same silhouettes. I am an advocate of uniforms, but there is an artful component of white supremacy woven into their history that must be confronted. A dress code, like in ballet, encourages uniformity. It is supposed to eliminate feelings of competition, but I often felt that it also encouraged an atmosphere of shame.

I tried to hunt down my old student handbook, but I guess after fifteen years, my family figured we didn't need it anymore. So I took a look at a similar school's website to see what they said about their dress code. "The uniform symbolizes respect for tradition, order, equality, and authority. Wearing the uniform proudly and properly is one of the central ways in which we communicate commitment to our Catholic values. Parents, please ensure that your children adhere to our uniform policy and our overall dress code. Students, please wear your uniform in a manner that reflects pride in yourself and in our school. Sacred Heart School expects students to be in full uniform every day. Uniforms must fit appropriately and be in good condition. If a student is not in full uniform, a note of explanation must come from a parent, and a uniform exception permit will be issued for the school day."

In other words, adhering to the dress code was a conditional requirement for attending school. The dress code also outlines what is acceptable for "civvies days," days when uniforms were not required. Here's a short list of things that were not allowed: shirts with logos or phrases, short or tight skirts, shorts that are too short, jeans that are too tight, shirts that are too cropped or too low cut, hats, high heels, pants with sayings on the butt (which, at the height of the Juicy Couture craze, was extremely problematic), and, my favorite, hoop earrings. It was through this framework that I was able to develop my own understanding of what was acceptable. As you may have noticed, anything that puts the body on display or expresses allegiance to a team or idea is a no go.

One's presentation at school is a preparation for the concept of professionalism, an idea steeped in white supremacy, that seeks to force conformity from people of color, reducing their own cultural influences, mannerisms, or dress in favor of a white standard. Most people are not exposed to this idea until adulthood. I can't say if that's an advantage or a disadvantage. Some companies—financial and medical institutions, for example—have dress codes like these. Military and ballet dress codes include stipulations about hair. Legislation has been passed to combat this and reframe the idea that natural or braided hair is unprofessional. On an unofficial level, some artistic and professional institutions have amended their definition and requirements for "nude shoes" or "nude tights."

By high school, I was already practiced in the art of it all, having been scolded for my uniform violations and made to feel ashamed about my clothing choices. I learned, though, and I used this knowledge to judge others, wielding my opinion as a weapon and cutting others down for not knowing better. I shamed them as I had been shamed. I knew what was expected of me, so I arranged myself accordingly. I was not to be a "distraction" in any way. I have no tattoos and the only thing pierced on my body is my ears. Granted, I have seventeen ear piercings, all acquired in adulthood, so that real estate is a bit crowded, but when I had around ten or so, my mother asked me when I would "stop mutilating my body." Which is to say, these standards were enforced at home as well as at school. Prohibiting hoop earrings—which are often seen as a danger since something can get caught and pulled in the hoop—is another quiet way of establishing a dress code of white supremacy. Hoop earrings are worn proudly in Black and brown communities. I wear hoops every day of my life now, but for years, I was aligned with the warped thinking that they were tacky. They were something I might get in trouble for wearing. In fact, as an adult horseback rider, my teacher repeatedly told me I was not allowed to wear my hoop earrings. And before you ask, yes, she was white. With so many influences in my life dictating what is appropriate, breaking out of that kind of thinking took a lot of personal work.

Contemporary fashion associated with Black culture is often deemed "inelegant" or "inappropriate." Many schools and offices have policies against hoodie sweatshirts, baseball caps, Timberland boots, and certain kinds of sneakers. This means many people need to code-switch in their dress: khakis and polo for school or the office, a tracksuit for your off time. These wardrobe markers can also be misused to identify someone as dangerous. For example, Black men who sag their pants have been demonized and characterized as "ghetto" or "disrespectful." Affluent and middle-class Black people hate sagging pants. Growing up, I heard many tirades on the subject from my grandfather. (He also hated my distressed jeans and couldn't believe I purposely paid for pants with holes and stains.) Sagging pants were how I identified a random stranger as a "thug" as a child, in contrast with my father, who favors a slim-fit jean.

The origins of sagging pants are murky at best. The style is loosely tied to gang membership and prison culture. At some point, it made its way to the mainstream, and this, like hoop earrings, became a threatening movement that needed to be policed into abolition. Sagging pants were such a widespread menace in the eyes of local governments that legislation was introduced to force men to pull up their pants, or else. The *or else* translated to fines or prison time, which is an extraordinary overreaction, but there are no limits to the determination of respectability politics. When asked about the phenomenon during an interview with MTV's Sway in 2008, then presidential candidate Barack Obama (yes, it had been such a big deal for decades that it seemed appropriate to ask a Black man running for president what he thought about it) said, "Brothers should pull up their pants. That doesn't mean you have to pass a law . . . but that doesn't mean folks can't have some sense and some respect for other people. And, you know, some people might not want to see your underwear—I'm one of them." This is something that I also might have said in 2008. It was certainly something I had heard my entire life. I was conditioned to believe that men who sagged their pants were untrustworthy, perhaps rude, and certainly not going to the right school or getting a good job because, if they were, their pants would be pulled up. If you asked me now, I would say I don't care what people do with their pants. What someone is wearing does not dictate the amount of respect they are owed. People need to be respected regardless. Dress codes are often designed to enforce white supremacy, and while I do believe they can have positive effects in schools, letting them spill over into private adult life is bizarre and unnecessary.

Uniforms can also put anyone who does not "fit" on uncomfortable display. If a body is somehow not a perfect shape for the uniform, like in ballet, it will be immediately apparent. For me, again, the problem was my butt. My butt created an exaggerated curve from my back to my legs, and it always—still to this day—makes skirts appear shorter in the back than in the front. This was true of both my school and tennis uniforms. In horseback riding, before breeches had the significant Lycra component that they do now, I kept sizing up to get them on, making me feel like I was fat, and still, the pants never fit since there was a huge gap between my back and the waistline, the same gap that denim companies like Fashion Nova and Good American have dedicated themselves to eliminating as more women get Brazilian butt lifts and are faced with the same problem I was. But back in 2003, no one was addressing the gap. You either fit or you didn't. And it was incredibly isolating if you didn't fit, so I just did my absolute best to make sure I did.

When we were permitted to be out of uniform at school, it was my time to shine. I put a substantial amount of planning into what I would wear on my "civvies" days. I was a little girl who loved to play dress-up, and I grew into a big girl who loved to play dress-up as well. I might have had a natural disposition for style and aesthetics, but as I devoted more and more time to learning about designers, styling, and the industry in general, my confidence swelled. I suppressed the knowledge that my life was all a giant costume party because, after all, fashion is a serious business. It may seem frivolous, but it's a complicated industry to navigate, and one that is especially predicated on looking the part.

Clothing has power. It helped me feel superior to others in an arena where I might not otherwise have been able to compete. Even if my skin tone was wrong, my hair texture was wrong, and my body was wrong, my outfit would always be right. I began to train my style muscles early, carefully laying out the night before what I would wear to school. I would map out which days I would not have to wear my uniform and hold my breath all year in anticipation for the opportunity to show off my sartorial prowess. Though I wanted my style to stand out, it was also, paradoxically, the one area in which I could exhibit a sameness with my white friends. If I could have the same clothes, we were the same. I knew I could not fail in that area because failure meant social suicide. Wear the wrong thing, and risk the harsh and swift judgment of your peers.

Clothing is an excellent tactic for unifying the version of yourself that you imagine with who you really are. Those who work in the fashion industry describe their organic love of clothing, often claiming they got into the business because they have always been "drawn to color" and "radical self-expression," that they have loved "art" forever and are fans of "extreme creativity." (It's that or their mother was a seamstress, which has become less common as the profession becomes an antiquated rarity.) This is probably all true-*ish*, but it is also a nice, gentle, PR-friendly version of my truth. I love clothing for all those tidy and acceptable reasons and also for the ways it allowed me to construct an idealized version of myself and my life, one that I actually wanted to be, instead of one that was assigned to me. I could build myself into a new person with each outfit. I could cover up my self-loathing in sequins or Chanel. I could creep closer to the top of the beauty ladder with each and every compliment I received. Being better dressed than, well, everyone helped me establish my worthiness. This is an ugly thing to admit, so no one does. It is much easier to say that we love the way cashmere feels on our skin, that certain colors can lift or dampen a mood, or that the texture of a garment can extract a distant memory—and there's power in all these things. There's some truth there, sure, but it's not the whole truth.

CHAPTER THIRTEEN

In order to take total control of my image, I had to become a necessary authority on clothing. I read, watched, and consumed anything and everything that might sharpen my expertise. Fashion was the gladiator arena in which I chose to compete, and there were so many fine nuances that required such fanatic attention, I barely had time to think about anything else.

By the time I entered adolescence, celebrity culture in America was reaching a fever pitch. We were moving away from dial-up to full-on unbroken internet connection. Headlines like "It Girls" and "It Bags" dominated publications like *Us Weekly* and *People*, informing rapt audiences where famous women were shopping and what they were wearing. I cycled through aesthetics quickly. First I experimented with the trashy and overtly sexy style favored by Britney Spears circa 2003 because it was the standard look of "Hollywood" and what I thought it meant to be an adult. I spent a lot of money at stores like Guess and Abercrombie & Fitch. I was partial to "ultra-low-rise jeans," which were absolutely miserable to wear as my hips started developing, and if there's one thing to notice about starlets of the early millennium, let's just say they were demonstrably lacking in curves. For a good six or so years, my ass crack was always exposed.

When that aesthetic was poorly received, I quickly pivoted. My prep school classmates were heavy into Ralph Lauren polo shirts, pearl necklaces and earrings, and J.Crew everything. The style staple of my school was a hideous shoe that still haunts me to this day: the Jack Rogers Jacks Flat Sandal.

For the uninitiated to the nuances of WASP taste, the Jack Rogers brand was founded in 1960 in Palm Beach, Florida, creatively sparked by the late great Jackie Kennedy Onassis, with whom I share a birthday. (Leos are always responsible for trends.) Palm Beach was the location of several of my Connecticut classmates' second homes, and I spent a lot of winter and spring breaks in Palm Beach, feeling awkwardly on display. Token status is conspicuous in a place like Palm Beach. The vibe there is aggressively exuberant, favoring another ubiquitous designer of the vacation locale, Lily Pulitzer, whose vivid depictions of shellfish always disturbed me. Everything matches in Palm Beach, and most girls coordinate their Lily Pulitzer dresses, skirts, or skorts with a Jack Rogers sandal, predictably called "Jacks" for short. These sandals are flat, with a wide strap across the bridge of the foot, and a thong portion for the toe where a round disc replaces what would be a more common "flip-flop" shape, giving the shoe its signature element. They are made of leather, and the wide stitching, often in contrasting colors, complements whatever loud prompt the Lily Pulitzer is usually providing up top. I have never understood the appeal of these shoes, and after years in the fashion industry, I can only conclude that their sole charm is that they are a physical embodiment of a hive mentality. Everyone at school, and I mean *everyone*, had a pair of these shoes. In college, a particular sort of sorority girl also wore them. As an adult, I see them on grown women at bridal and baby showers or springtime events, and it is a marker of one's rearing for sure. They are chillingly omnipresent. For all my desire to fit in, I never wanted a pair of these shoes.

I did, however, cave on some preppy status markers. I verbally bashed J.Crew as a defense mechanism because their clothes never fit me, but I still had pearl earrings and necklaces. I wore a ribbon in my hair every day of my sophomore year of high school. I had an assortment of colorful headbands and Tiffany's sterling silver jewelry. There was still a part of me that was drawn to the loud, bad taste embodied by brands like Von Dutch and True Religion, but when getting dressed, it's important to know your audience. And in Greenwich, Connecticut, there was no market for trucker hats. All this helped me fit in with my friends.

Each micro-community has its own signifiers of status and success and its own interpretation of beauty standards. In Westchester, this can vary from town to town or school to school. When I separated from my middle school friends, they were dispersed among other private schools, but none of them attended prep schools. That meant they wore uniforms and had decent educational advantages, but the school sport of choice was likely not field hockey—a distinctly ruthless sport played among affluent white girls—but something more accessible, like soccer or softball. Those friends of mine got french-tip acrylic nails and wore diamond studs in their ears, things that would have garnered whispers and eye rolls in the hallowed halls of my school. It was important for me to be stylish, yes, but the *right kind* of stylish. It would not have served me to embrace another kind of aesthetic, one that pushed too much upon the unspoken parameters of the class and privilege that surrounded me. I began to develop a phobia of wearing the wrong thing. Being underdressed is, frankly, such a nightmare for me that I developed a superior sense of taste to combat it. Since my skin already marked me as an outsider, I needed to make sure my clothing, mannerisms, and anything else in my control were reflective of the population to which I needed to belong.

My very rich friends always had huge birthday celebrations, like the kind broadcast on MTV's *My Super Sweet 16*. For one such occasion, a girl's dad purchased a massive block of tickets to Z100's Zootopia, a multi-artist pop concert, and had a chauffeured limo take a group of girls into New York City. I'm telling you, life in Greenwich is not real life. We traveled in our limo, behaving obnoxiously, as teenagers do without adult supervision, blasting music, and sticking our heads out the sunroof. All of us wore variations of the same outfit: a denim miniskirt and a semi-risqué top. It was a summer Friday afternoon on the West Side highway, and traffic was impossible. To ease our boredom as the limo creeped along, we tried to get the attention of our fellow motorists. We had mostly positive responses, as one would expect a car full of young girls would get. As we pulled up alongside a car near the Fifty-Ninth Street light, I rolled down my window to start a chat with our new comrades. There was a brown man in the driver's seat, accompanied by three friends of varying nonwhite ethnic origins. He glared into the car. "White bitches," he spat at us, but upon seeing my shocked face looking back at his own, neither of us knew what to do. I rolled up the window. My entire group was tickled with giggles over his anger, but I knew something was wrong. I just didn't know how to express what it was.

My ability to look, talk, and act like my friends helped me blend in with them in a way I felt was necessary, but I wasn't sure I wanted to be lumped in with "white bitches." I both did and I didn't. Those guys had no real schema for understanding my presence in that car. The man said it with malice, and yet, the reaction from inside the car was one of amused nonchalance. I don't think the girls I was with thought about that incident ever again. The same year, in 2004, the Wayans brothers released the satirical comedy *White Chicks*, loosely based on the popularity of the white-heiress archetype made infamous by Paris and Nicky Hilton. In the film, both Wayans brothers play federal agents going undercover as "white chicks" to thwart a kidnapping. They have to adopt behaviors like toting around small dogs, singing along to Vanessa Carlton songs, and dancing poorly—all things that, for better or worse, could have described my friends at the time. Vanessa Carlton's song "White Houses" became something of an anthem at my school, and whether it was clear that the song lyrics were about losing your virginity was of no consequence. We scream-sang that song every day of our lives for a year without irony, as *White Chicks* grossed over $100 million at the box office.

Meanwhile, I didn't know that I was allowed to like being Black. The people around me did a very good job at convincing me that identity was something to be ashamed of or something to overcome. No one would even say the word *Black* at full volume. It was always a whisper or a pause before deciding to go with "African American." Wanting to be Black or enjoying being Black was a concept supported by zero available evidence. Wanting to be white, however? Yes, how could you not? To be engrossed in this culture was to love even the elements people were poking fun at because, at the end of the day, it was abundantly clear that being a "white chick" was a good thing. Whiteness was something so precious and coveted that it is considered a compliment even when it is obviously meant to be an insult. It was, to these girls, literally laughable that being called "white bitches" could be meant to hurt their feelings. This made being proud to be Black particularly challenging. White was something you should want to be and express in your clothing, music, and canine choices. I couldn't be white, of course, but I could definitely dress the part.

CHAPTER FOURTEEN

Pledging allegiance to a clique is a dangerous game to play in an all-girls school, and my loyalties shifted frequently and often, depending on the payoff. As a fragile girl with an autoimmune disease and a visible disability, Isabelle garnered a lot of sympathy; she had one fully developed arm and one that, though functional, was essentially absent of muscles. And this is not to discredit anyone with an illness, but I do need to say that this girl often overemphasized her limitations, even saying at one point that she might not apply to college because she wasn't sure if she was going to live that long. She did indeed make it to college, and as far as I know, she is now a mother living on the West Coast. But an altercation with her was the first time I saw a girl weaponize her whiteness, and I was on the receiving end of the bazooka.

For a number of years, there had been increasing friction between me and Isabelle. In a way, we were intensely competing for the affections of the third member of our friend trio, an unsuspecting girl caught in the middle of our cold war. I don't remember what Isabelle did that finally pissed me off so much, but apparently, it was something unforgivable to a high school student. In any case, I made the grave error of taking my grievances to AIM, where I said to someone else, "Isabelle is so annoying I could kill her. I wish she was dead." It was, inarguably, a horrible thing to say about anyone, and an especially heinous thing to say about someone who is sick. But as I was a highly emotional teenager, prone, as I am even now, to exaggeration for effect, I am not that shocked at my radical statement. My friend told Isabelle.

The response was swift and severe. The next morning, I was straightening my hair, as I did every day, when my mom answered a call on our landline and was promptly informed that, pending an investigation, I could not return to school. At first, I didn't even remember the conversation about Isabelle, but the next day, as my parents and I drove up to the school building to have a meeting with the headmistress, I knew how serious it had become. We walked through the double doors, and the place no longer felt like mine. The meeting was at a long, dark table with the school administration on one side and me and my parents on the other. The atmosphere was charged and cold. All the evidence had been mounted against me. The girls had printed out weeks of AIM conversations, making me look like a relentless nutcase with a vendetta against Isabelle and she, of course, just a helpless, virginal kitten. Even worse, the school hacked my emails and found links to a photo-sharing website called Webshots. (Before social media, kids posted albums of their lives on private sites on the internet.) My Webshots included an incriminating array of snapshots featuring underage drinking at a basement party with boys from neighboring schools. In actuality, I had gotten drunk only a handful of times, but the pictures made it look like I was on a bender every weekend. To make matters worse, it was 2005, a time when "hard partying" socialites were making headlines all over the country, and I was being raised in a way that strictly opposed that type of lifestyle. I'd been caught red-handed. There was nothing I could say or do to deny what the evidence so clearly showed. Never mind that all the kids at school had Webshots profiles, which were deleted as news of my debacle spread. Never mind the rampant bad behavior of untouchably privileged white girls. I was the one caught holding the bag for everyone, and—this was the best part—it was because Isabelle was "scared of me."

There it was. The fatal blow. Isabelle probably *was* scared of me, but not scared that I was going to kill her. My mother was the type who banned my sister and me from watching *Power Rangers* because she did not want us to "play fight," ever. I had never so much as slapped anyone. I did not have a violent bone in my body. I sat out the boxing fitness craze because I don't like throwing punches, and I am lousy at it. None of this mattered. Isabelle's father, a notable oncologist, had treated the headmistress's best friend, and he said his daughter was scared, so something had to be done. I was suspended. I couldn't attend school for weeks, which, after my freshman-year concussion, was the longest I had been out of school. No matter that I was a straight-A student, polite, a well-mannered rule follower, or that I was a junior taking the SATs and considering my college options. This incident nearly derailed my future, and my intense drive for success was partially birthed out of the ensuing struggle. All the administration saw was an alcohol-drinking, fast Black girl threatening an innocent white one. None of the rest mattered. Beyond the humiliation of being out of school and everyone knowing why was the injustice of it all. I knew I was not a danger to her. I knew I was not a skanky teenage alcoholic. Worst of all, I knew I had been bested and set up.

It took a long time for me to see the racism in this situation. I now see it as more of a systemic problem than a personal one. I still donate regularly to my high school and show up at alumnae events. I consider my visibility as a graduate important, especially to those who label Black girls "scary." And I do also firmly believe that my education and experiences there had a huge impact on who I became in more positive ways than negative ones.

Ostensibly, the people in charge saw me as a threat. It was not just about what I had said—it was the package it was delivered in. I was asked if I had a weapon, if I had access to a gun. I don't believe a white student would have been asked these questions. And as for me, even now, at thirty-two, I have never held a gun in my life. Never even touched one. I don't skeet-shoot. I've never been paintballing. I am even lousy at laser tag. I don't target practice, and I certainly don't glamorize gun usage, but I have white friends who tote guns and flaunt their marking abilities, posing with rifles in Barbour jackets. This was not me, ever.

Later that year, one of my good friends took up shoplifting from Neiman Marcus, I think for no other reason but sheer boredom. When my parents found out, they told me that I immediately needed to cease my relationship with this girl, knowing that if I got into real-world trouble, they might not be able to save me.

What I came to understand is that Black emotions, particularly anger, must always be monitored and tempered in white spaces. The ability to express things like sadness, anger, or even passion is a gift that is granted only to white people. It is a privilege. What Black girls get, in addition to the crushing weight of perfectionism, is stoicism. That reflexive survival skill is where the "strong Black woman" stereotype emerges from. And this is not because all Black women have a super-human control over their emotions. It is because they know that their emotions will be evaluated on a different scale. It is not that I am strong or that I never feel anything; it is that I have been shown repeatedly that my emotions will be invalidated or misinterpreted, that they will have dangerous consequences. I am encouraged to hide them for protection instead. Sadness? Dismissed. Anger? Feared and reprimanded. Passion? Quieted. Nearly all the Black people I know who grew up the way I did have a habit of being very quiet in public spaces, knowing that crossing a certain decibel level will draw unwanted attention. White supremacy works deliberately hard at convincing Black people that feelings are off limits to anyone not white.

Historically, the image of Black people as angry or aggressive has been used as a defense for overpolicing and censorship. During the final match of the 2018 US Open, we watched Serena Williams exchange heated words with a referee, who ended up penalizing her for an entire game, eventually costing her the match and, later, fining her $17,000. What did she do? She slammed her racket down, something that was frowned upon as unsportsmanlike but is not an uncommon action in professional tennis, from either women or men. Then she told the referee he owed her an apology for suggesting that she was receiving coaching in between points, something that is forbidden. The incident happened so quickly as I watched from my phone in the back of a car between shows during September fashion week. Immediately, my instinct was to silently will Serena to "get back under control," to just do what was wanted of her, because I so badly wanted her to win. Even though her opponent was another Black woman, too much of this scene was stacked against her. All across professional sports, fines are administered as disciplinary measures, but the fines Serena Williams has faced have been extreme. In addition to this $17,000, in 2009, she was fined $82,500 for an angry outburst. Comparatively, in 2017, Denis Shapovalov, a seventeen-year-old, white, up-and-coming tennis player hit a ball out of anger, and it ricocheted, striking the chair umpire and breaking his eye socket. The umpire required surgery. Shapovalov was fined $7,000, which is $5,000 under the maximum fine, and might I add, the next day, there was no racist cartoon mocking him in the *Herald Sun*. The consequences of the expression of Black anger or frustration have always been severe and punitive.

My parents hired a lawyer to advise them on the incident that landed me in trouble at school. He told them to fight the suspension. I imagine he also pointed out the curious and overdrawn sentence I had received in relation to my white peers, that a suspension at this juncture of my education could jeopardize my college admission prospects, that I was never actually going to harm this girl. The school relented, and I was made to write an apology letter to Isabelle, and then another after the first was deemed not sincere enough. And after two months, I was back in school. The suspension was scrubbed from my record, and I was able to apply to and enter college without a questionable incident on file.

But before I could re-enroll in school, I had to meet with the school's psychologist, a white man whose evaluation, after one meeting, was that I was not a danger to anyone. I still had to receive regular counseling after this with a Black woman psychologist my parents hired. Her assessment: I was breaking under the pressure. The pressure to be perfect, and popular, and pretty, and good at everything. And I was clinging to the idea that it all had to look effortless.

What I said about my classmate when I was sixteen was horrible and wrong. It might even have been worse than I remember. Punishment was warranted, but the way I was vilified was extreme, and I have no doubt it was tied to racism. I watched my white peers flagrantly break rules and avoid punishment for years. And in that way, we were never peers, never equals. Don't worry—I am not a snitch; I didn't offer anyone else up as collateral. But I did experience a deep depression brought on by my frustration at the way all the systems seemed to be working against me while I was encouraged to believe they were not. I didn't know how to articulate the injustice of it or the complicated emotions all this brought up. Instead, I learned to invalidate my emotions, constantly question what I was feeling, and most importantly, never express anger—especially not in writing. This lesson would come with some complicated lingering side effects.

I haven't spoken to Isabelle since we graduated high school almost fifteen years ago. I would be surprised if anyone else but the two of us and the others tangentially involved even remember this incident. If anything, I am actually grateful to the girls from high school. They prepped me for a world where Karen culture would be the expectation, not the exception, where ascending above a certain station puts a target on your back. I am both smarter and better for having learned this at sixteen. I was never caught up in a messy situation like that again, and I know I won't be in the future. My initial instinct was to implode, but instead, I took this lesson and used it. It was my villain origin story; I was built by this moment. This is not to say people need to use trauma as a building block for their personalities. I wish none of it ever had to happen to me or anyone else. I wish Black girls were free to make the kinds of mistakes that don't result in life-altering consequences and that they were able to process emotions in a way that validates them and considers elemental factors like their age, experience, and pressures. But I am, in a lot of ways, proud of the fact that it didn't break me. I used it to show them just how high I could ascend and ensure that I would, going forward, always understand just how precarious my positioning was in white spaces—an outlook some would argue is perfect for a career in fashion magazines.

CHAPTER FIFTEEN

My entire educational experience was a fast-track train headed one way: college. From the time I was in preschool, I knew I would be going to college, and people would ask me, when I was as young as ten, where I wanted to go to school. In preparation, my parents made sure to do all the right things—the legal way, of course, not the Operation Varsity Blues way. I really was captain of my high school tennis team. The only padding on my college résumé was volunteer work; prestige programs like "medical camp," which was ten days of *Grey's Anatomy* cosplay; and a combination of athletic and academic interests. My parents hired an SAT tutor for me after I earned a low math score on my PSATs, I took a smattering of AP courses, and I attended a competitive high school with an entire department dedicated to coaching students through essays and applications. I didn't know that most people don't have tutors or that securing a time extension for standardized tests was difficult because everyone I knew had acquired a version of either or both. With all that preparation, having that fate endangered with a suspension was a traumatic experience.

I got a lot of well-meaning advice from people about where to apply and what schools I would do best at. No one ever suggested historically Black colleges and universities (HBCUs). There were Black girls who went to my school and chose to attend HBCUs, but no one in my graduating class did. There is real value in being educated in an environment where you do not have to constantly perform or defend your identity. There is a sanctity to Black institutions that must be maintained for the sake of preserving the cultural heritage that is continuously under attack, but I don't think I would have been emotionally ready to matriculate into an HBCU. And I did not want to attend school in the South. My attachment to my family kept me firmly within a four-state radius. I was given a list of the "best" schools in New York, Pennsylvania, Connecticut, and Massachusetts. I selected schools of varying sizes, all in the Northeast. Early on, I wanted to go to NYU because it was close to home and seemed fun, while Columbia seemed depressing—no offense. And after years of single-sex education, I was absolutely not considering the all-girls school Barnard. Many people suggested I go to a smaller university or college in the name of comfort, convinced that I would be culture-shocked to graduate from a class of twelve, then fifty-two, then twenty thousand; they thought I would feel overwhelmed by the scale of a large university. Spoiler: I ended up at NYU, and the anonymity I felt there was one of my favorite parts.

The college application process was a decade-long pursuit for me that culminated in me, a teenager, trying to reasonably make estimations about my deepest desires in order to set up the rest of my life. I got into every college I applied to except for one. (Brown, why didn't you want me?) I don't remember sharing that information with many of my peers. It was definitely not popular for girls to speak about their triumphs and accomplishments in 2006. It was "bragging," which was ugly. Still, somehow, the news trickled out. I was in AP English one afternoon, sitting next to my white friend who was not happy with her college prospects. I believe her dream school was Georgetown, and she didn't make the cut. She turned to me and said, "You're so lucky there's affirmative action." It was like I had been slapped. My heart rate quickened. I had imagined that everyone was talking about how I had only gotten into schools *because I was Black*. And, turned out, she believed it because she believed the most pivotal lie of American life: the words scribbled on the so-called Declaration of Independence, declaring that "all men are created equal." In this case, not men, but you get the idea. Because we are all "equal," we should be judged solely on our merits, talents, and accomplishments. In her eyes, my Blackness gave me a cheat code. In fact, we were actually nearly identical in terms of our qualifications, so perhaps my race did give me an edge in college admissions. That doesn't mean I didn't deserve to be admitted. For all the "colorblindness" privileged white women love to proclaim, she was pretty quick to point out that a college might want me—rather than, say, a legacy student, an athlete, or someone with dual citizenship—only to fill a diversity quota.

Gaming the system of academia is a hobby among rich white people, one this girl was bitter to have lost. Again, see the Varsity Blues scandal of 2019.

Planting a seed of doubt that erodes a Black person's self-esteem is a classic tactic of white supremacy. Suddenly, I was suffering from impostor syndrome, a condition characterized by feelings of unworthiness, and my case was acute, if not latent. I started thinking that I had been admitted to college solely because of my race, not because I was an excellent student, captain of the tennis team, on the yearbook committee, and a finalist in a national photography competition. Not because of my stellar admissions essay, excerpts of which would later be published on my college's website. Not because I was starving myself and sleep deprived from studying and taking the most challenging course load possible. Just because I was Black, and that's it. "Not that I'm racist or anything," she added after a beat, when I didn't respond.

In that same class, we read Mark Twain's *Adventures of Huckleberry Finn,* and our English teacher encouraged everyone to read passages out loud that contained the N-word—with the hard *-er.* "It's just a word," she said, downplaying everyone's visible discomfort. As the only Black girl in the entire class, the weight of the shame I felt pressed on all my internal organs simultaneously. What could I have done? The alternate reality where I had enough gumption and vocabulary to challenge that teacher was light-years away. She justified her actions to a 99 percent white room by explaining that it was a satirical work and, of course, "historical." We were to understand that Mark Twain was just *joking*, a convenient excuse for the acceptance of racism, and that it was so long ago, it almost didn't matter anymore. There was no nuance in the lesson to give context to the historical origins of the N-word, how powerful it was, and how hurtful it could still be. There was no way to demonstrate the thread of continuity that links Twain's "satire" to the idea that I "only got accepted to college because of affirmative action! Omg jk, jk."

Instances like this, in countless classrooms in my youth, made me feel humiliated to be the only Black girl. Some people have to grow into themselves. I had to learn to love and accept myself, and neither of those things seemed possible for me in those moments, especially when I was mortified to discover that people were discussing my major triumphs as the result of a diversity quota. I was ashamed. Suddenly, my Token Black Girl status seemed useless. Harmful, even. I was only good for making white people appear less racist. All my other skills and accomplishments, well, they were frivolous. Looking back, I wonder whether this is part of the reason I didn't choose to apply to HBCUs; I needed a metric to prove to both myself and my classmates that I could do anything they could do.

In a 2015 piece for the *Huffington Post* called "The Myth of the 'Good Negro,'" Nikki Johnson Huston, Esq., exposes the issues with being forced to absolve white people of their racism by your mere existence, even when they are engaging in blatantly racist behavior: "There is an unspoken code for many middle class or affluent African-Americans that we don't speak about race with people outside of our race because it always tends to end badly for both sides. Actually it only ends badly for us, because we are seen as angry and hostile—with comparisons to Al Sharpton—and it could hurt our careers."

People of color are conditioned to accept degrees of racism in white spaces because they fear the consequences of looking "crazy" for pointing it out. Really, looking crazy is the least of it. Losing your position, job, or housing may be more in line with the potential repercussions. Colin Kaepernick is a great example. White supremacy flexes all its power when attempting to squash dissenters, and this is true across many different industries and situations. It is why many still speak anonymously when exposing racism they have faced. Ditto sexual harassment or assault. Repeated N-word use feels like high-key racism, but if authority figures are presenting you with mental gymnastics to convince you that it is part and parcel of the classic American literary canon, who are you, at sixteen years old, to say otherwise? Those who put on blaccents and use elements of Black culture to get a laugh are also doing harm to Black people, but call it what it is, and you'll get labeled "too sensitive." You "can't take a joke." This further ostracizes you, and when the stakes get higher—when, say, a promotion, a raise, or a job opportunity hinges on your ability to "hang"—you might be surprised at what you can ignore. White supremacy is very cunning. It can adapt to fit many different scenarios, spaces, and moments in time. But the end goal is always the same: to uphold the idea that, in all things, white people are the best, the most deserving, and the pinnacle of everything good. And anyone who says otherwise should be destroyed.

The exhibition of people of color bearing their badges of white acceptance is, in part, due to conditioning as well. Institutions stifle cries of racism by making sure that, publicly at least, they are impressively committed to diversity: *Look, we have a Black!* It should not be a convincing tactic. It does little if language and policies do not change in a real effort to eradicate racism, if you still uphold white as the default, if you are satisfied with your Token Black Girl and shove her in front of the camera at every opportunity, and if, for example, you let a Black girl into your family and still allow her to be slandered and disrespected. (Yes, British royals, I am talking to you.) Those acts continue the traditions of racism and do nothing to mitigate its violent othering.

CHAPTER SIXTEEN

For my first two years of college, I was enrolled at Tufts University, a prestigious PWI (for the those who don't want to run to Urban Dictionary right now, that's "Predominantly White Institution") minutes outside Boston in Medford, Massachusetts, a sort of quintessential northeastern college town. I fell in quickly with a group of binge-drinking, casual cocaine–abusing white girls. My friends were mostly private-school kids who liked to imitate what they thought was adult behavior, even though we were just eighteen. Partying hard was the bonding ritual of choice.

Entering college was a strange culture shock. It was the first time I was around many different types of people. It was the first time I had met anyone who didn't have a shared history with me or a way of understanding me and where I came from. And it was the first time I was forced to absorb negative stereotypes of Blackness on a large scale. The town/gown relations of the community surrounding the campus were extremely racially charged. The microaggressions I'd experienced in high school and middle school became mega-aggressions. Once again, I found myself operating in service of white supremacy, while veiled racist policies in the name of campus "safety" made sure to effectively segregate the students from the Medford and Somerville residents. Within school itself, I found it challenging to articulate my history, I suppose because it was considered so unusual. Many students had never met a "Black girl who rides horses," and they weren't shy about telling me so.

My freshman year, a group of guys mocked me for still having tags on the clothes hanging in my closet. It was apparently "bougie," a signifier that I had spent money, and I should be embarrassed about that. These boys had no idea that I had worn a uniform for all my years of schooling before arriving at college. To attend class in jeans was a luxury. I used all the teasing to stiffen my resolve. I already knew what to do when I didn't feel accepted: be meaner.

In one of these instances, I told a lie that haunts me to this day, but since learning to "let things go," the ghost is tiny as a garter snake instead of the king cobra it was before. There was a girl I found exceptionally cool—Zara, pronounced *Zaw-rah* and not *Zair-rah*—who grew up in DC and attended a fancy prep school like mine. One day she was holding court in her dorm room, the essential location for the pregame party. Zara was white and extremely confident in ways that I could never be. She chain-smoked and did drugs and was unathletic. She had huge boobs and no butt and bony legs. She had a pretty face and long blonde hair with a shaggy side bang she sometimes cut herself. But the really sexy thing about her was her ability to be constantly at the center of everyone's attention. Growing up in DC, she had developed a comfort level and familiarity with Black people that even I couldn't muster. She knew DC area rapper Wale *personally*. She hung out often at "I-house"—short for the international house—on campus.

As per usual, I was the only Black girl in the room, but with Zara as the queen bee, the circumstances felt particularly delicate. I do not remember the exact circumstances now, but somehow the topic of braids came up, and somehow I said, for no reason at all except perhaps that I was possessed, that I had never had them. I suspect now that I wanted to distance myself comfortably from my Blackness. Every other white girl in the circle let this go without comment or thought, but Zara rang the alarm and called bullshit. "Every little Black girl gets braids," she scoffed, her worldly knowledge smoking me out of my hole.

"I don't know," I replied, determined to run with this ridiculous lie. "I just didn't." I shrugged for good measure, hoping to sell it with my nonchalance. Now, had I been born into Gen Z, this egregious falsehood could have been dismantled with a quick sweep of my social media, which would have shown me on multiple occasions, with, you guessed it, braids. Luckily for me, it could not be proven or disproven, so Zara and I just stared each other down until someone presented a more exciting topic for discussion.

Why I said that in the first place and then doubled down on it, I have no idea. I guess, in Zara's presence, it felt necessary to make myself appear as much like her as possible, even though we really did have several things in common, and there was no need to fabricate more. The one thing that we glaringly did not have in common was that she was white, and I was Black, so I tried to erase it. I was desperate to make my experiences mimic hers, and I was jealous of the way she was accepted and admired. Eventually, I transferred schools and fell out of touch with Zara, but lying to fit in with her circle is something that my anxiety-fueled ego wouldn't allow me to let go of. It's still a shameful scar on that part of my life. If I could go back as a more sure-of-myself woman, I would tell that group about all the times my mom braided my hair growing up and what an act of love it was.

But I was intent on fitting in at whatever cost, and I had already started to develop my judgment muscles. I started dispensing guidance to my peers on what was acceptable or not to wear. This authority gave me a fragile sense of control. The media was also encouraging these kind of pronouncements. "Who wore it best?" pages dominated the weekly magazines and blogs, encouraging audiences to draw comparisons between starlets. Being caught in the same outfit as anyone else felt like it would be absolutely deadly, so I spent a lot of time scouring stores for unique colorways of the same exact items my friends had. *OK, fine, Uggs, but make them bubblegum pink.* Red-carpet commentary and newly popular blogs like *Perez Hilton, Pink Is the New Blog*, and *Dlisted* had scathing criticisms of the young women they featured. But their cruelty was played for laughs. Likewise, shock-jock comics like Dane Cook and Tucker Max added an extra level of toxic masculinity and rampant misogyny to the young cultural ethos. I adopted their language easily when speaking about other women in my life. The same girls who were trashed in the media made looking and getting trashed trendy. Being drunk was a pivotal destination, and I spent a lot of time and energy both acquiring alcohol and drinking. How fucked up you could get was a badge of honor. That culture also made girls more vulnerable to sexual assault and less likely to remember the details surrounding it. The party never stopped.

My college years saw the rise of the "Zoe-bots," a group of impossibly thin actresses and socialites that were styled freakishly similarly by Rachel Zoe. Their look was all big shades, big bangles, and tiny bodies. My friends mimicked that look, and we judged each other mercilessly. I often found myself in court. This was the way of the world. When it came to clothing and beauty, we were brutal and bloodthirsty. I needed to ensure my superiority or suffer the constant anxiety of being found on the receiving end of a "don't."

Everything was Chloé Paddington bags and flavored Absolut. The way your jeans exposed your hip bones was just as important as the denim brand itself. At the time, denim brands were on the rise as status symbols in their own right. The price of jeans crossed into triple digits, and you could tell a lot about a person from the label on their derrière. Brands like 7 For All Mankind, True Religion, and Citizens of Humanity were dominant among my group of friends. When the quieter, label-less brands began to emerge—like Paper Denim & Cloth and J Brand—wearing them held the underlying assumption that you had already established your style dominance by wearing the flashy brands, and therefore felt so cemented in that position that you didn't even have to shout with your jeans anymore. People would just know.

The opportunity to leave behind my uniform and wear my own clothing felt like walking a red carpet. Some assume that attending an all-girls school quells the urge to dress up, if you're a straight girl at least, since there's really no one to attract. To me, this makes no sense. I cared infinitely more about my friends' opinions of my clothing than I ever did any boy's. I am sure I've never thought about a boy when getting dressed. Their taste or approval never interested me.

I went into college assuming I'd end up a plastic surgeon. I had even gone to that medical camp thinking I was prepping for a future career in a hospital. That ambition was derailed after my introductory bio lab, an 8:30 a.m. class that almost ruined my life. Instead, I felt beckoned toward a glamorous life that was advertised by *The Hills* and *The Devil Wears Prada*. Luckily, by that time, I was practiced at seeing myself in white women, so the lack of Black faces in those Hollywood fashion narratives held no obstacle. I had zero reservations about my ability to make it in fashion. I started working on my new plan immediately. I needed to establish myself as a fashion authority from the moment someone looked at me. The problem was, at the medium-size liberal arts university I'd chosen, not many people cared about clothes.

Tufts didn't have the WASP-y community I was accustomed to, and I was struggling to find my niche, so I made the decision to rush a sorority. Female relationships had always come naturally to me, but at Tufts, I was having a really rough go of connecting with the other students. Everyone was studious, but overall, they lacked the resolute commitment to appearance that I craved, both for validation and purpose. So I used those girls to sharpen my teeth, dispensing overt criticisms of what others looked like. The more I vocalized my opinions, the more people responded to my position as an authority. It was a real-life manifestation of "fake it 'til you make it." To my surprise, people began to defer to me, asking me what to wear or buy. It was fascinating and addictive. I craved the power that making decisions for others gave me, and in order to establish my dominance, I crushed a few souls in the process. Like any Machiavellian psycho would say, "It had to be done."

One poor, sweet sacrifice, let's call her Elise, fell into my trap. Elise was a petite blonde from Fairfield County and a fellow rushee for the sorority. Her style, which feels silly to say when speaking about an eighteen-year-old, was basic. She wore cutoff shorts and Rainbow flip-flops. She had a braided hemp anklet and probably a wardrobe full of preppy staple brands like Tory Burch and Vineyard Vines. She was pretty and small, so the clothing had no bearing on her popularity. I identified her as easy prey because she was often visibly insecure, and I still feel pangs of guilt when I think about how I incinerated her for sport.

One night, we were engaging in a rush activity that also happened to be a campus tradition: "painting the cannon," a peculiar ceremonial bonding experience. The cannon sat, covered in decades worth of paint, at the top of the hill overlooking the campus. Painting it required an all-night stakeout because pranksters would often wait until the cannon was abandoned and then paint over it. After you painted it, you had to keep vigil to make sure your work was not undone. On this particular night, Elise wore a pair of white leggings, which was not ideal attire for the activity at hand, but there was no itinerary for sorority rush. In her nervous way, she began asking the other girls if she should leave to go change. I despised girls who wore their weakness on their sleeve. I felt it was a brand of white privilege, and I took it as a personal affront. I'd never been afforded the luxury of being publicly vulnerable. The superhuman strength required to be the only Black girl around for miles had to be turned on at all times. The sheer effort I exerted feigning confidence was award-worthy. So the pathetic quivering that accompanied Elise's near-constant uncertainty incurred a disproportionate wrath in me. I snapped. "Well, you should never wear white leggings anyway," I said, defiantly staring her down, my five-eight frame looming over her tiny five-foot (if that) body. It was savage, even for me, and I watched shock and hurt flood her body as she gaped at me to see if I was joking.

Many other girls were in earshot, and they all lowered their eyes, feeling the secondhand shame that comes with watching someone get publicly flogged. I am not proud of that moment. I knew it was wrong. I wasn't able to make the connection to that feeling I'd had so many years before, when Kristen told me the Spice Girls weren't cool as I stood in a T-shirt emblazoned with their faces in front of all my best friends. At the time, I had no empathy for Elise. I heard her crying later to other girls.

I still feel bad about behaving that way toward Elise. I hope any bully would after the requisite amount of therapy and much-needed personal reflection. Personally, white leggings terrified me. They would put all my cellulite and extraneous flesh on clear display. On her, with her protruding hip bones and toned little legs, they betrayed nothing. It was simply a white pant. Years later, when white leggings became hugely popular, buoyed by a minimalist movement, I still wouldn't dare put them on. Back then, all I saw was an opportunity to further prove that I was an authoritative voice in fashion, even among freshmen on a New England college campus. The scale of my influence didn't matter to me, so long as I had some. I made Elise a sacrificial lamb, and it worked. In the end, it forced people to desire my approval, and I loved the chance to apply my fashion knowledge to real-life circumstances.

I doubled down on my shopping. The experience of trying on clothes and evaluating them was enchanting, and I wanted to re-create that feeling as many times as possible. Fashion was the perfect place to bury my self-loathing because it was a system that could always renew itself. Every week I would go into a store and there would be something new. And every time I bought something, compliments would follow. I could tell people looked at me with envy, and I loved it. Fashion protected me from my fear of being ordinary.

Why, yes, this *is* a new Marc by Marc Jacobs T-shirt. I pretended to be humble. It was important to be confident but not too confident. I was still Black, after all, and everything could come crashing down if I became, you know, *too* special. Still, I was thriving in my quest. Few people were at my level now, and like the voiceover asks on *America's Next Top Model*, "You wanna be on top?" Yes, I did.

This is exactly what a penchant for beauty and glamour does: It creates and fosters competition where there is none. It establishes power hierarchies and makes pliant subjects of its devotees, forcing us all to uphold its structures as we police both ourselves and everyone around us. I had no way of knowing that my behavior was perpetuating a cycle, making other girls and women feel inadequate so that they, too, might impose the same values onto someone else. It is so efficient in its manufacturing, no one can really determine when it starts working on you or when you start working for it. We were all so busy trying not to be the ones called out for wearing white leggings or merch from a passé girl group that we didn't have time to think about how it was all related. Beauty, perfection, fashion—all of it fanned out like a virus, covering every woman I knew. Women who seemed immune were immediately shunned, called out for their laziness, or assumed to be lesbians. Being totally outside the parameters of acceptable femininity was inexcusable if you wanted to fit in, especially with white people, where the ruling class is rich white men. It was one thing to drop the ball one time, or even occasionally; it was another thing entirely to decide not to play the game at all. I would look at girls who claimed they "didn't care," who displayed their disdain for makeup and clothing, with plaintive pity. *Perhaps they don't know,* I would think. Maybe they hadn't read enough *Vogue.* I thought it was my own personal duty to demonstrate where they were failing and how they could improve like I had. I knew I could recruit more disciples if I continued to impress people with my outfits and makeup. The pathology of constantly striving to improve oneself had worked so flawlessly on me, I genuinely thought that when I was critical, I was being helpful.

As the allure of this began to wane, I needed a platform bigger than a frat party to exhibit my exquisite taste. I needed a more legitimate platform where I could continue to inform women what they were doing wrong and how they could do things better. So I got an internship at a magazine.

CHAPTER SEVENTEEN

I say it like getting that internship was simple. It was not simple at all. Here's how the process went: I first had to decide where I wanted to work. Since I read basically every magazine every month, there was a substantial pool to work with. Not many eighteen-year-olds pine for unpaid summer jobs, which I didn't know at the time, but it ended up working to my advantage. I made an Excel spreadsheet of every single magazine I read, along with their contact information for internships. I then made a list of all the designers I liked, along with their contact information for internships. I was so attracted to the glittering facade of the industry presented by reality shows and movies that I wasn't actually sure whether I wanted to work in public relations or in editorial, so I figured I would try both and see what I could get. I had high hopes, but I knew the competition would be stiff. I came home from college for spring break instead of going away like my friends, and I focused on setting up in-person interviews. I took the train into the city and met with dozens of brands and magazines. One Friday, I went to *NYLON*. Its offices were in Soho. The publication itself was a bit more indie- and rock-focused than my personal tastes, but I was still a fan.

As I entered the Soho building, my heart was pounding. I was greeted at the doors of *NYLON* by two shar-pei dogs, one gray and one brown, owned by the publisher and editor-in-chief, a married couple. I knew immediately I had to get this job. (I mean *job* in the loosest sense of the word, since this was in no way a paid opportunity.) I interviewed with the office manager, a thin white girl with blunt, thick bangs in her early twenties. She introduced me to the beauty editor, and we had a quick, friendly chat, after which she offered me the internship on the spot. I was shocked. I had assumed it would be a more difficult interview process with several more hoops to jump through. The office manager gave me a tour of the place, then passed me off to the other interns, who took over touring duties and brought me to the mailroom. Minutes later, an editor walked in and dumped a bunch of *NYLON* issues into my outstretched arms, with instructions on where to send them. I was ecstatic that I fit in so well she assumed I was part of the team. In reality, I don't think she looked at me at all.

It was one of the strangest interviews I've ever had, but I was in. One of my core, inner-child needs is acceptance (thank you, therapy). For many people, the need for acceptance has to do with lack of parental love. That's where we get terms like "daddy issues" and "mommy issues." But I was comfortable and supported at home and felt very unstable in the world. Acceptance was such a precarious objective, often dependent on what I looked like and my ability to conform. In my world, where there was a disproportionate number of blue-eyed girls named Katie, this was tricky. I clutched my need for acceptance and dragged it around with me into adulthood, so much so that some of my happiest memories involve gaining acceptance of some kind. They represent a reliance on achievement, that my hard work and dedication yield a positive outcome. Getting into college, scoring an internship at *NYLON*—these feats underscored messaging that I desperately needed to hear: "Welcome, you are now one of us." Being one of *us*, by definition, means that you are excluding others. Not everyone can be an *us*. There has to be a *them*. I was so content to be in the club, and I needed to do my part to keep it exclusive. So I dutifully ensured that getting in was difficult, that staying in was difficult. I was protecting a ridiculous lie so I could pretend to be happy.

Even though I had made it over the sacred threshold of a magazine office, I still struggled to find acceptance. On my first day, I carefully selected a floral dress and ballet flats, which I paired with a Ralph Lauren boy's blazer (a tip I got from *Teen Vogue*), and marched confidently into the *NYLON* office. My little intern table—I can hardly call it a desk—was situated next to the fashion editor's desk. She was speaking to another intern, who had already been there for months, discussing what they did over the weekend. The intern, a white, five-eleven, size-negative-two chain-smoker, said she had gone to Topshop to check out the new Kate Moss for Topshop collection. The fashion editor replied to her that she shouldn't bother, that all the clothes were frilly floral dresses—"Very girlie and very not *NYLON*," she almost purred with a cool edge in her voice and her eyes trained directly on me. I gulped and scolded myself for choosing such a stupid, juvenile outfit. I'm friendly with this woman now, who has since ascended the ranks to a much higher position. I think she would cringe to know how this interaction affected me, but just like anything that caused me pain, instead of letting it break me, I took notes. I learned to deliver critiques in a similar aloof way, to force interns to audition for acceptance. I turned that experience into a learning opportunity, making sure I never made that mistake again and adapting that behavior to be useful to me.

In April 2020, Tyra Banks came under fire for some resurfaced clips from early seasons of *America's Next Top Model* that depict questionable conduct, to put it mildly. In one, Banks reprimands a contestant for refusing to close the gap in her teeth in the makeover portion of the competition. In a later season, she gives a model a gap. The most damning clip depicts the show setting up photo shoots for the wannabe models where they try on different races, essentially promoting Blackface, brownface, and yellowface. Looking at this in 2020 is cringeworthy, but a decade prior, it was a true depiction of everything the fashion and modeling industry was. Banks, who came clean about feeling the pressure to get a nose job at the beginning of her career, had already been through all of it and more. She was trying to tough love the next generation into successful careers, and to do so, she clearly adopted the language of oppressors. This industry has a way of passing on bad habits like that.

Policing the clothing choices of others felt like my ultimate calling. I had been doing it for years already, but the higher I climbed on the masthead, the more authority I had to deliver ferocious evaluations. And, as it turns out, that was encouraged. The same year I started college, Twitter was born. Twitter offered the opportunity to provide real-time commentary and build a following based on your opinions. Like the model that comic Joan Rivers provided for popularity and engagement, the nastier the comment, the more attention you got. It was a constant game of one-upping to demonstrate who was funniest, smartest, and first. The more cutting and ruthless tweets won out in terms of engagement. Following along in the tradition of blogs, Twitter was a digital discussion forum designed for people who wanted to lash out. And lash out they did. I would spend all my energy reading blogs and tweets, making sure my clothes were the "right" ones, and making necessary financial sacrifices—like trips and food—so I could look like I worked in fashion.

That first summer I spent interning for *NYLON* was formative. I did a lot of transcribing and research. I was given work by the beauty director, and eventually, they let me write little blurbs in the pages. All my blurbs got rewritten, save a sentence or two, and I would sob about being talentless and going nowhere, my feelings hurt that they didn't like my words. Despite my wounded pride, I remained determined. I rushed to finish my assignments in record time, then would try to find something else to do. I sorted the mail. I walked the dogs. I organized lipsticks, fragrances, and foundations. I steeled myself for the task of becoming more "on brand" for *NYLON*, a pattern of attempting to chameleon myself to fit wherever I was working was born. I learned a lot about expectations, branding, and more importantly, what it took to make a magazine—and what it took was a lot of white women. I was the only Black person at *NYLON* that summer. There were maybe two Asian girls, but as for Black people, it was just me. It was a familiar position, and I didn't think about it much. It mostly came up as a problem if I was given an assignment on a subject that even I, swaddled in all things white culture, had no frame of reference for, like punk or alternative culture, two major aspects of the *NYLON* brand identity. *NYLON* was pretty alternative at the time, and I was strictly and thoroughly pop.

Just as the acknowledged canon for artistic greatness is limited to white men, the canon for beauty is limited to white women. I did countless image-research projects on women like Debbie Harry, Jane Birkin, Marianne Faithfull, Twiggy, and Françoise Hardy. Women like these served as the guideposts for the look the *NYLON* reader wanted to achieve. They were in permanent rotation in our pages, and I dedicated myself to studying them. I had barely heard those names before that summer, but I became an expert in their biographies and faces. I wanted to succeed in my job, and to do so, I needed to know this playbook. These women were adults, but the inspiration was drawn from their teenage years. Since I was eighteen at the time, it never bothered me that women in their late twenties and thirties were using teenagers as beauty inspiration. That's what they wanted, and that's what I gave them. After about a decade of regaling the looks of prepubescent girls, it will eventually get to you. But as an intern, I was a peon and happy to do whatever I was asked. Who was I to question anything? I could barely say *Givenchy* the right way.

Studying was a go-to skill, so that's what I did. I studied pronunciation guides for French words I didn't know and became deeply invested in understanding the inner workings of the industry. Fashion is a dictatorship, not a democracy—it can't work any other way. The inclinations of a few are what drive many decisions. There aren't many opportunities to challenge leadership, even fewer when you are at the bottom. For the most part, just consider free will an illusion. Someone else will always be calling the shots, and when the personal and the professional bleed together so indiscernibly, people forget that they have a separate selfhood from the one that shackles them to their job.

That summer, I learned that the editor-in-chief and the publisher are at the top of the food chain. They get the final say on everything and tend to influence the culture of the office. With each new boss, you begin to attune yourself to their whims, pleasures, and displeasures. Every magazine has its own brand voice, which is how it can be identified in the market. It also has its own unspoken dress code for its employees, prompting a mini makeover with every new job in the industry.

Within magazines, there are interdepartmental rivalries. The fashion team reigns as the Regina George, so to speak, but each team can be snobbish about their area of expertise. The art department gets to stick their nose up about fonts. The photo department admonishes everyone over image quality. Everyone pretty much unilaterally hates the staff of the digital department, which is viewed as young and inelegant, but this has changed as traditional print advances toward fossil status. The features department has jurisdiction over films, music, and culture in general. But the fashion department is the worst because it works with the most visual and outward-facing medium: clothing. Back in the latter half of the aughts, it was important for everyone to look like they worked at a magazine, no matter which one you worked for and no matter which department you worked for. You wore your employment like armor. Just like you recognize a mail carrier by a postal uniform, you should be able to identify someone who works at a magazine by how they look. This can bring a lot of stress to an employee who is uniquely passionate about home decor but whose job demands a certain diligence when it comes to physical presentation.

Also, people were quite mean, almost as a rule of engagement. I still don't know whether this was a general consequence of everyone being overworked, underpaid, and slightly depressed, or more of a bizarre gag we all played on each other just because. Over the years, the culture has improved (being nice is cool!), but when I first started working in fashion, meanness was the price of initiation. In digital spaces, humiliation, slut-shaming, and judgment were the norm. That style of humor, writing, and blogging affected how I socialized or expressed myself. Being mean was *funny*.

We were not having a mental-health conversation yet; we were too busy enjoying Mariah Carey having a "breakdown" on *TRL*. Britney Spears shaving her head was late-night fodder, not cause for concern. It was a vicious portrait of who and what we cared about as a society, and magazines were a place where snobbery and elitism were born and fostered. It seemed wholly necessary to accept abuse as an intern, or witness it being flung at your coworkers. The pattern was to exert the full extent of your limited power over those who had even less. It was a warped way of working, where mistreatment was believed to produce the best kind of creativity, and kindness was deemed useless. Fashion hardened me even more, and I doubled down on the drive to succeed, wanting to climb even further since the higher you were, the more irreproachable you became.

Very few places operate like this now, partly because the money and the perks that required this kind of fanatical loyalty have all but dried up. It starts to seem crazy if you're a magazine executive who is lambasting employees for some free jeans and lip gloss, much less so if you're behaving that way because your position allows your children entry into a prestigious school, opens the door to an interest-free mortgage, and grants access to year-round car service. You start to do what you think you have to so you can protect that position.

People ask whether it was difficult to work at magazines, and the short answer is yes. I would endure the polite, delicate kind of racism that whispers and stings, just like in my adolescence. There were many politics at play, and if I thought high school was bad, navigating this new, complicated game as an adult without a rulebook was near impossible. But it was my job to make it look fun and easy. I was preserving the impression that the club was one people should want to suffer abuse to enter. Eventually, I believe that fissure between perception and reality, the one I'd been walking my whole life, drove me into a deep depression. But you don't get to complain about your glamorous job. As Meryl Streep's fictionalized character Miranda Priestly quips in *The Devil Wears Prada*, "Don't be silly, darling. Everybody wants to be us."

CHAPTER EIGHTEEN

By the summer of 2008, I was a professional intern. I transferred out of Tufts the first semester of my sophomore year because of the limited opportunities for continuing to intern in Massachusetts. I wanted to continue working in magazines, so I transferred to the College of Arts and Sciences at NYU and then the Gallatin School of Individualized Study when the school administration tried to put a cap on my internship credits. I found it counterproductive to sit in biology class when I was already working in the field I wanted to go into.

I was happy at NYU—or as happy as my low-grade functional depression would allow. My NYU circle was richer and more privileged than the one at Tufts. I made friends easily with jaded but driven girls—girls who declared partying venues "over," who could get free drinks or dinners, and who made out with celebrities. In this group, I was almost always the most cautious, and I was mesmerized by their devil-may-care/YOLO attitudes because I knew my rules were different. I didn't do drugs or blow off classes or even breathe easily. This isn't to say I didn't party; I did, but my new friends' lifestyles were almost straight out of a *Gossip Girl* plotline. We were the most glamorous, broke-ish students there were.

I scored my next internship at *W Magazine*. I secured my spot by borrowing a friend's Marc Jacobs Stam bag to impress the assistant who interviewed me. It worked. It was critical to look the part, even as an intern. I was so excited to have made the cut, to be initiated into such a high-fashion institution. That internship was where I memorized the addresses for designers like Oscar de la Renta, Calvin Klein, and Ralph Lauren. I will likely be able to recite these from memory for the rest of my life. It's where I finally found out how to correctly pronounce Givenchy, Loewe, and Balmain and sniggered at people who still struggled with little finesse. It takes no time at all to become a snob once you're sitting at the table with the cool kids.

It's also where I was trained in fashion's obsession with being thin. The assistants subsisted on cigarettes and Diet Coke. We wanted to be thin, made no money, and spent a dangerous amount of time working in an office that never ever allowed breaks. As a college student without an iota of knowledge on nutrition, I assumed I could eat whatever I wanted so long as I ate a very small amount. It was already my regular practice. So every day, I would have a toasted everything bagel with cream cheese. I would get it from a two-story deli across the street on Third Avenue. It kept me full for the whole day, or at least that's what I told myself, and most important, it was cheap. My food intake for an entire day cost me $1.75. Honestly, what could be better? We interns did our best to try to hide the fact that we needed to eat, take a break, or otherwise stop working because being seen as lazy, entitled, or uninterested had disastrous consequences.

Keeping the fashion closet neat and orderly was one of the responsibilities of the intern crew. The fashion closet was less a closet and more a massive room for clothing storage, also doubling as an office and occasionally a dressing room, a stage, and a shipping center. Because I was an overeager weirdo, I would sometimes come into the office early to organize things. One such morning, as I typed away on a Mac desktop with my bagel, an assistant whose style I idolized and a friend to this day, came into the closet. She checked that everything was fine with the racks, chatting with me about innocuous nonsense before turning to me and saying, "Wow, I mean, I'm really jealous that you can eat that. A bagel is like six slices of bread, you know?" And then she walked out, and I didn't eat another bagel for the next seven years or so. I also repeated that line anytime I saw someone with a bagel. To anyone I said that to, I'm sorry.

Trying to make it in the fashion business, you can begin to feel puppeted. The lines blur between who you are and the role you need to play. You need to act one way, dress one way, and look one way. Do you actually like that thing, or does your boss like it? No one even bothers to examine where grand creative direction originates; it's just made very clear that you study it, then live it no matter what, and that attitude extends way beyond style. Someone said bagels are six slices of bread to me, and I said it to countless other people. And before you know it, no one is eating bagels, and everyone is low-key starving and totally miserable.

Because I already knew what profession I wanted to pursue, I structured my education around that. I condensed all my classes into two days a week, whether or not I was particularly interested in the subject. The other three days I spent interning at magazines, which I took as seriously as if it were my full-time job. I did not go abroad. I did not go on spring break. I did not go on Christmas holiday or long weekends. I wanted to be available to work at all times. This flattening of my needs mimicked my refusal to feed myself, and it all worked out for me. I was a sample size when I ended up getting hired as a full-time assistant before I finished my senior year at NYU. I was lucky enough to be able to study at a school where I could make up my own major, and the one I designed was "Fashion Theory," a study of the coding of clothing from monarchies to the present, with a special focus on the ways fashion can communicate political afflictions, class status, and subculture allegiances—something I would be able to use later in my fashion career. Being an outsider gives you one tremendous gift: the gift of observation, of surveying and understanding environments that you are on the periphery of but not totally immersed in, and fashion magazines presented a really fascinating opportunity for study. Over years of interning, I began to understand the power dynamics and politics of working in fashion.

Magazines are kind of like people you might meet in life. *Vogue* is the mom, with the strongest and most historied presence. She's well respected and revered, but everyone thinks she has a stick up her ass, and they're all a little afraid of her. *Elle* is the cooler, younger sister to *Vogue*, but *Vogue* isn't worried because *Elle* lacks refinement. *Elle* chews gum and once had a skater phase. Everyone loves to hate on *Cosmo*, who is like your cousin who got knocked up in high school. *Vanity Fair* is your reserved but liberal-leaning uncle who wears glasses and used to go out for drinks with Tom Wolfe. *Town & Country* is your racist grandparent who abuses the help. *Glamour* is your little sister's best friend who you can't stand, rolling your eyes at everything she says. *Complex* is the guy you regret sleeping with who always texts you when you're home for Thanksgiving. *Harper's Bazaar* is your sorority sister who did a lot of coke in college, had a wedding that was way too big, and secretly voted for Trump. *The New Yorker* is the grad school professor you have a crush on. He is definitely too smart for you, but you still flirt with him sometimes to feel older and sophisticated.

When trying to make it in publishing, it's necessary to maintain a familiarity with each of these brands, and you must remember to alter your dress and behavior to properly integrate. When you get old enough, or more advanced in your career, you will simply shed the ones that suck and keep the ones that don't. That's just how relationships work. When I first started out, I wanted to be where anyone wanted me, but I was wanted only insofar as I could stand the unspoken and spoken commandments that allowed me to be there.

At my first paying job, my boss's boss, the creative director, a famously trenchant British man, told me and the other fashion assistant that we were "too milk-fed, like all American girls" and demanded to know why "we all looked like Reese Witherspoon." I, of course, look nothing like Reese, and neither did my Jewish coworker; neither of us were blonde, and both of us had several inches of height on the famously petite A-lister, but it didn't matter to him. He thought we were too fat and that we should know it. Of course, Reese Witherspoon is hardly fat, but that didn't matter to him either. We knew what he meant. We were both twenty-one years old, and this was our first job out of college. Wanting to do our best, we took the note, each of us dropping at least ten pounds from stress alone, then using the residual anger that resulted from our endless starvation to influence our interns, touting the benefits of not eating and romanticizing thin bodies. The objective of this chain of command is to make it known that being fat is unacceptable, and whatever is in your power to do to make sure you don't gain weight, you do at all costs. For a long time, I was sure my weight would affect my hirability. No one ever said this to me directly, but when I looked around fashion, all I saw was an abundance of thin women and men. For years, I didn't meet anyone above a size six who worked in fashion. So you tell me: Does it matter?

In the third round of a job interview at *Teen Vogue*, I met with the fashion director, who grilled me about what restaurants I liked to go to and what stores I liked to shop in. I was twenty-three years old and applying for an assistant position. I used to share a disgusting punch bowl at Brother Jimmy's and get blackout drunk off free shots at Dorrian's. At the end of our chat, the fashion director told me that what the team was currently missing was a girl with a "cool downtown urban vibe," and she hoped that could be me. This was true at most places I've worked; we weren't so much being hired as being cast. She was telling me the role she needed me to play, so I played it. Just like being Scary Spice or Jessi or Lisa Turtle, I just zipped myself into whatever role was required of me at whatever time it was required. I had no attachment to any of these appointed identities and certainly no ability to refuse, even if I wanted to. I made my body available for any and all projections, and I tried to accept each one so I could, in turn, be accepted.

The hypocrisy of the industry is staggering. We, by definition, must remain exclusive for esteem, but countless brands—both publishers and consumer-product companies—count "inclusion" as an integral part of their business, especially now. At every turn, you'll discover that's not true. Many size runs don't extend past what can be described as a generous medium, and fashion offices and magazines are overwhelmingly run by white people. Sure, in the last few years, there has been wider acceptance of different body types, skin tones, and racial backgrounds, but the acknowledgment that you need to broaden customer appeal in order to sell something is not synonymous with genuine respect. Changes to organizational structures or leadership do not extend past the surface level; we don't like to look under the surface in fashion. As for the publishing companies, well, the demographics there shouldn't surprise you. Fashion is a who's who of very rich people. They are thin. They are white. That's pretty much it.

Working in that environment, I never thought I could be rid of my eating disorder. My success was dependent on my ability to stay skinny so I could wear the clothes that impressed people and be promoted to keep trying to impress people until I died. Black women who seemed to have made it in fashion, like Genevieve Jones, Shala Monroque, and Michelle Elie, seemed well adapted to the pressures of the industry and were revered for their excellent taste. What else did they have in common? Their sternums protruded through their clothing. I don't point this out to shame them, but it demonstrates the kind of body that is acceptable in the fashion world. To a certain degree, a bony body can supersede Blackness, if you can wear the clothes well.

I hadn't developed a gauge for understanding when I was hungry and when I should feed myself. Since I was perpetually hungry, I assumed it was just a condition I had. I even told my therapist that I was prepared to live that way forever. I figured I would just live my entire life hungry, and I was happy to if it meant I would never get fat. Over the years, many ex-models, singers, and dancers have written about their eating disorders. Their jobs are in the public eye and especially vulnerable to the pressures of the oppressive beauty system. What frightened me most about reading those accounts—and, trust me, I have pretty much read them all—was a trajectory that saw women (and men, in some cases) being cured of their disorder and then gaining about one hundred pounds and becoming almost unrecognizable. That possibility was terrifying. A whole lifetime of dieting just for me to "recover" and get fat? Are you nuts? I wouldn't let that fate befall me. Zoë Kravitz was a notable outlier, who remained thin after declaring herself free of anorexia and bulimia. I accepted that I could change if, and only if, it would be like that. But the way my weight yo-yoed if I deviated from my ordinary routine told me that would not be my story.

As I spent more time working in fashion, I started getting invites to tag along to sample sales. The problem with clothing made for fashion, I would later learn, is that if you have a body that is curvy in any way, you will inadvertently draw attention to those curves, even when you don't mean to. I have lost a lot of sleep worrying about how my legs look in shorts, if heels are going to be "too much" on me, and whether to wear something that could be seen as too short or too tight—the slumbering influence of years in uniforms cropping up.

Once, when shopping with coworkers at a department store abroad, I found a pair of platform lug-sole boots by Alaïa. We loved Alaïa. Most everyone in fashion does. Those boots were on major discount, and I was ecstatic. I tried them on, and at five-eight, they pushed me north of six feet, easily. My coworkers told me I couldn't wear those shoes because they made me look too masculine. That's not exactly the phrasing they used, but it's the nice way I'll say it. They said such boots were only for tiny Russian millionaires like Miroslava Duma, a rising street-style star our age who stood at five feet on her best day. She later exposed her closeted racism in 2018, when she posted a photo of a celebratory bouquet she received upon arriving in Paris for couture week with a card that read "To my n*ggas in Paris." Needless to say I never looked at a heel that high, or at Miroslava Duma, ever again.

The fashion industry has a way of molding you, of letting you know the limits. On a surface level, we encourage "individuality" and "artistic expression"—to a point. The skeleton of what is acceptable does not really change. Some of the rules I absorbed those first few years included these:

- Stretch fabrics are tacky; everyone will judge you.
- Looking tacky, in any sense, is something to avoid.
- To some degree, it is still expected that one should suffer for fashion.
- We might not wear corsets anymore, but we have a newer and better corset: 100 percent cotton denim jeans. They are a penitentiary made of fabric.
- Jeggings are a joke.
- Formfitting things are reserved for models only or other similarly svelte forms that fashion people think regular people want to see, as to avoid your breasts "falling out" in front of a *Vogue* editor at dinner.
- Single-sole heels are always preferable, even if they are the most painful.
- Black is the best color to wear because it's easy, but it doesn't look great on a page, so everyone wears black and no one shoots it.
- If you're good at your job, the day will come where you won't have to pay for anything, but until that point, you must buy

everything so you can build up the reputation of being someone who is well dressed, and then, eventually, you will get
everything for free.

• Youth, money, and a bony body to hang it all on are all that
matters.

All the magazines drive these rules home, and then it's reinforced by
movies where twenty-seven-year-olds are cast as mothers of three, and
nineteen-year-olds are the love interests for forty-seven-year-old men. I
never thought it would be possible for me to break any of the rules, so
I tried to follow them as dutifully as possible.

CHAPTER NINETEEN

After graduation and my first jobs working in editorial, I took a break from traditional print media to work at a luxury retailer start-up. The entire ethos of the company—selling exclusive luxury—all but hinged on the foundation of white supremacy. Pleasing the powers that be involved catering to a very thin, very rich white woman, who, in turn, wanted to cater to other women like her. That mission was made explicitly clear. I reported to a woman whom I admire for her tenacious insistence on inclusion at every level and her dedication to making sure I was advocated for and protected. Her type of integrity is rare, and though she was white and thin herself, she made it possible for me to contribute creatively and be heard in rooms where I would otherwise have been ignored.

Her protection could reach only so far. It was my job to communicate the brand's message: that the best way to look was being swathed in expensive clothing while also being a size zero while also being blonde while also looking rich, but fun, but still rich. I was reprimanded for hiring models who were brunette, let alone another race. My immediate boss constantly went to bat over an Asian model, who we loved working with but who the founder later banned, saying she looked like a "mean old Chinese lady." After that, a dark-skinned Black model, also lovely, was banned, too, because the founder said she "did not look expensive" and that her look was antithetical to trying to sell luxury clothes.

I knew my skin and body must have repulsed this woman. I didn't look expensive, either, did I? It was the muted mockery that, when paired with what I had already experienced in childhood, properly eroded my self-esteem—a series of tiny wounds that set about decaying my sense of self. None of this would stop me from fighting for approval. I put the full value of almost every paycheck back into that site, accumulating clothing and attempting to elevate my personal image in the hopes of being accepted.

It was a higher-stakes version of high school, which is pretty much what working in fashion is like. My yearning for acceptance just got a little pricier. I flagrantly starved myself at this point, encouraged by the camaraderie of my coworkers, who would join me in eating a single banana and gleefully exchanging war tales about caloric deficits. We drank gallons of water, which would have been healthy if it weren't merely an attempt to keep our stomachs full and distract our bodies from starving. I chewed ice chips obsessively, which served both as a distraction for my anxiety and a way to satisfy my craving to chew what should have been food.

Another stressful aspect of the job was the requirement that it be publicly perceived as the greatest job ever, and this is true across the board for most jobs in media. For a fashion start-up, that meant I was invited to a lot of fancy parties and events. My wardrobe needed to match my new lifestyle. It is not financially possible to live in New York and maintain such a ridiculous level of glamour unless you are very rich, even if you never eat anything. Because I was becoming identified as a well-dressed person, I was invited by designers to borrow clothing. "Borrowing clothing" usually means samples, and samples are the pieces that are worn on the runway or by celebrities. They are the prototype of the clothing that will be later made in a full-size run. Samples are small. *Extremely* small. I admonished myself harshly when I tried on a sample and it didn't fit. I had access to clothing and designers the likes of which I had never seen before, and it was a brutal blow when the fabric wouldn't close around my hips.

Working at that start-up was like being fashion famous. The industry was excited about the company. In 2012, Instagram had just begun to tear at the iron curtain of fashion, opening up doors to the public that had been closed for decades. Behind-the-scenes content was a cute novelty that people wanted to be a part of. It was thrilling to be involved in something new bubbling up, and more importantly, working there was the ultimate stamp of approval, no matter how precarious my position seemed. From the outside, we were the quintessential popular girls: stylish and willing and ready to have a good time. We went to Paris, we did closed-door fittings with famous models and actresses, and we got our photos taken everywhere. It was my first experience upholding the facade of a brand at the expense of my own well-being. My success hinged on maintaining the performance, making sure that the reputation of the brand remained something to be coveted and relished.

Looking the part was crucial to success in fashion, and as a subsidiary extension of the *Vogue* brand, this company wanted to mirror *Vogue* in every way. There were adopted idiosyncrasies about how to handle shoots, passed down from some sort of generational and verbal rulebook, like "No shoes photographed on couches" and "Two girls can be featured in a single photograph, but not three"—really antiquated and bizarre commandments that were whispered in a professional game of telephone. One of these directives dictated what employees should look like, and the term "*Vogue* girl" was tossed around as an all-encompassing descriptor. If you closed your eyes and imagined what you thought a girl who worked at *Vogue* would look like, you would likely conjure an attractive, tall, thin, and white woman, but most importantly thin. Everyone we hired was filtered through this value system, even interns. As an assistant and then an editor, I was often tasked with conducting the intern interviews and overseeing their work once they were hired on. I wanted to give Black girls opportunities, but I was conscious of the optics. I tried my best to hire one Black intern, one white intern (or another non-Black ethnic variation), and alternate them over semesters so no one would be suspicious of my motivations. I had just left *Teen Vogue*, where a director had accused my former boss of "trying to turn the magazine Black" after she brought on too many Black employees.

One intern, a sweet, smart, plus-size Black girl, went on to work at actual *Vogue*. Our paths crossed again almost a decade later. She told me that when she inquired about full-time employment after her internship, I informed her that "what they are looking for is a *Vogue* girl." She interpreted this to mean white. I did not mean white; I meant skinny. But it doesn't matter because it was hurtful, and it was something she carried around for almost ten years—an interaction I barely remembered. At the time, I thought I was giving her a kind warning about the physical requirements of the industry she was entering, offering a generic euphemism that had become common language in my world. I didn't coin the term, but that oppressive language quickly took hold in my brain, and I unconsciously weaponized it to harm someone else. I wish that kind of cruelty didn't come so naturally. I never cared about being a "*Vogue* girl" or protecting what that image meant, but I did care about performing well in my job and doing what was expected of me. Unfortunately, this meant a further endorsement of white supremacy and asserting white supremacy's particular brutality over myself and others. I was, by this point, extremely practiced at both.

In my last year working for the start-up, we did a partnership with *Vogue* for the Met Gala, and I got to attend the party. The Met Gala, considered the "Fashion Oscars," is a distinctly exclusive event and is arguably the only reason *Vogue* is still relevant. You cannot simply *go* to the Met Gala; you must be *invited*. I was working, but it was still exciting to attend. The theme of the Gala was punk. I spent weeks stressing about what designer dress I was going to borrow and how small I needed to be to fit into it. My boss was getting a custom gown made by Thom Browne, so hers was going to fit within an inch of her life. I, a peasant, had to make sure my body could fit the clothes, not the other way around. The magazines I read as a girl had assiduously detailed dressing for your body type, but in Fashion with a capital *F*, only one type of body is acceptable. I had suspected that fact as a distant observer, but it became abundantly clear once I entered the eye of the tornado that there was one look: skinny. You either did it right, or you were invisible.

In the weeks before the Met, I starved drastically, abstaining from food so my bones could be on full display on "fashion's biggest night of the year." I committed myself to doing nothing but working and working out. I wore my eyes out searching through the runway shows on Style.com (yup, that long ago) for punk-inspired gowns that might work for the event. I happened upon a sequin and tulle dress from Theyskens's Theory by Olivier Theyskens, and I exhaled with celebratory relief when that size-zero sample (with stretch, come on) zipped all the way up.

For reasons I will never understand, I was assigned the job of "greeter" (although come to think of it, perhaps it is an ideal Token Black Girl job), which meant that I stood like a statue in the doorway leading to the dining room, ushering guests through after they were received by *Vogue* editor-in-chief Anna Wintour and her fellow cohosts at the top of the stairs. My position was largely unnecessary since waiters serving glasses of champagne stood directly next to the hosts, and there was really only one way to walk, so I don't know how anyone could have been confused about where to go next. Regardless, that was my duty, and I was both thrilled and terrified. I was, first of all, positioned very close to Anna, which required me to be on my best behavior. That meant no gawking at famous people or doing anything else unsavory. Second, I was on full display to each and every celebrity who walked by, and I could feel their eyes evaluating me, gauging how on or off brand I was for the Met. And third, I was the only Black one, so I knew that had I messed up at all, it certainly would have been remembered.

My heart pounded with panic the entire time, and since I was so malnourished, I am sure you could see my pulse beating against my ribs with a steadfast rhythm. I stood there for four and a half hours, in one single spot, while my legs shook from the strain of my five-inch-high Manolo Blahnik Chaos sandals. This is a single-sole, ankle-strap sandal, in case you're not a shoe freak, and it's not easy to remain immobile in them on a concrete floor for hours at a time. When the final guests, Beyoncé and Jay Z, walked through the doors a little after 8:00 p.m., I all but collapsed—as soon as I was out of the sight of anyone who could be mad about that kind of thing. The Met Gala staff—basically all the employees of *Vogue*—eat dinner in the basement, while the guests have their dinner upstairs (yeah, like *Downton Abbey*), and since eating was of no real consequence to me, I made my escape to my apartment about thirty blocks south of the Met and changed into white Chuck Taylors that were covered in spikes, a gift I got when I worked at *Teen Vogue*. They were extremely punk, and I was thrilled to be able to walk, if nothing else. I got in a taxi to go back uptown and was at the after-party before anyone even knew I was missing. The after-party that year was a Kanye West concert, and it was much more enjoyable in sneakers. I heard the real *Vogue* girls sneering and whispering when I walked back inside, something I'm sure they don't remember. "Oh my God, I can't believe she's in sneakers." I knew I'd probably fucked up, but at that point, I had pushed myself so far to look "right" at this party that I was just relieved to be in tolerable footwear.

Just like with hair and just like with my weight, I learned to sacrifice so much for clothing. When I was building my career, I purchased the most ridiculous items, wardrobe elements that I cringe to remember. I wasn't even sure I had a taste. I would just buy things that would get me the kind of attention I thought I needed to succeed. I had skirts I couldn't sit in, shoes I couldn't walk in, and stacks of sweaters I liked to call "tricky knits," which had to be specially cleaned and could never be in the presence of any jewelry since they would completely unravel at the slightest snag. Poetic, really. I was so uncomfortable in nearly all of it, and I hated being itchy and fidgety, but the compliments kept coming. The followers kept coming, followed by the job promotions and new opportunities. I had built a new nightmare for myself, one that was both beautiful and horrific because I had the life I wanted, in theory, but the continuous maintenance was torture. Still, I knew I couldn't stop. I was finally being accepted, just as I had dreamed about for years. People asked for my opinion about trends. They asked about my personal beauty regimen. They wanted to know where I shopped and what I was "coveting." I became addicted to the accolades. I didn't know how to get off the ride I had begged to be on in the first place. And I never thought I had the right to complain.

CHAPTER TWENTY

A few months after the Met Gala, my mentor departed from the start-up, and I started looking for a new job. Without her protection, I couldn't stick around. I was hired as the fashion editor at Elle.com and joined a ragtag team of young and scrappy internet women who became my favorite coworkers ever. I was twenty-five years old and in such a poor mental space coming out of working at the retail start-up that the camaraderie between me and the other girls at *Elle* was a welcome reprieve. I began expanding my professional interests, thinking more about cosmetics and hair. I was the only Black member of the team and became a de facto guinea pig, testing out products and experiences so I could report on whether a brand's promises about inclusivity were true.

It was not uncommon for me to find myself in a salon chair for a complimentary treatment. On one such occasion, I stopped by Hair Rules, a natural hair salon for Black women and our curly-haired allies founded by celebrity hairstylist Anthony Dickey, known affectionately as Dickey. At that point, I had graduated from just a few tracks to a full-blown weave, my natural hair totally disguised in intricate rows of braids under hair extensions. The entire procedure was extremely labor- and time-intensive, taking between six and eight hours for me to get my hair done. I was, in truth, tired of the process. I had spent years of my life waiting in salons under dryers, getting braided up, sewn up, coiffed, and curled just right, before I was finally set free with my done hair, only to return for the same process six weeks later. It started to pull me apart, having to sit in the salon chair as I watched my precious time dissolve away, like pouring water over salt. I was ripe for seeking a shortcut out of the system, and the stylists at the salon piled on me, telling me how beautiful my natural hair was and that I should embrace it. They bolstered my self-esteem, calling over their colleagues to admire my curls, gently suggesting, in their own way, that I "go natural." I consented to their pleas and let them toss my tracks in the trash. I left the salon feeling lighter than I had in years, my natural hair barely blowing in the wind, now that it had no chemicals in it to alter its genetic temperament. It was a simple blowout complemented by a single pass of the flat iron. Not bone-straight, but straight enough.

That was Saturday. By Monday, I was back in the Hearst tower, and like anyone with natural hair will tell you, you never have the same hairstyle twice. So while I struggled to re-create what the Hair Rules experts did for me not forty-eight hours before, I still had to show up at the office, whether or not I was satisfied with my results. I walked into my nightmare. My hair had poofed up, just like it would before I had a relaxer. It was straight-*ish* but still different from when I had a full weave. Ugh, the shrinkage! Unlike when I got my first perm (to absolutely zero fanfare), my coworkers' oohing, aahing, and fawning over my "new" natural look also came with some unwanted hands in my hair. This was in 2014, three years before Solange Knowles's indispensable album *A Seat at the Table* featured the song "Don't Touch My Hair," forcing white women (at least the ones semi-knowledgeable in pop culture) to do a double take before reaching out to a Black woman's tresses. I am not sure who was telling their all-white coworkers to back off, but it certainly wasn't me. I was still mute on race at the time, and I was not going to rock the boat at my dream job.

I shamefully let the petting and fawning continue, somehow managing not to burst into tears, but I was suffering. I felt so exposed as

I was blitzed with questions. *"So this is your real hair?" "Did you get a haircut?" "OMG, so cute, but is it going to look like this all the time?"* By 1:00 p.m., I had made an appointment with a hairstylist in Westchester, where my parents lived, and by 2:00 p.m., I was working from the salon, knowing I would be there for at least the next six hours while I got my weave reinstalled.

Sitting in the stylist's chair, I received a Google Chat from my boss asking where I had gone. I hadn't said anything to my coworkers; I'd just left. I'll never know if one of them ratted me out or if my boss's intuition led her to question me, but I still felt it best not to lie. "I had to go get my hair done," I typed back, confident it wouldn't really be a problem since I could do all my stories from the comfort of anywhere with Wi-Fi. I was such an obsessive workaholic that I would likely be doing more than I should wherever I was. This was not the right response. Apparently, leaving work in the middle of the day for a "salon appointment" was not allowed, as I learned from the Chat tirade my boss unleashed on me minutes later. I realized I sounded frivolous and nonchalant, but there was absolutely no way I could convey to that white woman how life and death this appointment felt. I apologized and tolerated my lashing with as much dignity as I could muster, after already having been emotionally pummeled all day.

The issue was not that my boss was callous or didn't have the capacity to be empathetic. In fact, the opposite was true. In many ways, she felt more like a racial crusader than I did. The issue was that I was deeply ashamed of having to explain the series of grave mistakes I had made: removing my weave in the first place, my failure to re-create the hairstyle, the inability to tell my coworkers to back the fuck off, and finally, my desperate flight to get back to a place where I felt more in control and presentable, with my fake hair sewn neatly onto my head. I couldn't possibly say all that because, on some level, I knew it was insane. It was easier to let my boss think of me as an impatient narcissist who made a poor judgment call. Just like the disappointment from my gym teacher, I knew this was something I must withstand.

When you work in media, being looked at can become part of your job description, and the outward-facing element of being the Token Black Girl is often exploited because the entire industry hinges completely on image. By the time I made it to being magazine editor, I was used to being trotted out like a cute little show pony. In 2014, I received a pair of Timberland boots as a gift, which I wore to an event I can describe only as a Republican alcoholic's paradise, also known as The Hunt. The Hunt is a giant outdoor frat party, so I was excited to test the boots' impressive all-weather capabilities, and while I realized that Timberlands were not a new or novel boot, they were new to my closet. I wanted to tell people about how cool they could look with outfits. This was during the "normcore" era, a time characterized by the growing popularity of items that were not designer branded but more practical and utilitarian. I put together a slideshow for Elle.com of some chic women of all races—and yes, I included the Kardashians, as was customary of digital media in 2014. The piece was a flip-book, meant primarily to drive page views, and not really an informational article, so I wrote up a snappy little intro about the boots and their place in fashion history. I name-checked Brooklyn-born Jay Z and Biggie Smalls, anchoring the style's origin with men in hip-hop, then tried to use imagery of women like Rihanna, Ciara, JLo, and Rita Ora to demonstrate how women made the boots their own. I submitted my story and went home for the night, honestly thinking it was a job well done.

At the time, my title was "fashion editor." I was an editor, but I also got edited. I don't know who edited my story that night—at least six people could have done it—but the piece that was published removed all mentions of the historical context for the boots, and what's worse, the tweet that accompanied the link said the boots were a "trend." It was a cultural-appropriation atomic bomb.

Worse still, when the angry tweets began to stream in screaming erasure and disrespect, the *Elle* Twitter account tagged my Twitter handle and hung me out to dry in front of the entire world. Yes, the best way to respond to calls for you to hire Black people is probably not to say, "Hey! Look here at our Black girl who's responsible for this story." The ensuing tweetstorm lasted for two days, and there are still people who think I betrayed the entire Black community by penning those three hundred words.

As the Token Black Girl in any situation, but especially a professional one, it's often difficult to shoulder the burden of positively representing your community within an institution in whatever outward-facing ways are required. This can make Black girls sacrificial lambs, as many people lack sympathy for Black girls, who, for whatever reason, choose to work or socialize with a lot of white people. This was true of Normani when she was the sole Black face of Fifth Harmony, enduring her coworker Camila Cabello's abuse. This was also true of Nia Sioux (née Frazier), the only Black cast member of the Lifetime reality show *Dance Moms*, who repeatedly got called a wannabe white girl on social media when she was between the ages of eleven and fourteen. This was true of Justine Skye, who in 2017 was photographed with her famous friends in London and simply labeled "and friends" by *British Vogue* when every white girl in the photo was named. I was too young to know what the public discourse surrounding Mel B was like, but I suspect it was equally unkind. It used to be true of Jordyn Woods, former bestie of Kylie Jenner, and there was still a portion of the Black population who wanted to scream, "I told you so!" when the Kardashian and Jenner clan tossed her aside. There is a universe in which becoming the Token Black Girl makes you a sellout.

The truth is I was doing my duty as an editor and as a member of the Black community to showcase the shoes and reference those who wore them first and best. It was important to validate the names of those men and women who originally made Timberland boots look good and acknowledge their contributions to Black and mainstream culture. I had included that list of hip-hop stars and rappers in the introduction, so when that context was removed, what resulted was a betrayal of Black readers, but it felt like a betrayal of my work too. And I was left holding the bag. I don't have a clue who was responsible for the edits, but all six of the women who could have done it were white. My only reasonable conclusion is they saw the copy about rappers; thought, *This is very off brand*; and deleted it so the focus of the story was simply shoes without context. This is part and parcel of the type of historical erasure that got the Twitter community so riled up in the first place. Cultural signifiers of Blackness migrate over to white spaces, where they are colonized and capitalized on for financial gain, and the edited Elle.com story fit into that erasure.

I had already responded to some tweets before realizing my copy had been altered, and when I checked it, my blood ran cold. By then, there was nothing to be done. Because I was employed by a white institution, one that had a hand in systemic oppression by way of erasure and promotion of Eurocentric beauty ideals, I was guilty by association. The feelings of having to defend my Blackness in childhood came roaring back. And then, of course, there was the inescapable reality that I was actually employed by this magazine and still had to do my job for them.

A 1993 *New York Times* article details the rise of Timberlands in Black and brown communities in northeastern cities and the measures the company took to make sure these boots were not marketed specifically to this demographic. Jeffrey Swartz, the company's executive vice president at the time and grandson of Timberland's founder, is quoted in the story: "In fact, he said he was pleased that a new market had sprung on its own. 'Their money spends good,' he said." It's triggering to read twenty-eight years later, but that quote recalls the reality that, for a long time, fashion relied on the cache of the Black community without offering the community any respect. In hitting "Publish" on that story, all of us at *Elle* were guilty of the same thing, and as the sole Black employee on the fashion team, I had to answer to both my bosses and Black people as a whole. This incident has haunted me for years. It called into question my loyalties and my integrity. As a result, I got labeled every hurtful thing you can think of: a "coon," a "Black white girl," an "Oreo"—monikers you will recognize if you are a Black person who's ever had the misfortune of being too influenced by whiteness.

I try to extend empathy and grace to people who experience similar situations as adults. When actress Garcelle Beauvais joined the famously all-white cast of *The Real Housewives of Beverly Hills* in 2020, she faced criticism over being "boring" and "wanting to be white." It is possible to aspire to assimilate to white supremacy so much that you lose your Black identity completely and become a harmful presence. Stacey Dash exists, for example. But there is such a lack of understanding for the pathology behind living as a single Black female representative in a white world. The more tokenized experiences are spoken about openly, the better off we will all be. While no one knew about my life or story back in 2014, I always felt I had something to prove. I had to prove to my white coworkers that I belonged in their white space and deserved my position there, and I simultaneously had to prove to a Black collective that I wasn't an insensitive asshole playing to win for Whitey.

CHAPTER

TWENTY-ONE

At the same time my Black card was getting snatched back on Twitter because everyone thought I was stuck in the Sunken Place, I was actually in Massachusetts on a press trip. A press trip is a sponsored trip organized for promotional purposes to foster a good-faith relationship in the hopes that you will want to write about the sponsors' products one day. On this particular trip, I found myself in Nantucket on an extended weekend, getting acquainted with some new brands—and partying.

It was summer, and as part of my "diet," I was not drinking. I was accompanied on the trip by editors from various publications who found my alcohol abstinence a fascinating oddity but useful in a destination like Nantucket, where they have been reluctant to embrace Uber. I was the designated driver. One night, we went to dinner at a casual restaurant, and I drove a full Cadillac (one of the trip's sponsors) to dinner, with the promise that I would later shuttle the same group to the Chicken Box, a live music venue and bar that's the real turnup. Our dinner patrons were Miraclesuit, a swimwear/shapewear hybrid that sells mass-market bathing suits geared at helping women hide so-called "problem areas," like tummies, cleavage, and hips. The head honcho was a woman named Sandra, a petite, artificially tanned, grandma type, and her husband, Stuart, a loud, six-five tank of a man who—and this is not an exaggeration—wore only custom full-sequined blazers. He had a dazzling one on sitting catty-corner to me at the long table where we prepared to share a meal.

The conversation started off innocently enough. I was surrounded by my fellow editor colleagues. Generally, people who both talk and write for a living make easy dinner guests. Stuart was (obviously) very interested in being the center of attention. Aside from his intrusive physical presence, he had committed to a class-clown persona, which seemed incongruous for a man who would surely have been classed as a senior citizen. He was seated at the head of the table, and I was immediately on his right, so I found myself on the receiving end of many of his questions and, I'll say, *colorful* jokes. I learned that he had two granddaughters, three and five years old, and that they were constantly fighting with each other. "Sisters," he said with a shrug.

I assured him that it would get better. "My sister and I used to fight a lot, but that all changed when I got my license and I could drive us to school. We've been best friends ever since," I offered, with all the sage wisdom of a twenty-six-year-old.

"What was it like driving to school from the ghetto?" he asked.

I was taken aback. I hadn't given him any indication that I drove to school either in or from the ghetto. I decided that the best course of action was to cut the topic off at the knees. "I didn't go to school in the ghetto," I responded. He asked me where I went to school. I couldn't tell whether my colleagues—who were listening in—were feeling the same discomfort I was, but no one else said anything. I told him I went to an all-girls school in Connecticut, which was a truthful, if generic, answer that I usually gave to strangers. He began to badger me about where and which school, and I finally broke down and told him that it was in Greenwich, which, of course, might as well come with a *cha-ching* sound effect. "So what do your parents do exactly? Do they work, or are they on welfare?"

At this point, I'd had enough. I got up from my chair and went to the opposite end of the table to tell my other Black girlfriend what was going on. Some polite shuffling was done to rearrange the seating, and the dinner continued, but the man's loud, boisterous posturing grated on me, even several seats removed. I have an almost perfect recollection of this evening because, unlike many other dinners I'd had in Nantucket, I was stone-cold sober. He was not. He proceeded to get drunker and drunker, and not a single person told him to ease up on the cocktails—or the racism. I think the term *ally* gained popularity in mid to late 2020, but in 2014, the idea that bystanders had a direct responsibility to come to the defense of someone in a hostile but nonviolent scenario involving racism was still somewhat of a novelty. I had no allies. I felt so angry and alone because no one told that man to shut the fuck up. He was the one picking up the dinner tab, so he had some power over the group, but if it meant I could have avoided this experience, I would have gladly shouldered the bill myself.

The night wasn't over. As we filed out of the restaurant and everyone got into their respective rides, he bulldozed his way into the Cadillac I was driving and sat himself in the front seat. He turned to me, grinning, and said, "Oh look, Chocolate Thunder is driving," which was, I guess, a nickname and private joke about me that he had with himself. I turned off the car and got out, saying, "Good luck getting to the Chicken Box, because I am not going." The ensuing drama put a halt to the entire night. A distraught Sandra tried to apologize to me on behalf of her husband, and a couple of miraculous fixers spirited the wasted Stuart away so everyone else could go to the bar.

If you've gotten this far in this book, you can probably guess I am especially sensitive to peer pressure, so I ended up driving everyone to the bar and staying until they were all ready to go home. Stuart was officially uninvited, but the evening was tinged with the stench of what happened and no one really knowing how to handle it or what to do. I got "supportive" hugs, and by that point, everyone was lubricated enough to slur "That was so crazy" at me. But no one really *did* anything about it. To eat, drink, and be merry in the fashion industry comes with a hefty price tag, and whether that means enduring sexual harassment or outright racism, there was an understanding that it just came with the territory.

When I got back to New York, I sent the PR firm that organized the trip an email about it, and later, when Miraclesuit reached out to me for a feature in *Elle*, I followed up with a similar recounting of the night, not so politely telling them that the feature would never happen as long as it was up to me.

I began to loosen the reins on the ideology that your work friends are family. It started to feel like cheapening the concept of family by including coworkers. My family, lucky for me, is stable, supportive, and loving. And using that kind of family terminology at work is emotional manipulation, simply a tactic of capitalism to get employees to feel guilty about having personal boundaries and taking days off. After that weekend, I felt hung out to dry by my colleagues, just as I had in the Timberland scandal. No one helped. No one came to my defense. And, if given the chance, they probably would have gone out with Stu and his wife again, if Miraclesuit was buying. Excusing the bad behavior of white men was already a practice I was all too familiar with, but working in magazines, that grace extended to anyone white, rich, and beautiful. Often my job depended on how many of those interactions I could stand.

When I started my tenure at *Elle*, it was the beginning of what some have dubbed the "White Girl Winning Era," when Sheryl Sandberg's *Lean In* was a national bestseller, and Taylor Swift was throwing infamously exclusive parties for other white girls with ridiculously low BMIs at her Rhode Island compound. It was a time when the phrase "Girl Boss" was used sincerely and not as ironic satire. Lena Dunham was rising in popularity, providing an "alternative" feminine presence for television. She had many problematic moments when it came to race, to say the least, but guess what? She rode that wave of success right from her HBO show to becoming a *Vogue* contributor, so now any person of color who has been harmed by her words gets to read them in print each month, cosigned by one of the most powerful brands in publishing.

At *Elle*, I was often required to interview and celebrate celebrities who had questionably racist pasts. Generally, these relationships worked because the magazine and the celebrity mutually needed one another. For example, our readership was obsessed with all things Blake Lively. In 2012, the actress married actor Ryan Reynolds on a plantation in Charleston, South Carolina. The property, called Boone Hall Plantation, boasts in their Instagram bio that they are "recognized as the #1 plantation in the Charleston area by *USA Today* 10 Best," which is a hilarious characterization to me, but it gets even better when they follow that up with "come see why."

Undoubtedly one of the reasons is Lively and Reynolds's nuptials, which, besides being featured briefly in *The Notebook*, is the property's only contemporary claim to fame. It took until the summer of 2020 for either star to publicly comment on their choice of wedding venue, but it rubbed me wrong for years before that. The careful and convenient manipulation of history for your own enjoyment is a privilege that few have. I know I couldn't be comfortable attending a wedding on a plantation, much less getting married on one, but lucky for Lively and Reynolds, they had zero qualms about stepping on the ghosts of dead slaves for some pretty pictures. Internet search results still yield praise for the gorgeousness of their wedding, with magazines and sites like *Martha Stewart Weddings*, *Elle*, *InStyle*, and E! Online extolling the glamour and beauty of the event.

Two years after their marriage, at the behest of pleasing the *Elle* audience, I used Blake Lively as an anchor for a feature where I changed my clothes ten times in one afternoon. I commended her stylistic choices in what became one of the top stories of my tenure at the magazine. It forced me to put my personal reservations aside in the name of traffic, an endeavor anyone who is a victim, I mean, *employee*, of internet journalism will recognize. The fact that Blake Lively might be a racist or, at the very least, doesn't care about Black people (trademark Kanye West, 2005) was of no real consequence. Our Elle.com audience loved her, so I had to love her, or I at least had to act like I did. And I did, over and over again with many celebrities over the years until it broke me down.

Almost every famous model we covered, from Bella Hadid to Hailey Bieber (née Baldwin), has an N-word scandal, or a colorful past with racism at best. And it's not just because Hailey married the white guy who remixed his own song "One Less Lonely Girl" as "One Less Lonely Nigga" in 2014. In 2018, the same year Bella Hadid was seen dropping the N-word at Coachella, a crop of problematic texts, direct messages, and public Instagram comments from Hailey Baldwin made waves on Twitter. Hailey made claims that she was a "different race" after a trip to Florida, casually using the N-word in digital exchanges. But the incident made barely a ripple in the fashion industry. The legacy family darling was still a model on the rise, and the next year, she was on the cover of *Vogue Australia*, reflecting on the "difficulties" she faced being five-seven in modeling. The feature was reported by Derek Blasberg, a white industry veteran who failed to examine any of Baldwin's past racially charged indiscretions in favor of the narrative that she was an underdog in the modeling world because she was short. Later that year, both Hailey and Justin appeared on the cover of American *Vogue*, celebrating their wedded bliss. A year later, *Vogue* released a statement about its commitment to fighting racism.

In 2017, Shia LaBeouf was recorded on video spewing the N-word, telling a Black police officer that he would go to hell because of his skin color. The actor apologized and, of course, took the required route to rehab, citing alcoholism and depression as the cause of his racism—not just regular racism mixed with alcoholism and depression. I worked with many women who joked about how "weird hot" LaBeouf was, admiring his unique outfits and applauding him as a real fashion innovator and purveyor of cool—if not good—taste. In June 2014, right before Stu asked me whether my parents were on welfare, my coworker at *Elle* published an op-ed with the headline "Why Do I Feel Bad for Shia LaBeouf?" To be fair, he had yet to commit his most heinous crimes, but this security blanket over LaBeouf was unsettling to me. In the article, my friend recalls an interaction she had with LaBeouf's former *Even Stevens* costar Christy Carlson Romano, in which Romano expressed displeasure at the memory of LaBeouf: "I can't recall the exact words, but the sentiment was that *he was the most. annoying. Person* she had *ever* met. Her face twisted up with disgust as she spat out the words. I should have been crushed, but I wasn't. I refused to believe it. I just assumed she was jealous." Of course, now we have more context to bring some clarity to the reaction, but I look at this as creepy foreshadowing. In February 2021, LaBeouf's Black ex-girlfriend, FKA Twigs, appeared on the cover of *Elle*, recounting the layers of abuse she suffered at his hands.

If you search LaBeouf's name on the *Elle* site, several articles will come up, almost all of them finding creative ways to excuse his behavior until it finally became impossible to call him anything but a monster. LaBeouf is an extreme example, but that same oversight and refusal to hold anyone accountable also happens on a much smaller scale all the time. Media and society are extremely quick to overlook offenses people make because we like them. And hey, as long as you wear the right clothes, fashion wants you. That's exactly the thing that's most celebrated about LaBeouf: his "unique look." The same cannot be said for anyone Black. I often have flashbacks to the ways I was disciplined as a child, the way I was nearly kicked out of high school for making one terrible comment, and I can't help observing with wonder the tornadoes of harm and destruction these rich white people can leave in their wake and still come out on top.

The industry collectively decides what is and is not a forgivable offense. Famously, disgraced designer John Galliano destroyed his own brand and legacy by going on an anti-Semitic rant caught on tape in Paris, in 2011. He was subsequently fired by both Dior and his own label, his fashions "canceled" and discarded. But girls like the Hadid sisters, and Hailey Bieber remain gainfully employed as some of the highest-paid models, repeatedly photographed by the paparazzi despite their multiple offenses. The industry consistently fails to hold them accountable for their actions. In fact, most of their press is largely positive, and it's hard to find anything that is not. An irrevocable damage is done to the psyches of people of color who have to write those positive headlines and altogether ignore what these celebrities have done in the past. Everyone makes mistakes, myself included, but the stakes and the consequences for mere mortals are not the same as for these anointed deities, who will continue establishing dynasties based on toxic power structures. To keep up with that level of pernicious dominance, a part of yourself has to be shoved aside so you can do your job and do it well. The audience wants what it wants, and what it wants is to not have their faves barbecued for mistakes they made in their teens and early twenties—or even, in some cases, beyond.

People often wonder why Black media professionals don't call out the racism they witness in their workplaces. It's because doing so would place a dangerous target on their backs, when even the smallest infractions can have dire material consequences. That person's job and ability to find new employment might be on the line, and once employees have been branded "difficult," they are shut out completely. In 2021, Janet Hubert, the original Aunt Viv on *The Fresh Prince of Bel-Air*, described how her professional reputation was derailed by the rumor that she was "difficult to work with." It is a marked fate for women of color who inhabit the juncture of two identities that come with distinct bias in the workplace and beyond. These women become "problem starters," and the result isn't just a week's worth of mean Instagram comments. For people of color, it can mean a disruption of their lifestyle that's so drastic, recovery is sometimes impossible. It is even more hurtful to walk that tightrope knowing your white colleagues are equipped with a parachute while you fall to your metaphorical death.

The fashion industry is not ready to have conversations about toxicity, misogyny, homophobia, or racism in the way they need to be had. Victims of harassment and sexual assault have their motives questioned if they bring their experiences to a legal platform. When Black people bring up racism in this context, they are told they are being "paranoid," or they need to "lighten up," or worse still, that "not everything is about race." So instead, we just absorb all that negativity. We swallow it and smile at lavishly decorated dinner tables with people who have racist conversations privately while publicly standing for equality.

CHAPTER
TWENTY-TWO

Lest you think that, as I matured, I abandoned my obsession with being thin, I did not. In fact, I learned to strategize and use my job to further that mission. In 2014, I decided I wanted to lose some weight, and like any good editor, I made my pursuit into a "story." When you pursue something as a story rather than as a personal agenda, it all but ensures that the endeavor will be free. My brilliant idea was to attempt to turn myself into a Victoria's Secret Angel, a quest I was already primed for by my youthful obsession with the VS Angels. My real intention, however, was to get skinnier. The Angels were a high source of web traffic for us when I worked at *Elle*, and people—me included—were particularly obsessed with their bodies. I attended the Victoria's Secret Fashion Show for work every year, an upgrade from being a regular television spectator. We did little backstage interviews with the models, but there was so much mystery in the way the machine functioned. I wanted to know more. So I pitched the idea to my boss and then to Victoria's Secret, and I was off to the races.

The first step in the journey was securing contact with celebrated nutritionist Dr. Charles Passler, who had famously helped Adriana Lima lose fifty pounds after she gave birth to her second daughter in order to make a triumphant return to the runway months later. Another coworker of mine had pursued Dr. Passler's services for "a story" but ultimately didn't get much out of it. I knew I could be more disciplined and, therefore, more successful, so I emailed his office and made a consultation appointment.

The first meeting with Dr. Passler served as a preliminary weigh-in. I discussed my relationship with food, he gave me some at-home urine tests to do, told me about the importance of external factors like sleep and stress on body weight, and after one hour, I went home. Three days later, I returned for phase two, where I brought the urine tests to him and he provided me with my first eating plan, which served as a "cleanse." I was not honest with Dr. Passler, as I had learned by that point that being honest about the way I ate to medical professionals set off way too many alarm bells. I was comfortable fudging my way through appearing to be a normal eater, and I told him just enough to let him know I wanted to lose weight, but not anything about my obsession with it.

Dr. Passler informed me that my body fat percentage was very high, and that if it got any higher, it could border on obesity. It was around 32 percent at the time, and the VS models averaged between 10 percent and 18 percent. LOL! This scared the shit out of me. He also told me my toxicology report was off the charts, indicating that I was putting toxins in my body faster than they could be released. He suggested that I stop drinking alcohol immediately. This scared me too because, aside from my occasional moments of diet-induced abstinence, drinking aided my bulimia by giving me an easy cover; plus, alcohol was a useful social lubricant. As someone who was more or less required to be out and about for work, I felt I needed it. Since he was the expert, though, and responsible for the snatched figure of a legendary supermodel, I felt it was in my best interest to do everything he said.

I quit booze, and I went on a ten-day no-sugar, no-dairy, no-meat cleanse. At first, I didn't lose any weight. I was angry and frustrated. I had a sad protein shake for Thanksgiving dinner, but I loved the fact I could drop "This is from my nutritionist" or "I'm working on a story" to prying family members who wondered why I wasn't partaking in the meal. Then, out of nowhere, I started to lose weight. Once I started seeing results, I trusted him implicitly. Dr. Passler "helped" me lose about twenty-seven pounds when I was at my thinnest. I continued to see him over the next five years, and the programs I did under his guidance grew increasingly more intense.

Dr. P said I was his star patient. He encouraged me to lose more and more weight, telling me I could slim down to the actual measurements of a model if I would just try. He gave a necessary authoritative voice to all the things I'd already been telling myself, but now it was doctor's orders. I loved the results I saw, and I would scream his praises to anyone who would listen. I talked about him obsessively. If it were the 1970s, I would have run away and joined his cult. I loved this man. We texted all the time. I told him about how lazy my friends were, that they would do things like eat cake on their birthdays (weak!) or have a beer when they were stressed (double weak!). I would hide with shame if I ever deviated from his plan, and I faithfully returned to his office every two weeks to be weighed and given my new instructions on my diet.

When I was within five pounds of my goal weight, which became a magic number that kept reducing as I would get closer to attaining a goal, he told me I still needed to work harder. He encouraged me to fast, eating only bone broth for days. He was impressed with how easily I could do this, not knowing that I had essentially been training for it my entire life. I sent many patients his way, either people who followed me on social media or personal friends. I even encouraged my own size-zero sister to see him at one point. And then, because I was obsessed and sick, I would go behind his back and try to do other programs on top of his regimen to speed up my weight loss. But as long as the numbers on the scale were down, he never questioned how. He just assumed that the plan was working and that I was behaving as instructed. He was the most important relationship in my life. I absolutely worshipped him.

As I got thinner, I got more attention in both my professional and personal life. I had a boyfriend, who I was sure I was going to marry, which served as confirming evidence that I needed to be skinny to be desired. I made more money than ever, which I linked to my super-human discipline and drive. On the surface, I was killing it. But the strenuous effort required to keep myself moving at that pace and make it look fun, easy, and attainable was untenable. I was in a bad place, and I didn't know how to get out. It had all spun so far out of control. I felt that I needed to keep this private infatuation with my diet because it served as fuel, as motivation for greatness in everything else. It kept me humble and striving, so I soothed and tended to it, and then I spread it far and wide outside myself.

I talked about food and nutrition and diets incessantly. I chronicled my nonmeals on Instagram. I wrote about diets online. I carefully monitored what other people ate and how much they drank. I never chastised them about it outright, but I might have subtly commented, and I silently added the information to the log in my mind, categorizing others as either committed or lazy. Friends often came to me when they wanted to lose weight. Slimming down for a wedding? I was your girl. Need to drop postbaby weight? Holla at me. Intentionally trying to make an ex jealous with an awesome bikini shot on vacation? I had you. Just as I had cultivated my authority on clothing, I became an accidental expert on weight loss. I, obviously, didn't always have healthy advice. I feel guilty for spreading that negativity, for my constant projection onto other women, and for the continuation of a cycle that nearly destroyed me. It got to the point where I would fantasize about being pregnant because I imagined that growing a fetus was the only way to be free from thinking about the flatness of my stomach.

I weighed myself at the start of each day, like a freaky prayer ritual, and was overjoyed when my jeans felt too big. That morning routine would determine whether I would have a good or a bad day. I never stopped thinking or talking about my size, and the crazy part was, despite being smaller than ever, I still wasn't fitting into samples like I'd envisioned I would. A big part of the reason I wanted a different body was so I could wear clothes better. My body was still totally wrong for my needs.

At every turn, I felt I was being rejected by the very structure I so desperately craved acceptance from. I did everything right, and it didn't matter that I couldn't squeeze my colossal ass into anything that didn't have stretch. It left me bitter and furious, so I went even harder with my methods. I would exercise at SoulCycle after eating nothing for two days, frantically trying to burn more calories so I could end the day calorie-deficient. I took the free gum on the way out of the studio, and on my walk home, I enjoyed the minty flavor and told myself it was dinner. I was so ashamed of the way my issues with food had swelled into this beast that I exerted further control over my diet by packing my schedule manically. I would attend two or more events a night, and since there was hardly food at any of them, by the time I got home, I would declare it too late to eat. If I needed to put on a performance and eat in front of my friends, I would carefully space out the dinners I attended and make a big show of being "hungry" for added effect. When I went on dates, I would feel increasingly paranoid about eating in front of strangers. Only when I was much more comfortable with someone would I eat the tiny fistful of food that I needed for adequate sustenance in their presence. I would let only men who could stand watching me do this stay in my life. That's the real reason I've been single for so long.

A guy I really liked looked me squarely in the eyes at breakfast one morning and said, "You know you have to eat, right?" He said it so sincerely that the memory still gives me chills. I furiously told him not to "food police" me. Others tried to gently feed me, and I would resist.

In my longest relationship, my ex said something once about how I didn't eat much at dinner and then, every other time we ate together, just proceeded to silently finish my food. That arrangement worked very well for me. I kept emotional distance from people so I could continue being bulimic. In 2017, I threw up on a guy when I was giving him a blow job after a meal. My gag reflex betrayed me because it was after lunch, and I habitually threw up once my belly was full.

I was incredibly ill, and yet, all the compliments I was getting pushed me to pursue more extreme measures. I was also convinced, in a material way, that being skinny was a key to professional success. My fashion cohorts would write, "Skinny legend!!!" "Skinny," "Snatched," and "Yes, waist" in my Instagram comments. They would grab me into hugs and tell me how skinny I was looking and congratulate me on a job well done. *Skinny* was the ultimate compliment from fashion people. It is the thing we are supposed to be, and if we aren't naturally thin and we work hard for it, we should be duly rewarded. No one will say it outright, but of course, being thin is the look.

In 2005, the summer before I graduated high school, the late designer Karl Lagerfeld published a book called *The Karl Lagerfeld Diet*, revealing how he'd lost more than ninety pounds. The book exposed Lagerfeld's own deep self-hatred and aversion to gaining weight. He detailed his low-fat, no-carb, twelve-hundred-calorie-a-day diet, which he dubbed "punishment." Up until his death in 2019, Lagerfeld served as the creative director for both Fendi and Chanel, two of the most prominent brands in fashion, where he had worked since 1967 and 1982, respectively. He had those jobs for longer than I had been alive. Later in 2009, he expressed anger at a German magazine that had vowed to shoot only real women, saying, "You've got fat mothers with their bags of chips sitting in front of the television and saying that thin models are ugly. The world of beautiful clothing is about 'dreams and illusions.'"

That kind of thinking and reverence for thinness is in the past. Because the concept of fatphobia has entered the lexicon, we are all magically cured of the idea that skinny is the only way to be. In August 2020, former child star turned lifestyle legend Drew Barrymore appeared on the cover of *InStyle*'s "The Badass Women Issue." In the feature interview, Barrymore reveals how she was living at home and coping with the pandemic. The entire feature is incredibly complimentary, presenting Drew Barrymore as a new-age messiah the way celebrity profiles often do, and then she slips in, when asked about how she takes care of herself, "I eat really clean and healthy, and I do an hour of Pilates at least four days a week. I have to work so hard at not being the size of a bus. And it's OK. That is just my journey. That is my karma. I don't know, maybe I was thin and mean in a past life." This is not to shit on Drew's journey. I have no idea what she has gone through. But the fact that the quote made it to print and still lingers on the InStyle. com website is exactly the way fatphobia still drifts on in this industry. The statement flew by unchecked; several people looked the story over and decided it was worth printing, which further contributes to the idea that fatphobia is not all that bad, really. After all, if "Badass" Drew is working hard at not being the size of a bus, then isn't that OK for us all? It is no longer as explicit as the way Kate Moss or Karl Lagerfeld have talked about their contempt for bigger bodies, but it is still present, faintly, disguised as "self-care" and repeated by the same people who genuinely say that loving who you are is the best accessory.

This is not honest. If you think because you have seen Mindy Kaling on a magazine cover or two that fashion people are all of a sudden devoted to the acceptance of women bigger than a size two, I hate to crush that dream for you, but they are not. That is not what's being said behind closed doors. I know because I have been in those rooms.

I have no problem saying that I still struggle with fatphobia. I have to check my behaviors and thought patterns all the time. Thanks to social media and my career in learning to package ideas in an ideal way for public consumption, I covered up my fatphobia by pantomiming health and wellness, in the same way I learned to pantomime happiness in being Scary Spice or "a downtown urban girl" when the occasion arose. When you consider what I have seen and what has not only been presented as the ideal body but also rewarded by my chosen industry in more ways than one, it is hardly a surprise that these poisonous and self-destructive beliefs persist in me. It's not something I can be cured of overnight. I can say all the positive affirmations I want to myself, but there will still be people who go out of their way to tell me how women (always women) should look and be extremely invested in their right to do so. Just like it took a long time to build a world where skinny was the most beautiful, it will take a long time to tear that world down. We still have to try our best.

CHAPTER TWENTY-THREE

I left my job at *Elle* when I was offered $25,000 more a year to work at *InStyle*, crossing me over into the six-figures club, which is a milestone I wanted to reach before thirty. I was twenty-seven. I was also in the throes of my first bout of professional burnout. I had just completed a viral story where I allowed my Tinder matches to pick my outfits for a week, when a female executive asked me what I was going to do next. I had overly commodified myself in service of my job, and it was wearing on me. *InStyle* offered me the opportunity to make more money and do less work, something I felt I desperately needed. It is the only move I have ever regretted making in my whole career. I went from Elle.com, an imperfect professional environment that did have bright spots of teamwork, mentorship, and inclusion, to *InStyle* magazine, which was easily the most racist working environment I have ever experienced. In the fashion department, there were only two other people of color: a white-passing Latina assistant and a fellow senior editor, who was of Indian descent. Our fashion director was an intimidating Italian woman who has since gone on to found a company that I can't figure out the purpose of, but based on its Instagram page, it appears to exist only to celebrate the beauty of white women. That's fitting because it's exactly what *InStyle* employees did under her guidance. In conjunction with another editor, it was my job to oversee the pages where we found trends based on street-style images (candid photos taken of stylish people on the street, usually before or after fashion events) and told readers how to re-create the looks with more affordable options. I loved those pages. They were a fun way to explore putting together outfits, and I always felt inspired observing the ways people choose to present themselves.

I'd matured at Elle.com and felt that it was important to experiment with being more vocal about inclusion—and by vocal, I mean I wouldn't say anything at all but would select images of Black women exclusively for my street-style inspiration pages in an attempt to make sure they were included. Month after month for a year, I was always asked to "find new inspiration," to "get better images," to "rethink the pictures." These notes were just a coded way of saying that Black women were not desired for the page, and the images were repeatedly rejected. I knew in my heart what was driving that rejection, but I refused to back down, and at the risk of looking bad at my job, I kept submitting these images and they kept getting tossed out. It was hugely frustrating, and it unearthed old feelings of rejection and longing for acknowledgment. I wasn't succeeding at my quiet mission, but it was not for lack of trying. This is, more or less, how Black women are erased from the pages of the magazines you read.

I had a somewhat childish notion that my presence as an editor there would give me the chance to change what I assumed had just been an oversight on the part of an overwhelmingly white staff to recognize Black women. It was no oversight. The fashion director didn't see any need to salute stylish women of color. If you look at the marketing for her new company, which she has complete creative control over, you can see exactly the kind of woman she seeks to celebrate: white and white only.

That is the racism that exists in fashion. Of course, if asked, my old boss will say she is not a *racist*. What she wants to be understood is that it is just who she wants to hire, cast, and acknowledge. It's *incidental*. It shouldn't be personal. It's about what is right for the brand, who *has the right look*—that's all. That's the script, and if you hear that over and over enough times, it seems believable. So if you got the right clothes and the right relationships and the right everything, you'd be in, right? Not quite. If you have the conviction that through hard work and dedication comes salvation, you imagine that all your weekend hours, neglected relationships, and silence in the face of disturbing amounts of prejudice would mean something. But none of it does. You're still not seen as valuable. You're here, but you're not here. If you actually get far enough to become a real decision maker, I can't even imagine the kind of trauma it took to crawl your way to that place. Eventually, I decided I didn't want it enough to even try anymore. Approaching the 2016 election, I just couldn't believe that my role in the world was telling women that the best thing to be was a carbon copy of Kate Hudson. I mean, no offense, she seems great, but there had to be something else, right? I weighed my options and knew that I didn't have that kind of fight in me.

The reality is when you work in an industry that is responsible for imagery that can potentially affect millions of people, you are constantly at moral odds with what you know is right and the requirements of your job. Since the industry favors white supremacy, it requires you to do the same. It happened to me when I first had to study the beauty goddesses for my internship at *NYLON*, and it had been happening steadily ever since.

In 2015, Valentino released a Spring/Summer 2016 collection that the house claimed was inspired by "primitive, wild Africa." Africa, not a country specifically, just the whole entire continent, the actual origin point of humanity, was just primitive and wild and a basis for fashion inspiration. OK. To add insult to injury, the runway consisted of fewer than ten nonwhite models. There were ninety-one looks.

The designers at the time, an Italian duo (Pierpaolo Piccioli, still designing at Valentino, and Maria Grazia Chiuri, who now oversees an aggressive brand of fake feminism at Christian Dior), defended their choice of words and their decision to move forward with this collection, telling Vogue Runway that it was a commentary on the recent uptick in immigrations and refugees from African countries seeking shelter in Italy. "The message is tolerance," they claimed, "and the beauty that comes out of cross-cultural expression." Except it was not tolerance; it was colonialism steeped in the history of Europeans taking anything they want from Africa and denying agency to African people while doing it. The *Vogue* writer who reviewed the collection, Sarah Mower (you guessed it, a white woman), glorifies the choices of the designers to "blend cultures": "Both designers pointed out that their respectful borrowings are hardly new; they are part of a history of Western assimilation that goes back to Picasso and Braque's embrace of African art in the 1920s, which, Chiuri said, 'was the birth of modernism in art.' It came over as most modern in this show."

Let's unpack this a bit. Valentino commits the fashion equivalent of looting in 2015, and *Vogue* calls it "modern." Oh, it's modern all right. It's an effective reproduction of what has been happening on a global scale for centuries, but now, it's to be fed back to consumers for thousands of dollars. And let's not gloss over the fact that she suggests that Picasso and Braque were in any way collaborative with communities they degraded and stole from for commercial gain and artistic respect.

You can try, but you will find little to no criticism of this collection. Go ahead, google it. You will likely find critical hot takes only on news sites like *HuffPost* or *Jezebel*, which are on the fringes of the industry. Valentino is one of the largest advertisers in print media, and that money helps fund shoots, parties, and the daily functions of a magazine. In other words, never bite the hand that feeds you. What's more,

Valentino is a cool kid on the block. Like I said, they have lots of money. They throw fun parties. I've been to them. They make nice things. You want them on your side. So everyone plays along and says how beautiful the collection is. Even independent fashion news site Fashionista.com has a kiss-ass headline: "Valentino Crafts a Beautiful Tribute to Tribal Africa on Its Spring 2016 Runway." Oh, is that what that was?

If you let it, the general apathy in the industry toward both historical and present wrongs will deaden your senses. It is crushing to witness, and even worse when these wrongs are praised instead of criticized. I worked at *InStyle* when the Valentino collection was released, and the staff received an email from our editor-in-chief at the time saying that Valentino was to receive no covers that season, a decision that I still respect him for. The other credits were at the discretion of the editorial staff, and our Italian fashion director—well, as you may have guessed—still wanted Valentino featured. So feature we did. This was a slap in the face to anyone who disagreed with what Valentino did on that runway. It was another way of letting everyone know how little the feelings of Black people mattered. And in six months, there would be a new collection, that convenient forgetfulness making it possible to breeze right past it.

Valentino made no comments on the backlash, and in a stunning show of defiance, they shot their spring campaign in Africa, featuring Maasai people as the backdrop. But, even without acknowledgment, they have learned. In recent years, their runways have been flooded with Black models. Naomi Campbell impressively led a crew of mostly Black models in the couture lineup of 2019. Still, that Valentino was allowed to press on from this scandal as if driving over a speed bump exemplifies fashion's tendency to forget anything unsavory and its dedication to embrace any- and everything new. It worked so well that designer Pierpaolo Piccioli declared himself something of a civil rights activist, stating to Business of Fashion in 2019, "I think if a message is aesthetic, it's stronger. The picture of those black girls wearing those dream gowns didn't need words. Streetwear is something different, but when people see black girls in couture, the highest point of fashion, the job is done. Images are more powerful than words. Change the face and you change the perception of people more than any slogan."

The job is done.

I did a Valentino campaign for social media at the end of 2020, then took the money they paid me and redistributed the entirety of the earnings to other Black women I thought were more deserving. I agreed to be their Token Black Girl for a fee that I wanted other women to have more than myself, women who might not have been asked had I turned the job down. It was my way of acknowledging that this industry is difficult to change, but in the little ways that we can, we must assert some power. I have been the Token Black Girl all my life, and I know when I am being used and to what extent, but at this point, I am going to make it work for me too.

The day I decided I'd had enough of working at *InStyle*, we had a staff-wide run-through for the front-of-book pages, which are the pages that contain the most variety in terms of price point and trends and are geared toward motivating the audience to shop. In the run-through, a white stylist and editor had photos of two models down on the floor, next to the clothes that would be used for the shoot. We were deciding which models we would feature in the pages. One was a white woman, a brunette, with greenish-brown eyes and very fair skin. She was what the industry would call an "every girl," pretty but not threatening, friendly looking, and just a tick above ordinary. The other model was a light-skinned if not mixed-race Black woman. She had a visible Afro and was more, in the words we would use in fashion, "edgy" or "directional." The truth is she could be an every girl too. In many communities, she is an every girl, but in the fashion world, where we don't actually want to honor the beauty of women of color, she is forced into the "edgy" box. The fashion director held both photos up in front of the entire staff of, as I said before, mostly white women, and dropped the Black model's photo back down to the floor, loudly declaring, "Well, we have Lupita on the cover this month so we don't need her." Heads bobbed in agreement. Never once had we said, "We have Jennifer Aniston on the cover, so we don't need another blonde woman on subsequent pages." Of course, just one Token Black Girl is enough to cover representation for months to come. Singular, all quotas met. We extolled the physical features of white women and ignored Black women entirely. It was an exhausting mission to try to make my coworkers see differently. After a year at *InStyle*, I left. I got offered a job at another internet-based start-up, and I took it.

My new job was content director of a Gen Z–targeted publishing property. The idea was to use social media as a means of distribution, meaning there was no website and no CMS, just handles. It seemed like a great gig on the cusp of innovation and something that would be fun to build. Fatefully, however, I had forgotten the lesson I learned in high school about needing to mediate my anger and personality so as not to appear menacing to white people. I got far too comfortable there, if you can believe it. I had experienced moderate success, so I started to think I could loosen up a bit. One month after I was hired to work at Clique Media, I was fired. My offense? A few, actually. The first was that they thought the content I posted on my personal Snapchat was inappropriate. My own channel, which had fewer than two thousand people watching it at any time, had rubbed them the wrong way. Too mean and too Black.

There is no way to overemphasize that Clique Media, a company founded by two white women, was interested in only white women (at the time). If there were a female version of *Get Out*, it would have been this. The first time I visited their offices in LA, every woman there was blonde, size two to four, and wore a variation of blue, nonstretch vintage denim with a white T-shirt, their hair neatly cropped to shoulder length or higher with a slight beach wave. It was spooky. The only other

Black woman I saw was at the front desk at reception—except I later learned her job wasn't reception at all; her job was actually HR.

The red flags at Clique Media were apparent from my first day. Without my knowledge or input, they had staffed a team for me, despite hiring me to be a director. They hired two nice, very junior girls, one blonde and one biracial. Then they asked me to fly to LA from NYC for a launch event right before a planned trip I had to Thailand. I had told them about my trip many times during the interview process. It takes a full day to get to Thailand, and I wanted to manage their expectations for travel while still trying to be a team player. I asked to upgrade my seat from economy to business on my flight to LA if they wanted me to be there for less than forty-eight hours so I could get some rest on the plane, and since I received no response, I just upgraded myself. When I got to the office and met them in person, I asked if it could be reimbursed.

Tensions increased when the executive leadership started having problems with the content I was posting on their channels. The issue with content that lives only on social media is everyone is constantly on social media, so the critiques were coming fast and furious. I got in trouble for posting a GIF of gossip legend Wendy Williams. "Wendy Williams is a mean girl," they told me, which arguably . . . sure. But it wasn't as if it were a clip of her dogging someone out on television. Digital meme-ing works by isolating a humorous moment and making it applicable to multiple things. I posted a photo of my chic friend with her two much older brothers for National Siblings Day and was immediately told to take it down because it was "off-brand." I suppose seeing two Black men on the feed was not something they wanted. It seemed like any time I posted about anything Black, it was an issue. Finally, they policed my personal social media to a point where I began to feel paranoid. When you are someone who shares a lot of their life online as a professional obligation, you can sense when people are treating you differently based on something you have shared. Sometimes questions like "How was your weekend?" get replaced with statements like "I saw you went . . ." and you know your time, both on and off the clock, is being heavily monitored.

The company fired me over the phone as I stood outside in Union Square, and by the time I got back up to the office, I was locked out of my emails and otherwise dismissed. They said they did not like some commentary I had made about celebrity children and a joke about Zika—a joke I made on my personal social media account. They would not give me another chance or let me demonstrate that I could improve based on their feedback. I was also informed that they found my request that my flight to Los Angeles be upgraded "totally inappropriate." They actually said the request changed people in the company's opinions of me. Just to make it clear, I paid for the upgrade myself. What I think is inappropriate is having quippy sayings published all over an office and website about "female empowerment" and giving copious advice about "asking for what you want," only to shut down a Black woman when she does exactly that. Shonda Rhimes left an almost two-decade contract at ABC over the fact that they wouldn't issue her an extra Disney pass; the straw that broke the camel's back was an exec asking, "Don't you think you have enough?" When I found that out, I had to laugh. Black women on scales large and small are being faced with this riddle every day.

I did what I thought was the classy thing and wrote the two founders an email apologizing, trying to smooth over what I thought was a misunderstanding. I never heard back from either of them. It was 2016, right before the election of Donald Trump, and his flagrant support of white supremacy pushed race relations to the forefront of every industry. In June 2020, Clique Media and one of the white female founders in particular faced criticism over fostering a racist and hostile workplace, none of which surprised me. As far as I know, neither of the founders has ever made a statement about their role in the racist environment at their company, but the way I was treated, monitored, and painted as a delinquent tells me all those accusations were true. When they do apologize and inevitably ask for the chance to do better, I'm interested to see whether they get it, the same chance I was denied.

Because of white supremacy, we find a way to accept and excuse racist behavior at every single opportunity. The most frequent excuses include "I was young," "I was ignorant," and "I was drunk." And if you, a person of color, do not "get over it" or "let it go," then you're petty. We are not allowed to demand justice for racist offenses because that justice does not exist. On the other hand, let a Black person get too heated, say something out of spite, or make a single mistake, and their life could be over. This is not an exaggeration. "Just get *over* slavery, already!" white people will comment on social media. But it's not about getting over anything when, in real time, people are both benefiting and suffering consequences because of racism, and many of us refuse to acknowledge the inherent injustices at play while proclaiming that everyone is "equal."

Even after brazen and audacious criminal activity—an armed invasion of our Capitol aimed at overthrowing the government like the one that took place on January 6, 2021, for example—white people expect to be absolved and forgiven for their crimes. In March 2021, a white radio host in Oklahoma was caught on tape calling a high school female basketball team "fucking niggers" because they knelt during the National Anthem, and he was not fired; instead, he released a press statement to affirm that he was "not racist" but just "had low blood sugar." And people accept these excuses. It is only Black people from whom we demand absolute and unveiled perfection. And that pressure produces an incredible amount of anxiety. The "work twice as hard to get half as far" mantra is only a part of it. The other part is an undying pledge to never mess up because the consequences will be worse for you no matter what. This, in itself, is violence.

When I lost my job at Clique, it was the first time I had significantly failed at anything. And I *felt* like a failure. I turned the volume way up on my self-loathing. Whenever I feel unworthy, I deny myself food. It is a way of literally making myself small and weak, and yet, at the same time, I felt that hunger gave me mental clarity.

The idea that being "palatable" as a Black person, that having a vocabulary and clothing and shoes, and so on, works to make you more acceptable to white people was finally exposed to me as a fallacy. So I decided to say "Fuck it" and just finally be myself. Four months later, I got hired at BET.

CHAPTER
TWENTY-FOUR

When I first started working at BET, I was elated. I had no emotional attachment to the brand because I had limited exposure to it growing up. I thought it would be a healthy departure, having scored so many "dream jobs" that later became nightmares at publications I was dedicated to out of sheer emotional attachment. I was not under the impression that working at BET would be any more than a job, a philosophy I now encourage. I am no longer defined by whatever brand I work for. It's freeing.

At BET, I was a part of a team of talented creatives who respected each other and wanted to work together. I am still in awe of the women I met while working at BET, their limitless potential and skill. At the time, the CEO was a woman, Debra Lee, and it felt, at first, like a hopeful new start. Black Girl Magic had started trending across social media, and I was all for its tangible presence in my life too. I worked for and with people who were supportive, who advocated for me, and who helped me make my ideas a reality. It did not stay that way, but initially, it was great.

When I got my job at BET, some people questioned whether I deserved it based on the Timberland snafu. I was nervous, conscious of the childhood trauma that told me I was "not Black." When listicles began to dominate as an internet content genre, I would click on headlines like "25 Things Black Mothers Say" and recite a silent prayer that I would recognize even just one phrase from my mother's mouth. I needed to find myself somewhere in "60 Things Every Black Girl Knows" as a way of forming a tangible foundation for my Black identity, one I'd been convinced had been broken in childhood, and then later by the Twitterverse. This fractured relationship to my Black identity was a major regret of mine that I did not have the maturity or wherewithal to deal with at that point in my life, but I have learned to forgive myself for the mistakes I made as I began to repair that fracture and the things I wasn't brave enough to push to change in the fashion industry.

In every industry, but especially fashion, there is an enormous difference between visibility and power. There is power in visibility, but it's not always a power you can control. Almost every one of my jobs has been very visible, and in a world ruled by clicks and likes, that seems great, but there were many, *many* times where I had no power. This is still true for many people working in positions across media companies, and it is vital to understanding how and why mistakes like Timberlandgate shake out in the public eye. As the Token Black Girl, your face may be on the building outside, but there will be meetings you are not invited to. Your words might be changed without your knowledge, and there will be things you agree to just because you feel you have to. And even when I was working at BET, with many other Black people, this was still my reality. I was a useful tool because of how I looked—in this case, photogenic and practiced at being used as a marketing tool—and that was exploited. It has always been my default to just put up with things until I get enough power to change them. Eventually, I thought, I will be the boss, and I will be the one making those decisions. But it's a difficult balance to maintain over several years. How much pain you can withstand should not be the barometer of how successful you can become. Growing up in predominantly white environments, I was uniquely equipped to handle those expectations because deference to the status quo had always been my reality, but I did not expect that kind of pressure in a Black environment.

It became quickly apparent in my work at BET that white supremacy was ever present, even in an all-Black setting. For starters, we had an office Karen, a white woman who would routinely confuse photos of Black celebrities and even cried, claiming she was being bullied by the other Black women in the office. I am serious. And because we did not work in a vacuum, the industry perception of BET as a brand hindered my access to certain talent and opportunities. I went from having invitations to all the industry events, parties, and celebrity interviews to having, well, way fewer. Because of these constraints, we ended up making a lot of concessions in our content, and still, we were able to produce work that I was extremely proud of. It might surprise you to find out who and what entities said no to being featured on BET. com. There are numerous political factors at play in those decisions, but because I had come from a world of prestige white entertainment and fashion, I was aware of what celebrities were willing to do for less than BET offered. I agreed to cover Rihanna's Fenty Puma launch at Bloomingdale's in 2017 and waited for more than three hours for a "group interview," only to find out that *W Magazine* had been given a one-on-one exclusive. Things like this happened every day. I had seen Black talent work with publications for sheer exposure, then tell BET they were too busy to work with us, which is more or less a euphemism for "not interested." It was a dizzying reality to straddle, one that I knew was anchored in the fact that mainstream books or networks that had greater access to white audiences, big-box advertisers, and the Hollywood powers that be were able to secure the kind of stories we were not. And we killed it anyway. That is the scrappiness of the Black community, finding opportunity where there is denial, opening doors for ourselves and building the best possible product no matter what.

As for my most useful contribution to the team, I was able to be an anthropologist of whiteness, filling the office in on pop culture history when necessary. Upon Brad Pitt and Angelina Jolie's separation in 2016, I became extremely useful in my ability to explain the genre of "white mess," an office favorite. It felt nice to have this part of me both acknowledged and celebrated, as opposed to being something I needed to keep secret for fear of mockery. There were still awkward moments where I outed myself as ignorant of something that everyone else seemed to know or understand. On a set in 2020, prepandemic lockdown, when we were still scrubbing down audio equipment and overusing hand sanitizer, my coworker declared, "It smells like Fabuloso," to which I stupidly responded, "What's Fabuloso?" This question produced a chorus of laughter from every Black and brown person within earshot, and—because we were on a BET set—that was everyone. My neck burned with shame, knowing I had made a faux pas, inadvertently drawing attention to an experience of Blackness I did not share. "It's like a dollar-store cleaner," my friend offered. OK, so it was a cleaning product, no big deal. My mom cleaned with something else, and though everyone laughed at me, I knew I was not going to be socially shunned because I had never smelled this thing. The rest of the crew volunteered their memories of cleaning with or smelling Fabuloso, and instead of the door being closed in my face, I was welcomed over the threshold. Then everyone just went back to work, difference accepted, public humiliation averted.

Despite this element of acceptance, there were issues at BET I was not prepared for. I was under the impression that working there would free me from some of the more harmful beauty standards I had struggled with at white institutions. And while there was not a collective diet culture at the office or the idea that there was only one acceptable hair type, anyone who works on the internet knows that you are beholden, first and always, to engagement and algorithms, where those beauty standards are constant. I felt immensely guilty about this, boosting Kardashian bikini photos and stoking the obsession that people had with the natural hair of women like Michelle Obama and Beyoncé. At the same time, the world I had just exited was publishing stories about "Boxer Braids" (read: cornrows) and continuing a tradition of violent erasure that was really not any more helpful to Black women than the content I was responsible for.

The public fascination with Beyoncé's hair is something that has become borderline parody. In September 2018, Beyoncé appeared on the cover of American *Vogue*, and her longtime hairstylist released a behind-the-scenes video that served as evidence that Beyoncé was indeed appearing without hair extensions. Stirring up fans and haters like only Beyoncé can, a debate about what was and was not her natural hair sparked online. *Way* less interesting than the conspiracy theory that she faked her pregnancy, but the conversation was at a fever pitch.

Honestly, who cares? Not a single celebrity alive has not used hair extensions, and it's become so commonplace that you can get them on Amazon and give yourself an at-home makeover. The obsession, however, with Black women's hair, how it is done, and what it can do is something that is foundational to the white supremacy beauty myth. And the natural-hair debate was always a Chartbeat topper on BET. com.

In Beyoncé's case, she has the added layer of being a representative for the Black beauty standard, which is a sticky position to be in. There is a stereotype that Black hair doesn't grow and that straightening your hair will result in irreparable damage, and while, yes, this may be true for mere mortals, Beyoncé is the daughter of a hairstylist and keeps a glam squad on call the way people with allergies do EpiPens. In some sick repetition of history, Beyoncé's daughter Blue Ivy is now being subjected to the same overbearing scrutiny. Overall, the hair of the Carter women defies stereotypes, and the level of fascination that results verges on disturbing. After that *Vogue* appearance and the subsequent tweets, headlines, and think pieces, I was sure many people thought more about Beyoncé's hair than Beyoncé herself does. While Beyoncé is financially blessed enough to afford the upkeep of her natural hair, the trickle-down effect for the general public is a pressure to adhere to this standard without the use of hair extensions, chemicals, or wigs while having neither the time nor the budget to do so. "Is that your real hair?" or "Why don't you wear your real hair?" are the kinds of triggering inquiries that tie shame to Black hair instead of celebration, and if those are the kinds of things you hear throughout adolescence and even into adulthood, it will not be easy to extract the feelings of degradation from the choices you make about your hair. By keeping these conversations alive, the beast is always fed.

When I was overseeing fashion and beauty at BET in 2016, we reported on a story where model Winnie Harlow, who rose to fame by embracing her skin condition, vitiligo, cyberbullied fellow model, Australian-born Duckie Thot. Thot had appeared in a campaign for jewelry brand Dinosaur Designs that featured her natural hair. The point of the photos, at least to me, was to emphasize Thot's beautiful dark and impossibly even skin tone juxtaposed against the colorful resin jewelry that is Dinosaur Designs' signature. To achieve this, Thot's natural hair was slicked back off her face and into a ponytail, as is customary for showcasing jewelry because hair can be a distraction from the product. Her snub ponytail only seems unusual because we are so used to looking at Black women with extensions added to their hair, rather than seeing their hair simply as it is. These images, while beautiful, sparked criticism from Harlow, who captioned a still from the campaign on Snapchat with the text "LMFAO! WHAT ARE THOOOOOSEEEEE cauliflower ass head."

Now, it doesn't take much imagination to envision what a cauliflower looks like and how that might relate to a Black woman's natural hair. Thot herself had already expressed her complicated relationship with her own hair. Earlier in 2016, she posted a now-deleted Instagram post that went viral, describing a harrowing experience she had on *Australia's Next Top Model* where she was forced to cornrow her own hair even though she didn't know how because her stylist didn't know how either. She wrote, "I was extremely upset and embarrassed that they 'didn't know how' to cornrow my natural hair when at the end of the day that's their job. I sat in front of the mirror silently crying before my shoot doing my own hair, cameras rolling while all the other girls had hair stylists . . ." Aside from the blatant discrimination at play here, which is rife in the fashion industry, the lack of knowledge is a huge factor for many Black women. In a 2016 interview, Thot tells *Teen Vogue*, "Being a black woman, we haven't really been taught how to take care of our natural hair—we've only been taught how to hide it." This is something Black women know intimately. As for Harlow, who has bolstered her own career as an advocate for anti-bullying, she issued an apology to Thot and followed up by telling her millions of followers on Instagram, "An apology has been made." Years later, her team requested that the BET story be taken down, and my bosses obliged for reasons I will never understand. Regardless, it demonstrates the brutality of criticism from within the Black community over hairstyles, type, and texture, and how that plays a role in power dynamics.

Almost all Black women in the public eye face a degree of scrutiny for their choices when it comes to their appearance, and especially their hair, which makes it difficult to focus on anything else. This eye is even turned to children. The mixed Kardashian offspring are being watched dutifully by the public to make sure that every single hair is always laid perfectly in place. Yes, they are Black and their mothers aren't, but they are also children and should be as free as any child to have wild, unkempt hair. The hair watchdogs are on everyone, from former First Lady Michelle Obama to athletes like Simone Biles and Gabby Douglas to Real Housewives. Mary Cosby, the sole Black cast member on *The Real Housewives of Salt Lake City*, was grilled about her wigs at the show's 2021 reunion hosted by Andy Cohen. The wigs did not meet the standard that Twitter wanted, and people dogged her out because of it, ignoring the fact that, even for a reality TV personality, having picture-perfect hair is not a contractual requirement. This is my biggest gripe with the hair criticism: the population of people whose actual job it is to have perfect hair is minuscule, but somehow, we have decided that perfect hair must be a requirement for Black women in any and all professions. Any offhand scroll through a social media feed featuring Black women will no doubt come with a healthy amount of hair commentary, from praise to ridicule, but here's what's never considered: that person's capacity to care for their hair in that exact moment, their actual job, whatever other life pressures might be weighing on them, and finally, that they might actually like their hair the way they have done it.

Olympic champion Gabrielle Douglas became a poster child scapegoat for hair hate while she competed on a global stage at the 2012 Summer Olympics. Never mind that she was seventeen, making history, and winning several gold medals, her hair displeased Black people who thought she looked sloppy and, the worst offense of all, like she was trying to be a white girl. In 2017, one Twitter user offered, "Gabby Douglas is that black girl with only white friends and bad weave," which is a sentiment I recognize, as it's been hurled at me often. If you become too hypnotized by white culture, you begin to unconsciously radiate it, and God help you if that's in a form of a messy bun. However, in Gabby's case and, later, in the case of her successor and perhaps the greatest gymnast of all time, Simone Biles, their hairstyles have a practical purpose and must adhere to a strict set of rules, which, like ballet or school uniforms, were never intended to include Black people. In fact, the official US gymnastics handbook specifies explicitly, "A neat and proper athletic appearance should be the overall impression with both warm-up and competition attire. The dress must be identical for members of the same team, with some exceptions for squads with both male and female athletes." It continues, "Hair long enough to be in the face or touching the shoulders of the athlete (male or female) should be pulled away neatly from the face and neck in a ponytail (no longer than six inches), bun, braids, or similar style. Whatever style, hair is not allowed to touch face, neck, back, nor shoulders."

As expressive as one might want to be with their hairstyles, these rules simply do not allow it. And who knows how their abilities might be hindered by braided or protective styles? Also, and I cannot emphasize this enough, *people can do their hair how they like*. I am embarrassed to even have to defend this. The fact of the matter is that both women overcame incredible obstacles to rise to the top of an unthinkably difficult physical sport, shouldered the hopes and dreams of the country, and exhibited extraordinary performances of grace and athleticism, all while being sexually victimized by a doctor they trusted to oversee their health and well-being. And at the end of the day, both of them have had to make numerous statements defending their hair. It's sad.

We must grant Black women the freedom to have messy hair and, at the same time, to also be fat, skinny, mean, nice, crybabies, or however it is they are. If I learned anything from that misguided stint as a Victoria's Secret Angel, it's that looking picture-perfect all the time is a full-time job. In fact, it *is* someone's full-time job, but it is probably not *your* full-time job. And even if it is your job, women still deserve nights and weekends off and occasions where we are not judged because our lace isn't perfectly laid. (Naomi Campbell suffered that fate when paparazzi shots caught her wigless on vacation.) It takes an unsustainable amount of time and money to live in filtered perfection.

In 2020, someone tweeted about me and my sister, "Danielle and Gabby Prescod had to have grown up extremely privileged the way their hair always looks." Skull emoji. And I get it, I do. Hair is important. Several chapters of this book are dedicated to it. And still, the policing, monitoring, and judgment of Black hair exclusively serves and reinforces white supremacy. I know that if I had perfect hair all the time or if I were still weighing my protein on a food scale, I probably couldn't have written this book. When I was younger and had perms, I didn't want to swim or overexert myself and get too sweaty. When I was hungry, I was tired and mean. We are missing out on life by upholding impossible physical standards, and even when we win gold medals or go on vacation, we can look forward to the opinions of the meddling public, the flaws of our hair, makeup, or bodies bringing into question our Blackness. Even at the top of your field, your appearance needs to be both nonthreatening to white people and pleasing to Black people, and that is practically impossible. In the grand scheme of things, the money and time we are dedicating to cosmetic upkeep can be a hindrance to our progress. Fielding critiques from naysayers can be just as cumbersome and draining.

Almost any content that invited people to weigh in on famous women's appearances was sure to be a top performer at BET, so even though I was no longer a token, I was still forced to endure daily commentary on how Black women should and should not look. And oftentimes, conflicting messaging came from within the company. I had bosses who commented on whether women with certain body types wearing bikinis was "appropriate." And nothing was off limits to the virtual BET audience; bodies, romantic relationships, natural hair, and diets were all laid bare for discerning spectators to applaud or tear apart at their discretion. Over my four years at BET, it became increasingly difficult to wade through our commenters' negativity on Black women's appearance while also dealing with opinions of the executive administration. All the while, I internalized these criticisms on behalf of all Black women and starved myself as both penance and a preemptive apology. How I looked was really the only element of the equation I had any control over. I knew if I could just get pretty and skinny enough, the world would fall more into balance.

CHAPTER TWENTY-FIVE

Through my tenure at BET.com, I continued to see Dr. Passler and evangelize his methods and philosophies wherever applicable. I had become increasingly desperate to lose more and more weight. I was asked to do more on-camera appearances at work, and with that new responsibility came an amplified anxiety about how big I might look. Eventually, I started to seek out more drastic weight loss solutions. I would do constant research on diets for "work," and I stumbled upon the concept of HGH shots. I started seeing a shady doctor on the Upper West Side behind Dr. Passler's back who would provide me with HGH and a diet pill called phentermine, which was basically an extreme appetite suppressant. It's legal speed.

It was not the first time I had experimented with diet pills. In 2012, one summer postcollege, one of my best friends and I thought it would be a good idea to try every over-the-counter option available. We were both high-profile assistants, her to a film actress and me to a fashion director. Our heart rates began racing at levels we didn't like, so we eventually abandoned our quest. But surely a prescription was something different, right? Except, in this case, it wasn't actually *my* prescription. No good doctor would ever prescribe me diet pills, and what this doctor did was even shadier. He secured the pills under other patients' names at a Florida pharmacy, shipped them to his office in NYC, crossed out the old name, and just handed over the bottle. I knew it was crazy to take them, but I could not stop. I was single again, and I felt, categorically, that the only way I could be loved was if I was very skinny. Never mind the notion that I was likely scaring men away by toting around bone broth on first dates. No, the reason I didn't have a boyfriend was because I was too fat, definitely.

I was visibly bony, but my five-eight frame still carried 130-ish pounds well enough, so I appeared healthy and fit to most people. And I was sure I could lose just ten more pounds. My hair started falling out, thanks to a combination of stress from work and a lack of nutrition. I stopped getting a regular period, a symptom of anorexia I reframed as a convenience. Who needs menstruation anyway? Like stopping for lunch, it just slows you down. I became irritable, set off by minor nuisances. I was extremely depressed. I had suicidal ideations. I pushed myself anyway. I was hitting up SoulCycle two to three times a week, Pilates three times a week, and doubling up on free workouts whenever they were available. In the meantime, I also worked constantly, on Slack as soon as my eyes opened in the morning and answering emails well into the night. I thought work could save me, but I had become much more jaded about my prospects of bridging the impossible gap between BET.com and the fashion industry.

In 2018, I participated in a *New York Magazine* story where editor Lindsay Peoples Wagner interviewed more than one hundred Black people working in the fashion industry. I am quoted both anonymously and not, and although I did not request anonymity, some did. Many were afraid of the kind of retaliation that being too honest can bring. The story surveyed everyone from designers to models to actresses to bloggers. It was an honest look at the more racist tendencies of the industry, and while it was a bombshell when it dropped in August 2018, not much has changed in the years since. Fashion has an incredible way of exacting a collective amnesia. Its mere existence is dependent on a quality of newness and regeneration that carelessly discards the old and forcefully embraces the new. This was what originally attracted me to clothing, since I was always trying to discard my old self, but it is actually one of fashion's most deeply rooted problems.

Fashion assumes that whatever happened in the past was the past. This is absolutely critical for ensuring that the industry continues with determined forward motion, never stopping, always pushing whatever is next or new. Phrases like "That's so last season" aren't meant only to make people feel self-conscious about their clothing choices, even though that is a useful side effect. The relentless insistence that everything become new in a constant cyclical motion is an ideology that buoys the entire industry. It is how people end up with ninety pairs of black boots. You always need to be acquiring the newer style, and with each iteration, the one before it becomes just a little more obsolete, even if it's still totally wearable. Once people secure all the things considered "wardrobe staples," the idea of variety is pushed upon them. *How about a leopard pencil skirt instead? Walk on the wild side. But don't forget, you still need the black. It's a classic.*

Regime changes at magazines and design houses mimic this reverent dedication to regeneration. When Raf Simons jumps from Jil Sander to Dior to Calvin Klein, fashion people discuss it with a hyperbolic excitement that rivals evangelical sermons. The same is true when a magazine gets a new creative director or editor-in-chief. The idea of change is both better and bigger than the change itself. In reality, not much changes at all. For example, if you are the kind of customer who has never shopped from Balenciaga before, it will not matter to you if Nicolas Ghesquière or Alexander Wang is steering the ship. You probably didn't even notice.

This is not a nihilistic or cynical view of the industry. I am someone who thinks fashion matters very much. I care deeply about creativity and clothing and how it is made. But the lies of the industry convert people into puppets and force us to all look at a mirage of paradise rather than the truth. This is how we come to feel that we can celebrate sixteen magazine covers featuring Black women in the same month for the first time in history as a victory, even though that same month, someone is anonymously quoted in *New York Magazine* saying, "People don't want to admit it, but there's still a contingency that you have to be the 'right' kind of black for fashion to fully accept you. They all look the same and are sample size . . . darker-skinned women with a different hair-curl pattern are being ignored. It's about the optics. And you think, how authentic is this?"

It is possible to be hopeful for the future, to recognize that change has occurred, while still being critical of the past.

In 2021, fashion industry website Fashionista published an investigative story on the rehabilitation of the Dolce & Gabbana brand. For anyone not in the know, Dolce & Gabbana has been ensconced in scandal for the last six or seven years, starting with a controversial homophobic statement from Domenico Dolce about gay families, stretching to cyberbullying of celebrities, and culminating in a racist advertising campaign that all but got the brand banned in China. Since then, the luxury heritage label has been slowly staging a comeback. First Lady Dr. Jill Biden wore Dolce & Gabbana to a presidential debate in 2020. First Black vice president Kamala Harris donned the label three times in her first month in office. For fashion people in the know, that raises eyebrows, but it has become increasingly easy to explain away these choices. *New York Times* editor Vanessa Friedman is quoted in the Fashionista story as saying, "This is a case where maybe we should do that more instead of leaping to simply call someone out; call them out *and* try to understand what's going on. Engage in that conversation and keep the conversation going, both so that we don't forget what happened and also so that we can use that to move forward as a broader sector." Unfortunately, this rhetoric does little to actually stop brands like Dolce & Gabbana from being racist or exacting their authority over more powerless people. Conversation is something white people often demand instead of asking for harsher consequences for racist actions. "What's going on" at many brands is simple: racism. The lines for accountability are blurry in this industry, and the fact remains that people are largely empowered to get away with bad behavior when they are rich or influential—and in many cases, they are both.

It is too convenient for a magazine to say, "This is the way we are now," touting a more inclusive cover feature without looking carefully at a past track record of exclusion or downright racism. It's why it ultimately didn't matter that I was the one with the byline for the Timberland story; it was content on the *Elle* website, an institution that has not examined its racist practices, and it was their responsibility to be aware and conscious enough to avoid putting out harmful content. The same goes for the people the media chooses to feature and promote. Should we ignore the racism of a plantation wedding because the couple looks great? If that's the case, then shouldn't we also ignore someone's race if they look great? That's not what happens. The double standard is an issue. The double standard is racism.

In January 2019, *CR Fashion Book*, a quarterly magazine founded by former *Vogue Paris* editor-in-chief Carine Roitfeld, celebrated Martin Luther King Jr.'s birthday on its Instagram page. They captioned a photo of Dr. King to commemorate his legacy and contributions to the world. A few hours later, they followed that up with a post celebrating the birthday of Carrie Bradshaw, the fictional protagonist from HBO's 1990s drama *Sex and the City*. As a person who does not exist, it's worth noting that Carrie Bradshaw cannot have a birthday. But, more importantly, just a few hours after exalting the accomplishments of one of the most influential civil rights leaders of our lifetime, it was a bit strange to see "Happy Birthday, Carrie Bradshaw." I posted a series of Instagram stories pointing out the incongruence of celebrating the birthday of a fictional character on the same day as an actual hero, a martyr. I had a moderate following in the twenty thousand range then, and it rallied enough of them that they made comments on *CR Fashion Book*'s original post. Instagram allows users to block or limit the comments under photos, so the *CR Fashion Book* team was able to step in and moderate (and selectively edit out) the anger, but the next day, I got a phone call.

I took the call in the women's bathroom at BET since I was sharing an office. On the other end, the digital director for *CR Fashion Book* told me that I needed to take my post down (no matter that it would delete in mere hours anyway since Instagram stories live for only twenty-four hours) and that my "attack" on *CR Fashion Book* was "unfair" because, "as a content person," I should understand that they "cannot spend the whole day talking about MLK," which, honestly, is kind of the point of the day. I was shaking, trying to defend myself without resorting to screaming. I told the person that as a "content person" I guessed I could understand that, theoretically, but I still, to this day, cannot wrap my head around any defense for posting a birthday message to a person who does not exist on the national holiday dedicated to the birthday of someone who actually *did* exist and changed countless lives for the better. This person suggested that I was "lucky" that I now had a job at BET so I could spend entire days on social media worried about celebrating Dr. King.

We ended at an impasse, and I was insulted and furious. I refused to take the post down, and he refused to admit any wrongdoing. In January 2021, after a year of discussions about the fashion industry's responsibility in fighting racism, *CR Fashion Book* neglected to post about Martin Luther King Jr. on his birthday. Instead, they put up an image from a fashion editorial, a photo of a model seated at a table with her hands folded, and captioned it, "Praying for more weekend," which is a strange choice of words because Martin Luther King Jr.'s birthday is a federal holiday that gives most office workers a Monday off, thus making it a long weekend. As far as I know, and because my sister worked there at one point, *CR Fashion Book* doesn't have the Martin Luther

King Jr. holiday in their vacation calendar, but regardless, as a brand that made some public declarations regarding their dedication to combating racism, the post seemed like a backward step, not a forward one.

That kind of flippant dismissal is a kind of gaslighting the industry as a whole is guilty of. People think I am "crazy" when I point out instances like this—that it seems petty and small to be harping on an Instagram photo. But, in my opinion, honoring Martin Luther King Jr.'s birthday is really the least an institution can do. It demonstrates to its Black employees that it is a priority for a company to recognize and celebrate Black leaders in a meaningful way. And if there is going to be an acknowledgment of his birthday and life, I think it should be respectful. At the very least, he's earned the right not to share his day with someone who was never even born to begin with.

I worked at BET, and because of that, I was insulated from having to deal with this sort of racism on a daily basis, but BET was just a Black island in a white sea. I still had to engage with the wider industry. I began to see how limited I was in the reporting I was able to do when fashion shows did not have any Black models or luxury fragrance companies wouldn't hire Black actresses as ambassadors. I could not do my job without the industry first addressing the inherent racism present in to whom it grants access. My refusal to put up with that constant gaslighting—conditions I had been subjected to for decades at the hands of white supremacy—helped me find the strength to decide I had had enough with it all.

CHAPTER

TWENTY-SIX

I get asked a lot about how I got "cured" from my eating disorder. I did eventually stop seeing Dr. Passler and start eating. But the truth is I am not really "cured." What I *am* is in recovery. I was forced to change. Having an eating disorder, in my experience, is the kind of addiction you have to work on challenging daily. Hourly, sometimes. And it is also one of those fundamental issues from which all others can stem. By refusing to feed myself and acknowledge my appetites, I was communicating to the world that I was without need, that I would voluntarily subsist on nothing, and that would be fine for me. Through observing my eating habits, I can finally understand the circumstances that led me to adopt the language of oppressive systems and wield them over myself and others. I did not have a way of valuing myself that allowed for understanding, caring, or nourishing. By denying these basic needs, I was able to extend that denial to other areas of my life.

I still do not eat in the way I imagine a healthy person does, but I try my best to respond to my body when it is asking for food or rest. I have worked on dismantling my phobias of foods such as pasta, rice, and bagels, and can eat them now with little to no guilt. This might seem like a petty victory to some, but the extreme degree to which I cherished and protected my disorder is legendary. There was a point, not long ago, when eating rice was something I was sure I could never do again.

My first real break with dieting came when I turned thirty, with no marriage prospects in sight, and decided to pursue freezing my eggs as an insurance policy. When the time is right, in the future, I figured I could have a family and mitigate some fertility anxiety as I aged. I went on the IVF drugs and had no idea what to expect. I promised myself I would not diet during the two weeks I was under treatment because I didn't know what my body was going to need. I was hungry every single second. I ate so much food, and the combination of suspending my restrictive diet with the hormone therapy made me gain about twelve pounds in two weeks.

During hormone treatment, you also can't exercise—at all. I tried because I assumed they meant no exercise for people who never really exercised, not me. The first day after I started fertility hormones, I went to SoulCycle, and it was a very bad idea. Thirty minutes in, I felt extreme cramping. I should have left, but instead, I shamefully rode "in the saddle" for the remainder of class. Afterward, I was worried I had upended my ovaries somehow. I didn't make that mistake again.

After my egg retrieval, which is full surgery, I felt out of it in my body. My lower stomach was enlarged because I'd been artificially plumping up my ovaries. Most people hope to get an embryo implanted after all that, but I got nothing, just a bunch of weight gain and some surety that, maybe one day, I would have a baby. At that point, I just didn't have the energy to go back to sipping bone broth for every meal. I paid one last visit to my Central Park West pill pusher and one last visit to Dr. Passler, who suggested a strict protein-and-vegetable program, and then quit going at all.

Over the next few months, I slowly gained upward of thirty pounds. During the pandemic, I gained fifteen more. Who knows what the number is now because, at the behest of my therapist, I finally stopped weighing myself. Initially, it was an absolute nightmare. I had to keep giving up garments I loved because, without carefully managing my calorie intake, a lot of my clothes no longer fit. This was and still is the worst part of recovering. I have spent years and thousands of dollars crafting my wardrobe and, by extension, who I was because of my clothes, and suddenly, it was all gone. I had to mourn the loss of my clothes, of my body, of my carefully crafted self-image, all in a very short time. I was letting go of everything I thought had been protecting me since childhood, all the armor I spent decades amassing. At a certain point, the loss became less and less important to me since living life actually became easier.

Like some sort of freaky seesaw, as I became heavier, other, more harmful weight started to lift. I could relinquish control of my schedule and relax all the things I was constantly hiding. I started becoming more honest in general and worked on appreciating my body for what it could do and not how it looked. This sounds cliché, but it was happening and it was useful. I also started to become a nicer person in general. Without the distraction of hunger, my fuse wasn't so short. I was able to be more patient, forgiving, and understanding. The more toxic parts of the industry I was working in started to reveal themselves, which, in my opinion, is all related to my personal healing.

As a part of my initial eating disorder recovery, I decided to take a more behind-the-scenes role at BET and drastically reduced projects that would require me to appear in photos or videos. That visibility would have added a layer of stress that was completely avoidable. As often happens in corporate America, BET had a change in leadership, and the new team signed me up to host a regular video show, which would have meant on-camera appearances several times a week. I refused, but the power struggle with the new team was the beginning of the end of my time there. Eventually, I quit my job at BET. In my last two years there, it became clear to me that I had to move on. It was disturbing to witness the blatant exploitation of Black creatives—especially Black women—in the form of overworking, denial of employment benefits, and an unusually abusive office culture. I also no longer wanted to be complicit in the constant monitoring of Black women's looks and behavior. I had finally begun to understand my own autonomy and that it was my responsibility to care for myself and advocate for my needs.

In college, I took a Western feminism course, and our reading prompted a discussion about whether the class would be OK switching bodies with someone else. Years later, when I was watching the show *Fleabag*, the main character and her sister attended a feminist lecture and the speaker asked if anyone would like to swap their body out for another. And just like *Fleabag*, I flushed with shame when I chose wrong in my class. The answer was unanimously no. Unsurprisingly, my answer was "Hell yes!" I was positively exhilarated by the question, thinking *Wow, oh my God, I have been waiting my whole life to walk around in Gisele's body.* The other ladies in my class spoke sentimentally, admiring all the things their bodies have done for them or allowed them to do. They said they knew their bodies and had protective stewardships over them. They did not want to abandon or trade them in for another. I, on the other hand, had spent so many years dissociating from my body, furious at all the times it let me down with how it looked, that I never considered how it had been useful to me, even generous, considering the repeated abuse I had subjected it to. It had never occurred to me that I *could* like my body. Not once.

In therapy, I practice a lot of "self-compassion" and "self-kindness," which I resisted at first. I was convinced that the concept of speaking nicely to and about myself would dull my senses and make me too soft for the world. The meanness I had built up served as a shield, a protection, and a fuel. I thought it was a necessary aspect of my life and that without it I wouldn't be able to generate success. And I was certain that without consistent self-regulated negativity, I wouldn't be able to stop myself from eating. Acknowledging that I want to eat, even acknowledging that I am hungry, is still a challenge. I had been shaped to believe in the ideals of capitalism: laziness is your fault, poverty is your fault, obesity is your fault. And I assumed I could just work my way out of any undesirable circumstances to find salvation.

While I wish I could have been presented with an alternative way of thinking sooner, the reality is I am a woman, and I have repeatedly been shown that people will assess your value based on how you look first and what you can do second.

People outside the industry insist that it is "getting better" and that we should celebrate the progress instead of focusing on the negative past. Hopeful changes in the past few years push the right messaging forward, yet I can confirm from directly inside the belly of the beast that real change is slow going.

When I finally decided to stare straight into the face of my eating disorder, I had to confront exactly why I have such advanced insecurities about weight, and a lot of it had to do with my genuine love of clothing. Twice a year, every year, my job requires that I sit through dozens of fashion shows and watch the clothing of the upcoming season be presented on size-zero teenagers. Without saying a word, designers are presenting their vision of how exactly they want their clothing to look and, by extension, how they want women to look. No designer would declare that they want to make women feel bad, but without necessarily meaning to, they do. As late as 2012, actress Melissa McCarthy exposed designers for refusing to dress her for the Oscars, stating to *Redbook*, "I asked five or six designers, very high-level ones who make lots of dresses for people, and they all said no." By keeping runways and ad campaigns and, frankly, sample sizes that way, fashion people perpetuate the old standards that have been in existence for decades, damaging generation after generation of women as we fail to ascend to the impossible beauty example of an underdeveloped girl.

All the onus for this culture is not on designers. Many factors contribute to models being cast the way they are: financial restraints, lack of resources, the way samples are produced, and so on. These are real obstacles. But just about every part of working in fashion is difficult. The industry needs to examine the extensive damage it has done to people's self-esteem, taking responsibility for our roles in amplifying archaic and harmful beauty standards. There is certainly no lack of research directly linking glamorized imagery to body dissatisfaction among women. We can't pretend we don't know. We can't pretend it doesn't affect the women working in the industry too.

There's another sector of optimists who believe that social media has done a lot of the work the industry could not, that it has provided people who exist outside the typical spectrum of beauty and fashion with the ability to reach millions. And they are partially right. Social media does give people the ability to find others like them. Entire communities are built online. The internet has helped me become more comfortable with myself. It's shown me other Black Harry Potter fans or horse girls or ballerinas, when, growing up, I thought I was alone. It has helped me find other Token Black Girls. Social media offers us the ability to connect within micro-communities and provides us with unprecedented tools for visibility.

The flip side is that apps like Instagram and TikTok rely on algorithms that eventually begin to mimic the larger world, and those algorithms enforce the exact same problematic beauty standards to a remixed beat. So while you may see a fat model or a girl with a skin condition seemingly "making it," their success is relative. Women are trolled on a daily basis by people who seek to shame them for how they look, the decision to edit or not edit a photo, and what they are covering up or showing off. It is a minefield of criticism and negativity no matter what you look like, but just like literally anything else, it is especially difficult for plus-size women and women of color.

Instagram has established a newer but still pervasive beauty ideal. The body of the typical Instagram model is curvier than that of a traditional model, with an emphasis on a smaller waist and bigger hips. A big butt and boobs are preferred. Plump lips are also a weirdly specific prerequisite. Being ethnically ambiguous or mixed race will allow you to thrive in multiple markets, but in general, a fairer skin tone will serve better. Youth is key, so having wrinkles or sagging skin—any sign of visible age—won't be lucrative. According to the algorithm, it would be advisable to have children when you're around age twenty-five so you can gracefully transition into the fashionable Instagram mom market.

Social media has essentially updated and remixed the rules that have been nailed to the giant wooden doors of society by the fashion and beauty industries. Overtly feminine features, youth, and wealth are all important signifiers we have been trained to seek out and desire, while characteristics that women of color, particularly Black women, have endured criticism over for centuries, like hips, lips, and a round butt, are all of a sudden regaled as the most attractive assets a woman can possess—just not on Black women. In other words, I am supposed to just toss out years of trauma about my body and facial features, years of shame over wearing hair extensions and wigs, all because another aesthetic—one that comes more naturally to me—is now popular on Instagram. Imagine all the time I spent in the mirror as a child practicing how to suck my lips in, just to have people pay money for them as an adult! I would like that time back. And white women are the ones benefiting the most from the new system, just as they do in the traditional beauty structure. Black female influencers are paid less, if at all, when being contracted by brands, even if they naturally possess the desirable physical qualities that attract followers.

Just as I starved myself for years to achieve the ideal body I saw on television and in magazines, women are spending enormous sums of money and suffering great personal pain for silicone butt injections, liposuction, breast augmentation, and various facial fillers in order to achieve the kind of look that is celebrated on social media. As with wigs, the more white women began to talk about these beauty measures, the more they became normalized and accepted. Now it's almost a fun game to try to guess who has natural curves or otherwise. It breaks my heart that women feel the pressure to surgically change their bodies, and to me, the struggle with this preoccupation and my struggle with food are the same fight. In both cases, women are taught that our bodies must be fixed and that, if given the power to do so, we should use it. We already know what that kind of thinking can lead to. It is the duty of the media, armed with extensive knowledge, to combat the ways this system hurts people and make sure representation and inclusion are not simply buzzwords, to ask more about why things are still the way they are, instead of simply accepting the rules as law and waiting for people to heal themselves as we continue selling them our poison.

There is hardly a taboo surrounding surgery among certain communities. It has developed into a cute bonding occasion for women—and sometimes men too! The same was true for my bizarre and restrictive eating habits. I knew I could be honest with certain people, like other fashion people, fellow former dancers, and strangely enough, male wrestlers. There was an understanding of the struggle and the necessity to protect the regimen. For the plastics people, the impetus to share their new procedures with like-minded friends and colleagues is irresistible. That is also a form of bonding, a connection formed by recognizing a shared commitment to youthful skin, a snatched figure, and minimal wrinkles at whatever cost. And then there are those who protect the secrets of their surgery at all costs. These people are the Kardashians.

After fifteen years of working in this business, I can tell you that you can stop all your questioning and wondering. If it looks too good to be true, it probably is. Many of your favorite leading men and women have had multiple things done to their faces and bodies. We shouldn't shame them for that; they are just as much players and pawns in this game as we are. We also shouldn't pretend that things are real when they are fake, and this goes for everyone. Do not say you "did a lot of squats" when you very well know that you underwent four fat transfers. It is just as damaging as people who claim they eat whatever they want and simply "work out a ton" when they are measuring their avocado slices and haven't had sugar since their tenth birthday. Do not claim you got your lips from obscure genetic heritage when you know very well they are full of Juvéderm.

Honesty, as hard as it is, will save us from this fresh hell we're cooking in as we airbrush everything on pages, then on big screens, then small ones, then even smaller ones, for the rabid consumption of the unassuming public. You'd think we would be smarter by now, knowing all that we know, but for the most part, we believe what we're told, even if what we're told is an offensive, bald-faced lie that defies all logic. We have to start telling people the truth. It is simply the only responsible thing to do.

Coming to terms with my own ability to be honest has been sickeningly difficult. I've tried my best in these pages because the only way to start is with yourself. I have spent years hiding the parts of myself I knew were ugly on the inside, just as much as I have spent concealing my outer flaws. If it still feels like I'm hiding something, the truth is:

- I wear Spanx with almost everything.
- I am, despite a hefty amount of inner work, disappointed in myself when I have to go up a jean size.
- I have said awful fatphobic things, and I am guilty of spreading fatphobia.
- I am never satisfied with my reflection.
- I always think I am doing everything wrong.
- I can't do my own hair, and I like to wear it messy.
- I can't jump double Dutch.
- I have never seen the movies *The Players Club* or *Brown Sugar*, and I don't care to.
- I fantasize regularly about living in a Nancy Meyers film, even though there are no Black characters.

All these things make me who I am. We are all a mess of contradictions, and we feel them crashing together as we move through the world. It is not enough to simply declare insecurities without trying to figure out their source because—I promise you—they will keep coming back up. We have to learn to live with them, and to make space for others to do the same.

AFTERWORD

I look back at my life and worry that so many of my personal relationships have failed because there was always something huge missing. That missing thing was *me*—me being my actual self instead of a fake robot who just wants to please everyone. I was always hiding something, always trying to dress up and disguise parts of me that were not likable. For a long time, that had to do with my Blackness. I felt that I could outperform racism, assimilate, and ignore it away. Then, predictably, there were Black people who thought I "acted white" and was a snob. I'm not exactly a snob, not in the ways I used to be, even though I've spent a lot of time admiring and acquiring nice things. That quality has nothing to do with wanting to be white. I have examined my relationship to white supremacy, and I can confidently separate my proclivity for luxuries from the influence of whiteness. Some will argue that capitalism and white supremacy are two heads of the same monster, and while I hear and honor that analysis, I still want to sleep on high-thread-count sheets.

Though it should be obvious by now, it still must be said: being Black is not a monolith. There is no rule book dictating how to show up as Black in the world. Over time, I have learned to accept the parts of my Blackness that are unique, to understand it's OK that my experience is different from the next Black person's, just as theirs is different from the next, and so on. And since I was brainwashed to think it could only be one way, it took a lot of work to get here. I have to forgive myself for denying the parts of me I thought would be rejected by my own community and, equally, the ones I thought would be rejected by white people. The complexities of race in America are not limited to a single experience, and it's my hope that we can craft a world where the media rallies in an effort to show that we can have many Black experiences.

In 2017, I made a public pledge to read only books about or by Black people, as I had become all too aware that the things I found entertaining were too influenced by whiteness, and it had been that way for all thirty years of my life. I had to relearn history. Despite a lifetime of education that cost upward of six figures, there were so many things I still did not know. And since I spent a good amount of my academic energy studying up on fashion, beauty, and models, I ended up with little knowledge about the cancer of systemic racism, even though it was something that was affecting me directly. But as I got closer and closer to my professional goals, everything else mattered less. I don't want another generation of kids growing up being served garbage about how kinky hair is bad and a big butt makes you a slut. Blackness is so demonized that we end up on an endless quest just trying to prove our humanity. And still, white people end up caring more about bees and dolphins and being vegan than they do about Black lives. They are desensitized repeatedly by the media and, from birth, affirmed by the notion that they are special, entitled, and perfect.

Black women deserve a place in the beauty canon. It sickens me how normalized it is in this industry to have entire stories that do not include any mention of Black women. Runways with no Black models. Casting calls that say "no ethnics." It happens all the time. Yes, *still*. And this is because white women control the lion's share of content, and white men control the lion's share of the money. They are responsible for the casting and the hiring and do not see the value in making sure that Black women are, at the very least, appreciated.

Returning briefly to the Doll Test, in 2010, CNN attempted to re-create the study, surveying children of varying racial backgrounds instead of just Black children. The results were the same as in 1940, suggesting that, though schools are desegregated, racist biases still encourage children as young as four to see Black as bad and white as good. University of Chicago professor Margaret Beale Spencer consulted with CNN, serving as the lead researcher on the project. She published her conclusions, finding that "white children, as a whole, responded with a high rate of what researchers call 'white bias,' identifying the color of their own skin with positive attributes and darker skin with negative attributes. All kids, on the one hand, are exposed to the stereotypes. What's really significant is that white children are learning or maintaining those stereotypes much more strongly than the African-American children."

And what happens to white children? They grow up to be white adults, consciously or unconsciously living in the way that makes them the most comfortable, always at the expense of someone Black. A four-year-old child is not a full-blown racist yet, but as we are all living under the system of racism, you can bet that bias and prejudice are baking. People, white people specifically, are extremely quick to declare themselves "not racist." It's a reflexive reaction to the accurate suggestion that they are racist. The funny thing is it doesn't matter who *is* racist and who isn't because the *world* is absolutely racist. If, for example, a population of people are drinking a contaminated water supply for generations, it would be reasonable to predict that this population would be sick. Their children would be sick. Their children's children would be sick. How can someone be "not racist" and have grown up reading books like those in the Sweet Valley High series or *Rain* without question or complaint? How can someone emerge "not racist" when they don't think anything of the headline: "Meghan Markle: Straight Out of Compton"? Magazines still exist to tell white women that they are the best and the most beautiful. It is not possible to emerge from a contaminated world with your thoughts completely unaffected.

I should not have to work to change any of this on my own, especially since, as the doll study shows, white bias is largely responsible for the way the world is interpreted. I should, instead, be joined by my sisters of any race who have ever felt invalidated, who know exactly what a crushing rejection based on your looks can do to self-esteem. But just like when Stu ridiculed me at that dinner party as my white friends and colleagues looked on, I do not feel joined by the white people I grew up with.

As I get older, I reflect more about the way my life has developed and the ways it will continue to develop. I still have many white friends who do not have any close friends of any other race. I see it when I am at their weddings, baby showers, and birthdays. Aside from their domestic help, their children will likely not interact with a person of another race, either, thus leaving the cycle free to continue. Eventually, these people's kids will meet a little Black child and inevitably make them feel inferior about their skin, hair, body, or something else. I worry about this often. That's why having conversations about race and racism matter to me. If you are not consuming media that is actively antiracist, you can be sure that it is somehow racially biased in favor of white people, and these issues will continue to be problematic for future generations unless that is changed.

After a lot of podcasts, retreats, and therapy, I've learned if we're ever going to get anywhere, we have to shed shame. The shame I felt about being Black and then the subsequent shame I felt about not being Black enough were both a hindrance to me. I needed a safe environment to feel like myself, and I got that for a fleeting moment when I decided to work at an all-Black company.

When I made the decision to leave behind traditional fashion publications, I was afraid I was disappointing people, but I had no more fight left in me. It had been squashed by years of suppressing anger over injustices, enduring racist interactions, and being forced to smile through it all. I was burned out. And all that had bled from work into my personal life. Leaving felt a bit like giving up, but that turned out to be some old, racist thinking. White media gives you legitimacy. Anyone who pretends otherwise is lying. The prestige of the *New York Times* and *Vogue* excites people.

In her memoir, *Negroland*, Margo Jefferson recalls how she felt when the publication *Ebony* was founded: "A separate world of Negro beauty and glamour did exist when *Ebony* arrived. I studied its cream, beige, tan, buff, brown, and sepia models. My favorite was Dorothea Towles . . . I admired her, I envied her, but I didn't worship her as I worshipped Suzy Parker. She was in *Ebony*, not *Vogue*. My white friends didn't know who she was. Diana Vreeland didn't have to know or care." Brand recognition and legacy are hugely important, especially when the entire world is governed by white supremacy. I have always taken a perverse pleasure in occupying a space that I know was never meant for me, knowing that my presence probably pisses people off. This is why I go to all my high school reunions, so all the old white ladies of Greenwich can see my face and know that even though they think they are very, very special, we all came from the same place. This is also why I felt like I was giving up when I went to work at a Black brand—but even there, I was presented with a new set of challenges. At BET, it was more difficult than ever to secure Black talent, who were swayed by the allure of the white media. I had to work to get invites to things I had been going to for years. Once I started working for a Black brand, the fashion industry decided I was irrelevant. That also stung, but honestly, it is still easier than having to break bread with actual racists.

Even though that feeling of exclusion was difficult to stomach after decades of hard work, it's more difficult knowing that people with extremely racist pasts are drooled over by fashion media. It's more convenient for them to just forget, to rely on that collective amnesia, to let beautiful and rich people apologize and chalk racism up to youth, stupidity, or substance abuse and just say, "Let's move on." But this is a continued affront to employees of color. Imagine the corruption in excluding Black media from access to talent and events, while the racists have several seats at the table and millions of fans. It's absolutely exhausting to work in that system. Black content creators and models are paid less, are worth less, and are made to know that by brands. They are seen as inferior and made to understand that. The messaging to them becomes "we need you, but we don't want you. The racists, though—we both need and want them."

There are white friends of mine who do not watch Black television programs that I love, like *Insecure* or *Atlanta*. This fact feels less stressful to me now that my world is bigger and I have a circle I can discuss Black things with. I also have a wide social media network. I can, for the most part, choose what to engage with. But in 2021, HBO Max is resurrecting the white emporiums of *Sex and the City* and *Friends* (a cultural touchstone from which I cannot seem to escape) so we can have Republican lawmakers push litigation around banning Critical Race Theory, while they continue to watch "classic" programs without any people of color.

It is absolutely critical that we improve our media literacy, that we start to train ourselves to read messages conveyed to us, whether overt or not. Understand what it means that the press attacks Meghan Markle and praises Kate Middleton. Combat your own biases constantly. Diversify what you watch and consume, especially if you are white. Do not feel threatened if Black women are celebrating themselves; join in. If something feels off, say something. Do not make it a handful of people's job to be constantly fighting this fight. They will get tired. They will lose. Reinforcements are necessary.

Early in 2020, a video went viral featuring a little Black girl who was four years old. She is getting her hair done as her hairdresser records the process on her phone. The little girl turns to the camera when she catches a glimpse of her reflection, and says, "I am so ugly." The hairdresser tells the little girl that she is beautiful, and that she should never say that about herself. The girl starts crying, as do, I'm sure, all the viewers. She is a baby. It's hard to even comprehend how she came to understand the concept of ugliness, much less to see herself as ugly, but that is a critical time in a Black girl's development, where an idea like that can stick. For me, the idea that I was fat stuck, and I spent a lifetime running from it. What if we could be taught to love ourselves the same way Jessica Wakefield from Sweet Valley High looked in the mirror and knew she looked perfect?

One of the tools I use in therapy is to look at a photo of my younger self, age three or four, and try to say the things the voice in my head says: "You are fat." "You are unlovable." "No one wants you." "You are stupid." "You can't do anything right." "Fix yourself." Honestly, it's incredibly powerful. You would *never* say those things to a child, and if you would, then perhaps don't have kids. It brought a lot of clarity to realize I am always going to be that same little girl, and every time a new trigger comes up, I have to show up for her the way a loving parent might. I try to show up for her and for all the other girls who can't show up for themselves yet.

Of course, the other thing I want is for everyone to stop putting so much pressure on looks in general, but considering I sat in coronavirus quarantine crying about my manicure and my lack of eyelash extensions, I realize that the battle is going to be tough. I am still infected by the disease that requires me to look a certain way at all times in order to accept myself. I know I am still in the belly of the perfection beast, even if I have begun to pry open its jaws. In this culture, it is not enough to have working bodies and healthy lungs and teeth. We instead become consumed with how we can make these things perfect, as opposed to just being grateful that we have them at all.

Even as I say this, I know that, because of racism, it will always be a more difficult climb for Black women. I know Black women will always be under scrutiny for how they look, no matter how good they are at what they do, from both inside and outside the Black community. You can say all the right things and go to all the right schools and win all the right awards, but until people (and subsequently, the media) are retrained in the way that they examine and evaluate Black women, we will continuously be subjected to a demoralizing kind of patrol that tells us we need to outperform, outdress, and outshine—and it still will never be enough. How are we supposed to accept ourselves if the obstacles to progress are constant and at the hands of the enormous vehicle driven primarily by the press?

My questions are directed to the people I know have the power to influence who and what is represented in the media. Are you interested in making these things worse or better? Do you see how no representation and negative representation can have the same result? Are you willing to acknowledge the ways you benefit from this system, even if you are not a direct participant? Are you willing to acknowledge that mistakes have been made, and even if they have nothing to do with you, they still have everything to do with the way the world is structured today? Dignify me by saying you understand that things might be harder for me, and that you understand how you might be guilty of making them harder. I shouldn't have to beg anyone to have to see these issues, but since I know how ignored they are, I felt compelled to write this book.

Although I will shallowly admit that knowing women are paying thousands for the lips and butt I was teased about for years does give me a punitive sense of justice, I don't want to see anyone become a human pincushion. Whatever cocktail you're made from is made for you, and only you. And it's the media's job to accurately reflect the world we live in, not distort it. That's why I try my best, with whatever little power I have, to shake up and break up toxic beauty standards and encourage people to be more influenced by abilities than aesthetics.

I might never be satisfied with what I see in the mirror. But I post photos of myself, and even if I see a roll I don't like, I don't edit it out. I go on dates, and I don't wear any makeup. Now I like the parts of myself most that have nothing to do with how I look, and I make caring for myself a priority. This has made me a gentler person overall, one who no longer accepts abuse or abuses others. It is something I have to work on all the time. I have to constantly pull myself out of barbarous spirals of self-criticism, which is why I am adamant about encouraging everyone to take a step back and look at the way this environment endangers us. Let's account for the harms that have been done to us. And let's share in the collective responsibility of correcting them.

ACKNOWLEDGMENTS

Writing this book was challenging and at some times super lonely, but I did not do it alone! And so now I have to let everyone know how much they meant to me and this process. Nothing really will ever feel good enough, but I will try my best!

Firstly, I have to thank Mommy and Daddy, and yes I still say Mommy and Daddy, because I am forever their child and that's what I call them. Thank you, Mommy and Daddy, for providing me with safety and love. Your endless support has allowed me to develop in ways that I hope make you proud. I also hope that this wasn't too difficult for you to read and know that I wouldn't change anything. You gave me the absolute best life, and I am so grateful that you love me the way you do. I always say that the world would be a better place if more people had parents like you.

To Gabby, I am the luckiest person to have you as my sister, my soul mate. I know I would not be the person I am without you. Thank you for being my sounding board as I was writing this book and for living the Token Black Girl life with me. I guess I was never just THE ONE, was I? Thank you for being there.

To my extended family (Uncle Lewis and Aunt Louise, Uncle Warren and Aunt Shelly, and Uncle Ronald and Renee), thank you for your support. I always had a very robust and Black cheering section so thank you for always making the time and showing up.

To Jessica, my literary agent (who I have still never met in person!), thank you so much for your tireless work in bringing this book from proposal and rough pages to finished product. Thank you for answering all my questions about contracts and terminology with patience and clarity and for your belief that this could be a real book! I am so grateful that you are the agent who made all of this happen.

To Laura, my editor (who I have also never met in person!), thank you for taking a chance on me and buying this book. Thank you for your vision and commitment to making this dream come to life for me. Thank you for making me feel heard.

To Camille, my other editor (who I have also never met in person! Writing a pandemic book is definitely weird!), thank you for your questions and your honesty and how hard you worked to help me express myself in a way that is honest and authentic. I am so grateful to have worked with you, and I'm sorry I hit you with ninety-six thousand words at first.

To everyone at Little A who is working so hard on this project who I have only seen via a screen, thank you and I hope I can consensually hug you and tell you in person very soon!

To Taylor, thank you for giving me a chance to be your intern when I was all of nineteen and keeping me! You gave me such a meaningful example to follow. You always advocated for me and I saw that. I am forever grateful for your friendship and love.

To Shiona, I know how hard it was for you, and I am in awe, always, of your strength and tenacity. Thank you for taking me in when I was so lost and broken and for your leadership and courage. I am also lucky to call you a friend.

To Leah, I never thought I could do this, but somehow you always believed. Without your advice, I never would have written anything ever. You helped me find my voice. I am sorry for all the things I kept from you and for what I didn't know how to say, but I am always thinking about how I didn't know how to put the accent mark in the right place in Céline and you hired me anyway.

To my former bosses Jermaine, Damian, and Meggan, thank you for letting me do work that I found fun and fulfilling and creating an environment where creativity was fostered and nurtured. Thank you for your guidance and supervision.

To my Elle 2.0 team (Sally, Natalie, Justine, Kate, Julie), apologies for airing out all our dirty laundry and also for bailing when it just got too hard. This is still the most special team I have ever worked on, and I am so proud of all of us. No one else will ever really understand like y'all. I loved our years together and the work that we did. And I am so happy that everyone is blossoming personally and a professionally like I knew you would. I love to watch you all shine.

To my BET/219 ladies (Brook, Ashlee, Iyana, Jaz, Tira, Shalaeya, Tweety, Lainey, Essie, Jocelyn), wow, we really really really went through something together. I am so so so thankful to have had the privilege of working with you, and I am so honored to be in this company of women. You are all brilliant and so strong, and though everything did not go as I wanted, we all still made it work anyways. I thank you for your support and positivity and friendship. Thank you for everything.

I always say NO INDUSTRY FRIENDS! But I have so many and I appreciate all the laughs and the love over the years. Thank you for ditching drinks for SoulCycle classes and letting me count my almonds and cry and rant about Chartbeat. Thank you for the connections and opportunities and endless style inspiration. You know who you are, but I am listing you anyway because I know you know how nice it is to read your name in print and mastheads are just over. (Sue, Winnie, Amelia, Mercedes, Chrissy, Nikki, Julia, Tiffany, Yash, Ron, Laron, Kevin, Aurora, Blair, Emily Schumann, Marta, Charlotte, Alex Gobo, Nate, Nadia, Federica, Gabby Katz, Martha, Glenny, Christy, Christyanna, Tashon, Matt Kays, Stephanie Strauss, Chase Weideman, Savannah, Strugatz, Brendan, Arianna, KNC, Solange Franklin Reed,

Tamu, Tyler Joe, Travis Paul Martin, Sandrine, Ade, Ayanna, Devan, Bianca, Brooke Devard, Nicolette, Serena, Justin, Rebecca Ramsey, Kathy, Garrett, Will, Abby, Sergio, Serena, Angel, Dren, Coco, Breezy, Alyssa, Kendall, Simone, Barbara.)

To my CSH girls (Eli, Gen, Molly, Liz Franco, Maggie Connors), thank you for being my friends for so long! I really love you and I mean it. Sustaining connections over this many years and life changes is difficult, and I can't thank you enough for being in my life.

To Katie Schloss (girls who went to school in Greenwich know that a Katie *must* be followed by a last name, because if not . . . which one??), I couldn't have done this book without you. Your consistent belief in me and your eternal optimism helped me tremendously. You went so out of your way to push me to try to connect me with people who gave me good advice, and I can't even believe your stamina for it, but I am so grateful.

To all my teachers and therapists, thank you. As you can see, I have grown a lot, but it is only because I had some critical help.

And lastly, to Harry Potter Prescod, because Mariah Carey thanked every dog she's ever owned at the end of her book so it normalized it for me. Harry, an angel, thank you for trotting alongside me on punishing runs when I didn't know where we were going. Thank you for conspiratorially eating all the things I was not going to eat. And thank you for your protection and your affection, even when I smothered you. If I ever do get a tattoo, it will be for you.

ABOUT THE AUTHOR

Photo © 2021 Scarlet Raven

Danielle Prescod is a fifteen-year veteran of the beauty and fashion industry and graduate of NYU's Gallatin School of Individualized Study. A lifelong fashion obsessive, she was most recently the style director of BET.com. With Chrissy Rutherford, Danielle cofounded 2BG Consulting, which aids fashion and beauty brands and influencers on their anti-racism journeys. She dedicates her time to researching how feminism and social justice intersect with pop culture. An avid reader and writer, Danielle also loves TikTok, the arts, staying active, horseback riding, and exercising at any hour of the day.